# PLAYS FROM BLACK AFRICA

# Plays from Black Africa

*Edited and with an Introduction by*
FREDRIC M. LITTO

❧❦❧

A MERMAID DRAMABOOK
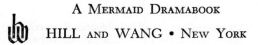
HILL AND WANG • NEW YORK

Manufactured in the United States of America by
The Colonial Press Inc., Clinton, Massachusetts

# CONTENTS

# CONTENTS

# INTRODUCTION

Some years ago a book appeared with the title *The Frontiers of Drama*. In many senses the present anthology could well claim that idea in a subtitle, for nowhere in the world is there as fresh and vibrant and effective a drama as that of contemporary Africa—even if largely unknown to most theatrically literate persons. To come into contact with plays written by men and women of Black Africa is to discover a frontier that combines the centuries-old cultures of the African peoples themselves and the European culture of the colonizers, whose influence in Africa must also be measured in centuries. To this extent these plays may be read as social documents, and social scientists will find considerable anthropological and folkloric evidence throughout the volume. But it was not for their purposes that the plays were written. In fact, these playwrights may distort myths and mores in order to achieve their real goal: to create viable works of dramatic art. Students of literature and drama will find that many African writers have reached this goal, that their creations deserve to be evaluated with the same seriousness and by the same standards that we apply to modern writers in the West.

It will be some time before a cadre of "authorities" on African drama will develop opinions possessing the awesome weight of older bodies of literature. Here is yet another frontier. While the amount of critical literature on African plays remains small, this drama can be appreciated without critical prejudice by all interested persons. In fact, this collection will serve a useful educational purpose: these plays can be studied in order to apply theory to playwrighting practice in a critically free and uncluttered atmosphere.

It is almost impossible to speak of an "African" drama;

we must discuss it by regions or countries. And even these divisions will not be entirely satisfying, because language groups in Africa, as elsewhere, have always been more potent realities than political units. In the Arabic countries north of the Sahara the traditional Islamic abhorrence for dramatic representation seems to have been put aside. The Arab Theatre Conference held in Casablanca in November, 1966, included representatives from Algeria, Libya, Tunisia, Morocco, Syria, Lebanon, and the United Arab Republic. (The proceedings were published in *The Afro-Asian Theatre Bulletin* [Lawrence, Kansas], II, 2 [February, 1967].) It promises to be the beginning of a fruitful venture.

In Egypt the leading playwright at present is Tewfik Al-Hakim, a celebrated man of letters whose *The Tree Climber* was published by the Oxford University Press in 1966. Algeria has produced Mouloud Mammeri, whose revolutionary play *Le Foehn* has drawn critical praise, and Emmanuel Roblès, some of whose half a dozen plays have been translated into Arabic, German, English, Spanish, and Rumanian. Morocco's Kateb Yacine has received attention through Parisian productions of his *Le Cadavre encerclé* (Paris: Editions du Seuil, 1959) and other plays. General surveys of the North African theatre with excellent documentation can be found in Jacob M. Landau, *Studies in the Arab Theatre and Cinema* (Philadelphia: University of Pennsylvania Press, 1958) and in Arlette Roth, *Le Théâtre algérien de langue dialectale, 1926–1954* (Paris: François Maspero, 1967). The French-language theatre of North and West Africa is covered in Lilyan Kesteloot, *Les Écrivains noirs de langue française: naissance d'une littérature* (Brussels: Université Libre de Bruxelles, 1965), and the same author's *Anthologie négro-africaine* (Verviers: Marabout-Université, 1967).

Farther to the south the stages of the Congo (Kinshasa) are dominated almost exclusively by European plays by French and Belgian writers. By contrast, in the Malagasy Republic off East Africa, the poetic French-language plays of Jacques Rabemananjara (who was recently appointed that country's Minister of Foreign Affairs) have long been well received.

Rhodesia and Portuguese-speaking Africa have not produced significant theatres as yet, but South Africa has at least two different types of dramatic activity. The Afrikaans and English-language theatres are for white-minority audiences and are characteristically European. A newer movement, which Herbert Shore has called one of "experimental realism," is now about a decade old. Its plays deal with the social problems of South Africa, occasionally using racially mixed casts performing before racially mixed audiences. The Serpent Players, in Port Elizabeth, is the most noteworthy company of this theatre, and the fact that it is under constant attack by the government does not seem to dissuade its members. Its leader is Athol Fugard, a white South African whose excellent play on apartheid, *The Blood Knot*, has been successfully produced off-Broadway and in Chicago. (An American paperback edition was published by Odyssey Press in 1964.) Tone Brulin's *The Dogs* and Basil Warner's *The Strong Are Lonely* are other plays of this genre. Many of South Africa's best writers are in exile, among them Lewis Nkosi and Alfred Hutchinson, whose plays are contained in this anthology.

In East Africa Tsegaye Gabre-Medhin, the director of Ethiopia's Haile Selassie Theatre, has already written more than seventeen plays in Amharic. One was recently translated and published in English: *The Oda-Oak Oracle* (London: Oxford University Press, 1965). Rebecca Njau, Kenya's first female playwright, has received critical acclaim for her poetic tragedy *The Scar* (Moshi, Tanzania: Kibo Art Gallery, 1965). David Cook of the University of Makerere and Miles Lee of Radio Uganda are at work editing for Heinemanns an anthology of short plays from East Africa.

But it is in West Africa that we find a true explosion of theatrical activity. Three of the four university drama programs on the continent are in West Africa—at the universities of Ibadan (Nigeria), Ghana, and the Ivory Coast. (The fourth is in Tanzania at the University Col-

lege, Dar es Salaam, under the direction of Herbert Shore.)
Drama also exists in this region on the professional and
community theatre levels. Surely the most important playwright of all Black Africa is Wole Soyinka, who was born
in Nigeria in 1935. To date he has written ten plays (several of them produced in London, four off-Broadway, and
a greater number in the college theatres of Nigeria and the
United States), a novel, a host of poems, and two film
scripts. Readers may find his work in his collected *Five
Plays* (London: Oxford University Press, 1964). John
Pepper Clark, also of Nigeria, and of equal importance in
the English-language theatre of West Africa, is discussed
below. Duro Ladipo is a Nigerian who writes in Yoruba;
his short folk operas, which are plays of great merit, inte-
grally employing drumming and dancing, have been translated into several European languages (in English: *Three
Yoruba Plays* [Ibadan: Mbari Publications, 1964]) and performed in Berlin and London. Kola Ogunmola and Obo-
tunde Ijimere of Nigeria also write on folkloric themes, and
Obi B. Egbuna has written a good comedy about Nigerian
student life abroad. The popular traveling folk-opera theatre of Herbert Ogunde is a professional unit that performs
with equal ease in remote villages and metropolitan cen-
ters of Nigeria. Ogunde has solved the problem of losing
his well-trained actresses to marriage by marrying them all
himself. Joe de Graft and Christina Ama Ata Aidoo of
Ghana and R. Sarif Easmon of Sierra Leone have all published plays in English which have been performed in West
Africa. Efua Theodora Sutherland, the head of the Ghana
Drama Studio, is discussed below. And Guillaume Oyono
of Cameroon has seen his French-language play *Trois
prétendents . . . un mari* performed in English at the Barn
Theatre in Stony Point, New York.

By all reports, the most popular foreign authors performed in African theatres are Sophocles, Shakespeare,
Molière, and Gorki, and their plays are done in their original languages or sometimes in the regional vernacular languages. As early as 1920 Shakespeare's *Comedy of Errors*
was translated into Tswana by Solomon T. Plaatje, and in

recent years outstanding translations have been done of *Henry IV* into Tswana by Michael Ontepetse Seboni and of *Julius Caesar* into Swahili by Tanzania's distinguished president, Julius K. Nyerere (London: Oxford University Press, 1963).

Many plays which are planned as primary-school readers are written in English, French, and the vernacular languages throughout Africa today. Among the most successful West African authors of this genre are Saka Acquaye, D. Olu Olagoke, Edward Braithwaite, and Michael Dei-Anang. Another form of "educational" dramatic literature, though not intended for children, are the Nigerian popular chapbooks that are written, cheaply printed, and consumed in the market places of Onitsha and Oshogbo. Although of little literary distinction, the books have the double purpose of improving the English of rural Nigerians recently arrived in the cities and familiarizing them with city social etiquette. They are written in a difficult pidgin English and have such delightful titles as *How to Get a Lady in Love*, *Rose Only Loved My Money*, and *Why Some Rich Men Have No Trust in Some Girls*. The most prolific writers in this form are Felix N. Stephen, Speedy Eric, Thomas O. Iguh, and O. Olisah (very likely all pen names). The latter two have also written chapbook plays on the careers of Kwame Nkrumah, Patrice Lumumba, Moise Tshombe, Jomo Kenyatta, and Sylvanus Olympio. There is no doubt that these little plays will eventually be important in studying the history of ideas in Africa, and two good studies on them have already appeared: Donatus I. Nwoga, "Onitsha Market Literature," *Transition* (Uganda), IV (February, 1965), and Bernth Lindfors, "Heroes and Hero-Worship in Nigerian Chapbooks," *Journal of Popular Culture* (Lafayette, Indiana), I (Summer, 1967).

Some knowledge about Africa and the value systems of its many different cultures would be of considerable help to the reader of these plays. It was, in fact, my original plan to have each drama prefaced by an Africanist anthropologist's statement concerning the traditions involved in the work. But since this documentation proved impossible to arrange, the plays must, and can, stand by themselves. Persons wishing to produce one of them on the stage, however, will doubtless want to do substantial library research on the particular culture from which the play comes.

Just as some of the meaning of these plays will be hidden to the Westerner, some attitudes and literary techniques are shown that would surely be foreign to an African audience ignorant of twentieth-century international dramatic literature. We may well ask, then, to whom the African playwrights address their plays. Most African literary works are still published in London or Paris and therefore are directed to an international audience. Conscious of this, the African writer may slant the content of his work to attract the interest of the publisher's editorial advisers, sensationally depicting wherever possible the exotic tribal customs and religious rituals of his own or a neighboring people. John Povey, in "Canons of Criticism for Neo-African Literature," *Proceedings of a Conference on African Languages and Literatures held at Northwestern University, April 28–30 1966* (Evanston: Northwestern University Press, 1966), has noted that many Western and African critics have accused African writers of being too documentarian. Yet he argues that though he would not wish to defend a literary work conceived by its author as a piece of anthropology, i.e., a work in which "characters may exist largely in order to expose the details of their unusual background, not as human beings," such emphasis on local color may be necessary because the writer cannot assume much information in the part of his reading audience. This problem does not, I think, hold for the plays in this volume, nor for that matter, for most African drama. The very nature of the dramatic form, as opposed to the heavily descriptive narrative, almost precludes it.

The arts have always been an integral part of African society. They have not existed for their own sake or as essentially decorative elements, as in the West, but rather for the sake of man and society. As a result African critics place great emphasis on the functional worth of an art object: how is this play "good" or appropriate for the present social situation of our people?* There are critics who say, too, that the modern African writer cannot, like the traditional tribal poet, express the "collective African soul," but is limited to his individual voice, which merely expresses his own experiences and interpretations of mankind. What we encounter in these arguments is in part a variation of a critical principle widely held in the emerging countries of the world: any work of art that does not display the "reality" of the country's social milieu is nonvalid. While this belief may act as a kind of strait jacket, restraining writers from treating themes other than those related to contemporary social ills, it may be claimed that such literature can increase the cultural integrity of a people and probably even help eradicate those social ills. For the African writer totally immersed in the European tradition, however, literature and the theatre become self-justifying and completely independent of nationalistic and other external values. Each writer must ultimately make the difficult decision as to the audience he wishes to reach, and whether he will accept, reject, or modify its critical standards. And what of *négritude*, that attempt to resurrect the African past and discard what its believers consider as worthless in European culture?† Its influence is confined almost entirely to the French-speaking part of Africa, and it is generally disdained in English-speaking Africa. Wole Soyinka has put it succinctly: "A tiger does not have to proclaim his tigritude."

With the exception of the unique folk opera, African dramatists have for the most part used European dramatic forms. But almost to a man they have made the content of their plays distinctively African in setting, theme, and spirit. The following list of themes found on the continent is only a brief and tentative sampling:

* See, for example, *Le Théâtre négro-africain et ses fonctions sociales* (Paris: Présence Africaine, 1958), by Bakary Traoré, currently the editor of *Le Mali* in Bamako.

† See Leopold Sédar Senghor, "Negro-African Aesthetics," *Diogenes* (Paris and Montreal), No. 16 (Winter, 1956).

1. the conflict between the old (tribal) and new (urbanized) way of living
2. alienation upon the return to a birthplace
3. rejection and acceptance by oneself and others
4. the conflict between blacks and whites
5. symbolism taken from folklore
6. the "white-man-listen" message
7. superstition and backwardness in the country
8. the stories of the past against which the new values of the nation may be measured
9. corruption among politicians and civil servants
10. materialism
11. the problem of sterility
12. feminine emancipation
13. the conflict of generations

More than thirty Black African nations have gained their independence in the past decade, and assassinations, military coups, rigged elections, and corruption are not unknown in their dramas. In most of these plays, too, the image of the white man is not a pleasant one. His portrayal ranges from the innocent white who cannot possibly understand what the black man is thinking, or even appreciate his sentiments, to the truly antagonistic white government official, who through his ignorance of tribal customs, or his English or Boer pigheadedness, brings death and destruction to many people.

The English language used in these plays and in the literature as a whole is not that spoken in America or Great Britain. It is African English—a language which is effective English but which also captures African speech idioms. English is a second language for all of these writers, and they bring to it a distinctive phraseology and grammatical structure born in the cities and shanty towns of Africa that may at first startle more conventional writers of the tongue. Ezekiel Mphahlele, the South African novelist, has said that African writers are "doing violence to standard English," by which he meant that they are bringing a new experience to the language. In using the English language with such originality they are enriching it. If one occasionally discovers a cliché, the result of a cultural and time lag in language, it is usually less important than the entirely novel and vigorous way the language is used. This is particularly the case in the sensuous imagery of the poetic plays of Clark and Soyinka, who are doing more to bring poetry back into the English-language theatre than the most important playwrights in the West. The Modern Language Association's conference originally called "British Commonwealth Literature" changed its name in 1967 to the "Conference on World Literature in English," in order to include writers in Asia, Africa, and the Caribbean who are using English for literary expression. The group is also planning a reader for use in high schools containing selections from such literature. Purists who claim that there will always be only one true English litertaure forget that two centuries ago American independence gave rise to a second dialect in English and ultimately to a second distinct branch of literary expression in the language. They forget, too, that the situation of multiple national literatures within a nation is now commonplace: Canada has literature of English and French expression; India can count its literature in fifteen different languages, including Indo-English; and even Yiddish literature, studied across national boundaries, allows for certain linguistically distinct currents within the mainstream.

More writing for the theatre is bound to come from Africa in the years ahead. The drama, significantly enough, is perhaps the most suitable form of literary expression for the African writer. As Michael Crowder has suggested in "Tradition and Change in Nigerian Literature" (*Tri-Quarterly* [Evanston, Illinois], No. 5 [1966]), it offers the otherwise isolated African artist direct audience contact and response and the opportunity to bring together literature, music, singing, and dancing—links to the oral literature of his tradition that are unavailable to the novelist and poet. While Western readers and theatregoers may miss certain esoteric overtones or levels of meaning, I believe that on the whole the plays which follow meet the requirements of dramatic and theatrical effectiveness. The writers of this young, energetic, and ambitious literature have succeeded in expressing individual cultural experiences that are at the same time universal. Their settings may be African, but their emotional communications are international. It is no coincidence that a good, localized work of art is always internationally understood. Some things do not change; it is just the way they are seen that does.

Those who wish to gain a broad critical picture of contemporary African literature in general should see: Janheinz Jahn, *Muntu, An Outline of the New African Culture* (New York: Grove Press, 1961), and the same author's *A Bibliography of Neo-African Writing* (New York: Frederick A. Praeger, 1965); Anne Tibble, *African-English Literature, A Short Survey and Anthology of Prose and Poetry up to 1965* (London: Peter Owen, 1965); Ulli Beier, ed., *An Introduction to African Literature* (Evanston: Northwestern University Press, 1967); Gerald Moore, ed., *African Literature and the Universities* (Ibadan: Ibadan University Press, 1965); and J.A. Ramsaran, *New Approaches to African Literature* (Ibadan: Ibadan University Press, 1965). Trying to keep up to date with theatre activities in Africa and the relevant scholarship is a difficult task for Westerners. The only publications that regularly carry such news are *World Theatre* and *The Afro-Asian Theatre Bulletin.*

The present collection of plays from modern Africa was formed with the double intention of introducing the play-reading public to the best (by Western standards) dramatic writing in Africa today and providing theatre companies with a selection of highly stageable plays from Africa. Many unusually good plays had to be excluded because of the inability to locate their authors for permissions, or because of the limitations of space. All of the plays are by Negro authors, and all were originally written in English. There are serious and comic plays, full-length and one-act plays. In subject matter, I have attempted to choose plays which in part represent the concerns of modern Africans: the problems of the "transitional" person torn between the differing values of the traditional tribal society and the modern industrialized world; the dilemma of sterility; the mixed blessing of the presence of the white man in Africa; and the struggle of man—against the elements, against the inexplicable and mysterious powers in the universe, and against corruption among his fellow men. These concerns, of course, are not merely African. And these plays, speaking across national and natural boundaries, tell us something of what it is to be human.

I should like to acknowledge here the encouragement and advice given during the last five years by the following friends and associates: Alan Taylor, Alan Merriam, and Roy Sieber, all of Indiana University; Rosamond Gilder, Herbert Shore, Henry Wells, and other members of the American Educational Theatre Association's Afro-Asian Theatre Project; John Povey of U.C.L.A. and Robert Armstrong of Northwestern University; Joe Adedeji of Ibadan University; and my University of Kansas colleagues Robert Cobb, Clark Coan, and Thomas Buckman.

F.M.L.

*Lawrence, Kansas*

# THE RHYTHM OF VIOLENCE

*by*

## LEWIS NKOSI

*For Janet, Frances, and Margot,*
*who made South Africa bearable*

© Oxford University Press 1964

# THE RHYTHM OF VIOLENCE

*by*

## LEWIS NKOSI

*For Janet, Frances, and Margot,*
*who made South Africa bearable*

© Oxford University Press 1964

# CHARACTERS

JAN
JIMMY ("WHITE BOY")
JOJOZI
KITTY
PIET
CHRIS
TULA
JULIE
LILI
GAMA ("AFRICAN BOY")
SLOWFOOT
MARY
SARIE

"AFRICAN BOY" and "WHITE BOY" are the same characters as GAMA and JIMMY before they are referred to by name.

NOTE: For those unfamiliar with Afrikaans, the approximate phonetic sound for the letter *g* in the Afrikaans expletive *Ag* corresponds to the German guttural *ch*.

# THE RHYTHM OF VIOLENCE

## ACT ONE

### SCENE I

*The city of Johannesburg in the early 60's. It is just before sunset and the sky is an explosion of orange colours. The city has burst into a savage jungle of multicoloured neon lights, fluorescing nervously with a come-hither bitchiness of a city at sundown.*

*The foreground of the stage comprises the waiting room of the Johannesburg City Hall. What we see of the city shows through the huge glass windows which open to the city square. Through the windows we can see the silhouette shape of an African standing on a raised platform and gesticulating wildly, as though he were addressing a meeting. From left, near the back of the stage, is a door with a flight of steps leading to other chambers on the top floors of the municipal building. A door on the extreme right of the stage provides an exit to the street.*

*In the waiting room there are benches and a table piled high with magazines for visitors who wish to browse. On the right, a few paces back from the door, is a public telephone. The waiting room has been temporarily turned into the headquarters of the South African police who are mobilized to watch the African meeting in progress. The first clue we have of this is a police hat, a machine-gun, and a revolver in a waist-strap, all lying on the bench in the empty room.*

*The action begins with the sound of jazz rhythms, curiously nervous, and at times decidedly neurotic; even when subtly controlled and easygoing, the beat suggests a tenuous quality of insanity and nightmares. Jazz sounds will be used throughout wherever possible, interpolated between dialogues whenever it seems dramatically necessary.*

*When the play opens, the neon and the traffic lights, seen through the high windows, are going on and off to the rhythm of jazz music, also helping to emphasize the hysterical quality of the scene.*

*Finally, the music softens into a subtly controlled, provocative beat and then subsides completely as the roar of the offstage crowd, holding a meeting in the city square, mounts to a crescendo. There are shouts of the slogans "AFRICA!" "FREEDOM IN OUR LIFETIME," etc.*

*Presently, a young policeman in khaki uniform sallies from left, down the flight of steps, to the anteroom. He is weighted down by a heavy machine-gun which he carries menacingly with one hand while with the other he holds a big bone from which he is nibbling a piece of meat. He rushes to the door on right; but as he grabs the door knob, another policeman, somewhat older than he, emerges from the left and shouts nervously at him.*

PIET. Jan! Jan! Wait!

*The young policeman turns. He has a handsome, florid face suffused with a passionate zeal of youth. From time to time the scene is acted with a dreamlike unreality, a constant effort on the part of the people involved to detach themselves from the reality that engages them.*

JAN [*facing the older policeman*]. What is it, Piet?

PIET. Where are you running to, man! [*They speak in heavy German-like accents peculiar to South African Boers.*]

JAN. Ag, man, I though these Natives was starting trouble already!

PIET. Now, take it easy, Jan! You heard what the Major said. As long as they don't start anything, stay out of sight!

JAN [*dubiously*]. Yah, I know. [*Furiously.*] They drive me out of my mind! Yelling "Freedom!" "Freedom!" "Freedom!"

PIET [*pacing the floor*]. Me, too!

*JAN places the machine-gun on the bench and sits down next to it, giving his entire attention to the bone at which he nibbles. His back is against the window and the city square.*

*A voice from the square is heard enunciating clearly.*

VOICE.

Sons and daughters of Africa!
Everywhere on this continent black men are stirring!
From Cape to Cairo, from Morocco to Mozambique,
Africans are shouting "Freedom!"

That one word, friends, strikes fear in the hearts of the
white people of this country. At its mention they clutch
their guns!

JAN, *who had quickly clutched the machine-gun when the
voice was first heard, grins sheepishly and replaces the
machine-gun on the bench and returns to his bone.*

JAN. Ag, they're just talking. What can they do without the
guns!

PIET [*with less conviction*]. Natives love talking. It's their
habit!

JAN [*nervously*]. How many of us are here?

PIET. Two hundred men at the ready to shoot down any
bloody-son-of-a-bitchin' kaffir who starts trouble! [*He
takes the revolver which has been lying on the bench and
straps it around his waist, then sits next to* JAN *on the
bench with back to the window and facing the audience.*]

JAN. You think that number is enough?

PIET. We are armed and the kaffirs haven't got guns!

JAN. That's right, they haven't got guns!

PIET [*stands up and points at the silhouette in the square*].
That's Gama up there shooting his bloody filthy mouth
off! Thinks he's something, black bastard!

JAN. We ought to be out there at the square just to show
them we won't stand no nonsense!

PIET. No, that's no good! They like showing off when they
see the police!

JAN. Piet, what do you think they would do if . . . [*He
abruptly drops the question.*]

PIET. If what happened?

JAN. Ag, better not talk about it! They'll never do anything!

VOICE [*enunciating again*]. Friends, I ask you: What do

these stubborn men trust when they flout the whole world, when they continue to keep you in subjection against all reason and advice? I'll tell you what they trust: guns! They think they can handle trouble! But can they rule by the gun forever? [*There is a resounding "NO" from the crowd.*] That's right, friends, the answer is: NO! They can only keep you slaves so long as you want to remain slaves.

JAN [*has grabbed the machine-gun and is walking about nervously*]. Bloody bastard!

PIET. It's all talk! Talk! Talk!

JAN [*sitting down and nibbling at his bone again*].   Yah, what can they do without guns!

*Longer pause.*

PIET. Black Sams! Why don't they do somethin' so we can handle this once and for all! They're wearing me down, man, wearing me down!

*The telephone rings and both men grab their guns nervously, then rush to the telephone.* PIET *talks.*

PIET. Yes, Major. No! No! It's all quiet. Yah, they're just talking, making sound and fury! No, I beg your pardon, Major, I didn't mean to make a joke! Yes, sir. Yes, sir. We'll keep an eye on them, sir. Yes, sir. Good-bye, sir. [*Turning savagely to* JAN.] Well, how do you like that! We can't even make a joke about it anymore! No time for jokes, he says! Everybody behaves as though the Natives was just about to take over the country!

JAN. Was that Major Ludorf?

PIET. I'll kiss my arse if it wasn't! [*Looking across the square.*] How long are they goin' to keep this up anyway?

JAN. Till somebody has guts to stop these demonstrations, goddammit! Natives start talking like this and before you know it they are in control!

PIET. It's the blerry English and their City Council! If this was a Boer town, nothing like this would ever happen! We'd stop those blinkin' bastards before they'd even have time to open their traps!

JAN. The English don't know nothing about handling Natives! Look what happened in Kenya! Look what happens in Rhodesia now! That's what they get for mollycoddling the Natives!

PIET [*sitting down*]. Hey, Janie, give me a bit there, man! Never had anything to eat since this morning. [*Wearily.*] They are sure keeping us busy!

JAN. And give it back. [*Gives him the bone.*]

PIET [*munching*]. Hey, Janie, you ever shot a Native before? [*Makes panning movement with the bone.*] Ta-ta-ta-ta-ta-ta-ta!

JAN. [*grinning*]. Yah, it's kind-a funny, you know, like shooting wild duck!

PIET. The first time is not easy though!

JAN. Telling me! The first time I shot a Native dead I got sick! Just stood there and threw up! His skull was ripped apart by the machine-gun! I stood over him and got sick all over his body!

PIET. Ugh, man! Got sick over him! It's not enough you rip open a kaffir's skull! You must get sick over him too!

JAN [*pacing the floor*]. When I got home, I still got sick!

PIET [*walks over to him*]. Hey, you look as if you want to get sick again! Now, remember, I'm eating! It's not nice!

JAN [*angrily snatching the bone away*]. And who said eat all of it?

PIET. Ag, man, don't be like that! What's the matter with you?

JAN. What's the matter with you?

PIET. Okay, don't shout! You're nervous!

JAN. Who's nervous? Here, have all of it if you must. Pig!

PIET. For Christ's sake, Janie! Shoot all the damn Natives if you want, but leave me alone! I was only eating a bone and you start talking about shooting Natives an' looking as if you want to get sick. Then I ask you nicely, Don't get sick! Now, what's wrong with that!

JAN. I'm not goin' to get sick! That's what's wrong with it!

PIET. All right! All right! You aren't goin' to get sick! You were only telling a story! Don't jump on me!

JAN. You are always making a fool of me!

PIET. You're just a sensitive son-a-fa-bitch!

JAN. I'm a human being! And I'm just as tough as you are!

PIET. You're nervous, man; calm down!

JAN. Who's nervous!

PIET. I meant you're sensitive; now don't go an' jump on me again.

JAN. That's right. I'm a sensitive human being. That's what my grandma always said I was. Sensitive.

PIET. I'm not. I'm academic.

JAN. What does that mean?

PIET. Means a bloke who is a realist. No emotion. I can shoot any number of Natives without getting sick. No emotions! I shoot them academically.

JAN. Nice word . . . academically.

PIET. I got it from a sergeant down at Marshall Square. He used to say, when you get into a fight with Natives, don't let your feelings run away with you. Be academic. Shoot them down academically.

VOICE [*enunciating from the square*]. For years we have been waiting for action from the Congress leadership. For years we have heard nothing but speeches and rhetoric. Friends, today the young people are seizing the reins, and we promise you plenty action! [JAN *and* PIET *seize their guns and stand attentively at the window.*] Whether the struggle will turn into a violent one or not, we say that depends on the South African police. In any case, the issue is an *academic* one. [JAN *looks at* PIET *and grins. That seems to relax them; they sit down.*] Today, here and now, we pledge ourselves to act! Before you all we resolve to strike a blow against apartheid! From now on, we are serving notice on these arrogant men that we can no longer tolerate white domination, subjugation, and repression at their hands. When the blow will be struck, I don't know. It may be sooner than they think.

Tonight! Tomorrow, or the following day, but the blow shall be struck!

JAN *jumps up.*

JAN. That is incitement! He can go to jail for that!

PIET. Take it easy, man! The Secret Police are taking notes! They know what they are doing.

JAN. They're always twiddling their thumbs until it's too late to act. Then we have to do the dirty job!

PIET. Gama is just a fool student! Going to a white man's university has gone to his head. Now he thinks of himself as bloody Lumumba or Nkrumah!

JAN. Just an ape with a big mouth. There won't be no bloody Nkrumahs here! We can take care of them.

PIET [*played with dreamlike detachment*]. The sun is going down.

JAN. I don't like to see the sun setting.

PIET. I don't mind the sunset. . . . It's the sunrise I hate. The beginning of a new day.

JAN. What's wrong with the beginning of a new day?

PIET [*pacing the floor*]. "What's wrong with the beginning of a new day?" he asks! I don't know! Why should I know!

JAN. What's the matter with you? You're getting jumpy!

PIET. I don't know what I'm shouting for! Forget it.

JAN. Okay.

PIET [*reflectively*]. A new day . . . it's always uncertain. Sunset is all right. . . . May get a bit cold after, but it's all right!

JAN. My son loves sunrise. He loves to get up and catch the rays of the sun on his small hands and play with it. My old man used to say, "That kid is playing with his future." Funny thing to say to a child!

PIET *moves to the window to catch the pale rays of the setting sun with his hand. He plays with them for a while. As he plays absentmindedly, we hear the sad strains of jazz.* PIET *turns to* JAN *finally.*

PIET. It's so beautiful on the hands and yet you can't hold it.

JAN. What is it you can't hold?

PIET. The rays of the setting sun.

JAN [*stubbornly*]. I hate sunset!

PIET. Why? Sunset is pretty.

JAN. Pretty? . . . Sun goes down! Gets damp and cold, and some of your future goes too.

PIET. Nothing lasts forever. If the sun never set, the day would be unbearable.

JAN. But there would be no future to worry about.

PIET [*as an idea strikes him*]. Hey, that's funny! That's a funny idea! And maybe we wouldn't grow old either.

JAN. We'd just go on ruling this land and the Natives would do like they're told! Forever!

PIET [*grinning happily*]. And we wouldn't worry about tomorrow.

JAN. That's right! It would be a long, long day. Time just standing still!

PIET. And we'd go to work maybe and come back and eat and make love and just go on working.

JAN. Ag, it's just a dream, man.

PIET. Yah, I suppose so.

JAN. Even if there was no future, some damn fool would invent a future.

PIET. That's right! Some damn stupid professor or Communist fool would invent Time. And sooner or later you would have a call for lesser working hours and cries of more wages from the bloody Natives . . . and then riots.

*Blackout.*

## SCENE II

*Same as Scene I.* PIET *and* JAN *are occupying the waiting room. There is a knock at the door, which interrupts their conversation. A young African, looking shy and uncertain, makes his appearance. He carries a pile of signed petitions in his hand. At the sight of the two policemen he comes to a stop near the door. The police stare at him open-mouthed.*

JAN. Good God! Piet, do you see what I see?

PIET [*staring at* TULA]. No, Jan, I don't. What do you see?

JAN. Look closely, Piet. You think it's just my eyes?

PIET [*straining his eyes*]. I think it's your eyes, Jan.

JAN. I could swear I saw a kaffir standing by the door. Now, I'm not so sure. Look closely, Piet. Don't you see some kind of animal standing by the doorway?

PIET [*long pause*]. Now that you say so, Jan, I can see something.

JAN. What does it look like to you, Piet?

PIET. You really want to know, Jan?

JAN. I really want to know, Piet.

PIET. It looks like an ape to me.

TULA *stands there, not daring to move any further.*

JAN. Thanks, Piet, that's all I wanted to know because that's exactly what it looks like to me. A goddam ape! [TULA *gathers enough courage to approach the two policemen.* JAN *waves him to a standstill.*] Don't come any closer, kaffir. There's already an awful stink in here! What do you want?

TULA. I am a representative of the Left Student Association, and I've been delegated to submit these petitions personally to the Mayor's office.

JAN. Piet!

PIET. Yes, Jan.

JAN. You hear that?

PIET. No, I didn't hear it, Jan.

JAN. Kaffir, say that again so the baas can hear you.

TULA. I represent the Left Student Association, and I've been asked to deliver these petitions to the Mayor's office.

JAN. Piet!

PIET. Yes, Jan.

JAN. Are you listening?

PIET. I'm listening, Jan.

JAN. This Native boy here says he's come to deliver petitions.

*From here the scene is played with affected boredom, which conceals a streak of potential violence.*

PIET. I heard him, Jan. Maybe he don't mean any harm, Jan. Ask him again if he's sure he wants to deliver anything.

JAN. Boy, are you sure you want to deliver these petitions?

TULA. That's what I came for, sir.

JAN [*jumping up*]. Watch your tongue, kaffir, when you talk to me! You hear? Don't provoke me!

TULA. No, sir, I didn't mean to, sir!

JAN. You better not, kaffir! I'm baas to you! Don't "sir" me! I'm no bloody English!

TULA. Yes, baas!

JAN. Okay, let's start from the beginning. You came here to present the petitions. Is that right?

TULA. Yes, baas.

JAN. Your organization got complaints to make. Is that right?

TULA. Yes, baas. We've decided to register protests about the colour-bar in the major social and cultural institutions of the city of Johannesburg.

JAN. Piet, did you hear that?

PIET. No, Jan, I didn't hear that.

JAN. This boy here says his organization got a complaint.

PIET. I don't think he would say such a thing, Jan. Are you sure this boy said that? Ask him again, Jan. This boy looks reasonable to me. He almost looks too smart for a Native. I'm sure he would never say such a thing. Ask him again.

JAN. Boy, you said that, didn't you? You came here to pro-test against something.

TULA. Yes, baas, on behalf of my organization.

JAN. That's right. [*To* PIET.] This boy, Piet, has come to protest. What's the fancy word you used, boy? To *register* protest?

TULA. Yes, baas.

JAN. That's right. This boy, Piet, has come to "register" protest.

PIET. To register protest about what?

JAN. I don't know. About the colour-bar! [*Scornfully.*] . . . "in the major social and cultural institutions of the city of Johannesburg." Am I quoting you right, boy?

TULA. Yes, sir. [JAN *stares evilly at him.*] Yes, baas.

JAN. I thought you were forgetting, boy. I told you not to "sir" me!

TULA. I'm sorry, baas!

JAN. So I *am* quoting you right. Piet, I'm quoting this boy right. This boy has come to register protest about the colour-bar in the major social and cultural institutions in the city of Johannesburg.

PIET. Doesn't he like the colour-bar? Jan, doesn't this boy like the colour-bar?

JAN. I don't know, Piet. Maybe he doesn't. Maybe he was led astray by other student Communists.

PIET. Ask him, Jan, just to make sure. Ask him if he doesn't like the colour-bar or something.

JAN. Boy, don't you like the colour-bar? Take your time. Don't say anything you don't mean. Maybe you don't like the colour-bar?

TULA. No, baas, I don't like the colour-bar. My organiza-tion is hostile to any kind of colour-bar.

JAN [*suspicious*]. "Hostile"? What's hostile?

TULA. It means my organization is violently opposed to apartheid or the colour-bar.

JAN. Opposed! Why the hell don't you say so? You like the fancy words, don't you?

TULA. No, baas.

JAN. Okay, I'm not against the fancy words myself. So we'll use your big word. Your organization is "hostile" to the colour-bar?

TULA. Yes, baas.

JAN. Piet, this boy here is hostile to the colour-bar.

PIET. That's very unfortunate. Very unfortunate! [*He stands up and walks to where* TULA *is standing.*] Boy, you don't like the colour-bar?

TULA. No, baas.

PIET. Would you like to marry a white girl? [TULA *is caught unexpectedly by the question. His honesty prevents him from giving a simple answer.* PIET *flares up suddenly.*] Yes or no? Boy, can't you answer a simple question?

TULA. That would depend on many things, baas.

PIET. Like what?

TULA. Well, sir, like whether she is the right girl to marry. Whether she is intelligent or——

PIET [*interrupting*]. Look, boy! You think you're smart, eh? You think you're clever?

TULA. No, sir!

PIET. Well, you're not! You're a damn stupid Native if ever I saw one! Stupid! [*He holds* TULA *by the lapels of his coat and is shaking him against the wall.*] All Natives are bloody stupid! You hear that? You can go back and tell that to your organization. [*He seizes the petitions from* TULA *and scatters them on the floor.* TULA *moves toward the door.*] Wait a minute! Where do you think you're going? [*He takes out his police logbook, which he holds ostentatiously in front of him.*] What is your name?

TULA. Tula.

PIET. Tula? Your second name, kaffir!

TULA. Tula Zulu.

PIET. [PIET's *jaw slackens*.] Ah, I see. Is Gama your brother? The fool who's always shooting his mouth off at meetings? Speak, boy! Is that damn fool out there your precious brother?

TULA. Yes, that's my brother.

PIET. Well, get the hell out of here! And you can tell your brother he won't get away with anything! Tell him we're watching him! Tell him that! And get the hell out of here! [TULA *gets out*.] Bloody kaffirs! They're all Communists before they even learn to say ah! Janie, you keep a look out while I go and get some coffee for us.

JAN. Okay, Piet.

PIET [*going out through left*]. It will soon be cold.

JAN *sits alone. We hear a weird jazz melody accompanied by strong drums, evocative of death ceremonies. JAN moves about uneasily. The setting sun is playing on his face, since it is coming directly through the window out of which he is sometimes peering.*

*Blackout.*


## SCENE III

*Same as before. JAN and PIET are sitting on the bench, drinking coffee from big mugs.*

JAN. Ah, twilight!

PIET. And soon it will be night.

JAN. It's hateful!

PIET. A man needs some sleep! Damn it!

JAN. And that's the danger! . . . Sleep . . . Anybody can go to sleep on this bloody continent but the white man. Always he must stand guard!

PIET. We're standing guard over the future.

JAN. I know, but whose future? Ours or theirs?

PIET. Ours! Why do you say that? So long as we stand
    guard, there is no danger.

JAN. I don't know, Piet! All I know is this is wearin' me
    down, goddammit! While we stand guard, we cannot
    sleep! It's wearin' me down, I tell you.

PIET. Look, Jan, this is US or THEM!

JAN. Yah, I know, but it's still wearin' me down.

PIET. Always the white man must be on the alert. There's
    nothing else we can do!

JAN [speaks softly to himself]. Sometimes I wish all this
    was over somehow. . . . To walk in the sun once more!
    To walk in the shadows of the trees and under the moon
    at night . . . goddammit, to relax. Just to relax!

PIET [agitated]. Will you stop shouting!

JAN [aroused from his reverie]. Who is shouting? I didn't
    shout.

PIET. You didn't? Ag, maybe it's just my ears. Hell, I
    don't know what's wrong with me today.

JAN. It's nerves, man, nerves!

PIET. Are you implying that I'm frightened of THEM?

JAN. I'm not implying anything.

PIET. Maybe you are! Maybe you are not! But if you think
    I'm frightened, you are fumbling around in the dark,
    because I'm not! I can handle any number of Natives!
    Any number! Ten! Twenty! Fifty! Hundred! You think
    you know me! I'm a terror to Natives!

JAN. Hey, what's the matter with you all of a sudden?

PIET. I just don't want you to imply anything! Maybe
    you are nervous; I'm not! [A glint in his eye.] Once when
    we were on patrol in Sophiatown, THEY came! I tell
    you THEY came! It was night. Dark. And their shadows
    were darker than the dark itself. I was separated from the
    others! Alone! You understand that? Alone! You ever
    been alone with Death staring you in the eye? Well, I
    was! I started firing from my sten-gun. But those Natives
    kept on coming! It was like eternity, and the dark shad-

ows kept coming like the waves of eternal night. . . . Ah, but a sten-gun spits death much stronger than a thousand Natives! When it was all over, I couldn't stop shooting. I was no longer in control of my fingers. The sten-gun kept barking in the dark . . . against shadows . . . anything that moved. I began to think that even if my son had appeared there, I would have kept shooting away. . . . [*He calms down at the thought.*] I don't know what I am saying.

JAN. *I* know.

*Pause.*

VOICE [*in the square*]. Tonight! Maybe tomorrow!

MOB [*yells back*]. Why not tonight?

VOICE. Who knows, maybe tonight! Maybe tomorrow! Or the next day!

MOB. Tonight, why not tonight?

VOICE. We must learn to use their language. Say neither this nor that. Keep them guessing! That is why I say to you, "maybe"!

JAN. What does he mean? These Natives are playing with fire.

PIET. It's Gama. . . . He is all mouth and nothing much else.

JAN. He talks dangerous words.

PIET. He learned to talk like that at the big university up there on top of the hill. But he's all talk.

JAN. I hear the Government is going to stop them from going to the white universities.

PIET. High time too.

JAN. Think of that! I never even went to a university.

PIET. A white man does not need to go. Whatever that fool up there says, he's still a Native. He can't change the colour of his skin.

JAN. Yah! [*Laughs.*] God, he can't! Some even use face creams to try to look lighter than they are.

Piet. And straighten their hair! Honestly, it's disgusting! Don't they have pride?

Jan. No, whatever they say, they all want to be white. They all want to marry white girls. You know, sometimes I lie awake at night and try to imagine what it would be like to be born black, and I start having nightmares. 'Stru's God, I'm glad I was born white!

Piet. To be black! A curse, I tell you, it's a curse! Honest, Janie, what would you do if you woke up with a black skin?

Jan [they have shifted into a playful mood]. Ugh! Then I would start moving from my neighbourhood.

Piet. You'd have to move very early in the morning before the neighbours get up. . . . Which black township would you go to? Alexandra?

Jan. Too many goddam thugs there. Every day some black bastard is murdered there.

Piet. Western Native Township? It's not bad.

Jan. Ag, it stinks. You can't walk down a street without getting a mouthful of dust. No, not Western, for Chrissakes. Native townships stink.

Piet. If you turned black, you would have to live somewhere. Orlando, maybe. Or Meadowlands!

Jan. Hey, better not joke about this. I get pimples just thinking about it. [Pause.] I'll tell you what, though. Natives don't mind these places. Natives can live anywhere! No joke, Natives are a marvel to me!

Piet. That's right, but you would be a Native too, and therefore, you wouldn't mind!

Jan. And suppose Natives go on strike?

Piet. Hey, suppose that? Would you join in, Janie, just like a goddam troublemaker?

Jan. I would have no choice in the matter. . . . Hey, an' you know what? I would be the leader! I'm a born leader, so I would be a Native leader, right there in the forefront, fightin' for rights! Christ! Can you see me wearing a black face and leading all the damn Natives down to City Hall, shaking my fists and speechifying like hell. I would be a terror to all the goddam whites in this city!

PIET. And I would be a police major, Janie. I would stand there with my men armed to the teeth an' say, who is the leader of this procession?

*They slowly submerge themselves in the roles they are playing.*

JAN. I, Tom Lundula, am the leader of the procession. . . . Hey, that would be a good name for a trusted Native leader! A militant Native leader! [*Savouring the name.*] Tom Lundula!

PIET. Well, Tom Lundula, step forward and let me have a look at you. [JAN *steps forward stiffly.*] You look an intelligent Native to me, Tom Lundula. Maybe I'm wrong, but you look like a well-mannered Native who knows his responsibilities.

JAN. I'm flattered that you think so, sir. Under different circumstances you and I would be good friends, but this is hardly the time!

PIET. As I was saying, you look like a moderate Native who knows the laws of the land. And you know that leading thousands of Natives into the city like this without a written permission from the Chief of Police is a punishable offence.

JAN. We know the laws of the white man, Major Ludorf. We've made a career out of studying the laws of the white man.

PIET. I thought you were a clever Native, Lundula. I thought so. Also I knew that even a clever man can be misguided at times. You know, wrong advice can be given to him, which leads him into the ways of folly.

JAN. Sir, you mistake our mission. We come not to get advice from the Chief of Police. We come here—I and my people—come here to present demands to the City Hall, and unless those demands are met, not one of my men is going back to work.

PIET. Be careful about your tongue, Lundula. A clever man like you should not let his tongue get out of hand. . . . Last year you led a demonstration and the Mayor's flowers got trampled down by thousands of your men, but we understood the nature of your desperation. This year there will be no understanding if you lead your men any further than where you are.

JAN. You will not let us proceed to the City Hall, sir, to present our grievances?

PIET. It is my duty to prevent trouble in the city. There are riots all over Africa these days. A tiny thing can grow into a conflagration. Do you understand that word: CONFLAGRATION? It means big trouble. And things like riots are like a disease in Africa. They sort of spread. We are here to see to it that the disease should not spread to these parts, Lundula. In South Africa Natives are happy with things as they are so long as the likes of you leave them alone. And my job is to see to it that you leave them alone.

JAN. Sir, we intend to proceed to the City Hall. My men will be peaceful and orderly. We are peaceful and non-violent people, sir. We don't believe in shedding blood. We don't like the sight of blood, sir. It makes us sick. If you will let us proceed, sir, we will present our demands and then go home in a peaceful, non-violent fashion.

PIET. You will advance no further than where you are, Lundula. Those are orders!

JAN. You realize the gravity of the situation, sir?

PIET. Up to now I've been talking to you like an equal, Tom Lundula, but I'm running out of patience.

JAN. If there is violence, sir, you will assume every responsibility for it.

PIET. If you go home, there will be no violence!

JAN. I and my people don't like violence, sir. As you see, we are unarmed. Your men are armed. That is because we don't like the sight of blood; it makes us sick to look at blood.

Piet. Tom Lundula, I give you and your men three minutes
to get the hell out of here. Three minutes! If you haven't
dispersed by then, it will be my painful duty to order
my men to clear the streets!

Jan. Three minutes, sir! How can twenty thousand people
disperse in three minutes?

Piet. That is your problem to solve! You brought them
here. Now you can take them back!

Jan [*in a pompous manner, as he imagines an African
leader would do; he faces an imaginary African crowd*].
Sons and daughters of Africa! As always when we try to
present our grievances to the oppressors, to these fascists,
we always meet with arrogance, stupidity, and plain
brute force! Today as before they will not let us proceed
to the City Hall; they will not let your foul breaths defile
the Mayor's parlour; they will not let you, and they are
threatening to shoot if you will proceed any further.
   But, I will tell you this, friends: there will be a day
soon when they will want to listen to you, when they
will want to talk to you, but that will be too late! I
know they will say I'm inciting you and put me in jail
for it; but when a man says that someday it's going to
rain, is he inciting it to rain or is he merely saying what
will come to pass? No! . . . That is why I say to you
someday you're going to raise your fists against your dic-
tators, against these fascists, against your children's and
your oppressors!

Piet [*shocked*]. Jan, you were carried away, man! You
spoke just like a Native Communist.

Jan *grins shyly; he is embarrassed to find that he is no
longer acting but has identified himself with
the African cause.*

Jan. Ag, man, that comes out of listening to them speak
for too long. [*Pause. Jazz music again.* Jan *moves to
the window.*] They're still at it!

Voice. The time, friends, has come to strike a blow against
the oppressors! And the blow, I promise you, shall be
struck! Maybe tonight; who knows? Maybe tomorrow,

the following day, or the day after; but the blow shall be struck! There are those who accuse us of being anti-white, but lest anybody should misunderstand the nature of our struggle: our fight, we say, is not against the white man but against the evil laws, which in South Africa, unfortunately, are symbolized by the white skin. It is no longer possible to hate the whip and not the one who wields the whip!

PIET [*with the same detachment as before, but more mechanical this time*]. That Native just won't stop talkin'. He's all mouth and nothing much else.

JAN. Natives love talking. It's their habit.

PIET. But what can they do? They haven't got guns!

JAN. Yah, they'ven't got guns.

PIET. Nothing will ever come out of this. It's just big talk.

JAN. They want to panic us, but they have nothing with which to back their threats.

PIET. If they ever start anything, we'll teach them a lesson they'll never forget.

JAN. What can they do without guns?

PIET. Yah, what can they do?

JAN. Just talk!

PIET [*savagely*]. Damn it, I wish they would start something! Anything! So we can handle them once and for all. They are wearing me down, too, wearing me down! [*Blackout.*] They are wearing me down! [V*oice heard in the dark as the curtain falls.*] They are wearing me down, goddammit!

# ACT TWO

## SCENE I

*The same evening.*

*A dingy basement clubroom which serves as headquarters of a group of left-wing university students. The club is divided into two sections by a waist-high panel wall, the back room being on a slightly higher level than the front. The back room is used as a kitchen with a bar on the right-hand side. Liquor and food can be served to the people in the front room through a cubbyhole. The back and the forerooms are also linked together by a single door in the middle of the panel wall.*

*The foreroom, where most of the action takes place, is furnished with settees, chairs with broken legs, and some with their backs missing. There is a table with a telephone on the extreme left. Near the foreground, on left, stands a big phonograph. The walls are plastered with pictures of student riots, marches, and protest slogans. The peeling walls are inscribed with huge letters shouting: VERWOERD MUST GO! FREEDOM IN OUR LIFETIME! INTERRACIAL SEX IS A HISTORICAL FACT! etc. There are also photographs of jazz musicians, famous writers, actors, as well as avant-garde pictures which are distinguished by their strong African motifs. On either side of the stage hang big African masks. A door on the extreme right provides the main entrance.*

*When the curtain goes up, the stage is completely dark. First we hear the throb of cool jazz. Then a figure, recognizable only by the lighted match-stick suspended in utter darkness, moves into the foreground area through the panel door of the back room. Another light comes in the same way, and the two figures chase each other in the dark. They stumble and curse and laugh all at once.*

VOICE. Gama! Gama! [*Both lights have gone out, and the stage is dark.*] Gama, stop playing the fool! Gama, what's the matter with you? Come'un!

*The two dark forms can now be seen by the trickle of light which illumines them. The second figure tackles the first one, and the two roll down on the floor in a spectacular wrestling match. As more light picks out the grunting figures, we can now see that one of them is a husky, tousle-headed young man, looking more like an Oxford under-graduate than an English South African. He is grappling with a powerful African young man about his own age. The young white man is wearing a round-necked sweater, and both are wearing jeans. While they horse around the floor, a white girl with long dark hair hanging over her strongly featured face comes in through the entrance on the extreme right of the stage. She is carrying a huge basket stuffed with bottles of beer and other foodstuffs. At the sight of the girl the African young man gets up and hugs her.*

AFRICAN BOY. Mary, you sweet flower of European woman-hood! [*She smacks him on the face.*] Hey, what kind of humour is that?

MARY. I warned you about calling me a European woman! You're provoking me again!

WHITE BOY. That's right! Gama, you're provoking Mary again.

MARY. He's always provoking me!

GAMA. All right, I'm sorry!

WHITE BOY. You're always provoking Mary!

MARY [*turning savagely on the white youth*]. Why don't you shut up!

WHITE BOY. I dare say!

GAMA [*hugging her again*]. My apologies, ma'am! No of-fence was intended to you!

MARY [*kissing him*]. You call me that again an' I'll break a beer bottle over your head!

GAMA. All right, I'm sorry! What a horribly sensitive little
bitch!

MARY [*slaps him again*]. When you call me that, I always
know you're mocking me!

*This time she abandons herself completely to his embrace
and kisses. He rubs her behind in a vulgar manner.*

JIMMY [*closing his eyes*]. Look at that! Isn't it horrible?
The youth of our time is sunk in vice!

MARY. Why don't you go into the other room and help
yourself until Kitty arrives.

JIMMY. No part of the world is any better! Not even young
Africa.

MARY. Would you like me to help you?

JIMMY. Young lady, watch your tongue! You're speaking
to a young man of background!

GAMA. That's right! Mary, watch your tongue when you
talk to Mr. James MacBride here! He is a young man of
distinguished background. A young man of impeccable
background! Isn't that right, Mr. MacBride?

JIMMY. That's right.

GAMA. That's right . . . hmmmmm, what did you get?

MARY [*smacks his hand as it reaches for the basket*]. Don't
touch the basket! You two are not to drink until the
others arrive!

JIMMY. Rubbish! We have priority claims!

MARY [*taking the basket away into the kitchen*]. Soreheads!
What makes you think you have priorities over others?

GAMA. Because, my dear——

JIMMY. Because, sweetheart——

GAMA. . . . we are in the forefront of the African struggle
for freedom!

JIMMY. That's right! The frontline of battle!

GAMA. And we are catching fire! Isn't that right, Mr. Mac-
Bride?

JIMMY. Absolutely!

MARY [*suddenly tense*]. How did it go?

GAMA [*screams hysterically*]. A-a-ha-ha-ha! How did it go?
How did it go? [*Grabs* JIMMY *and they do a mock waltz.*]
How did it go?

MARY. Damn it, I'm serious, Gama.

GAMA. Mr. MacBride, will you enlighten the young lady
here as to the execution of our mission?

JIMMY. I should think it hardly advisable to enter into such
details at the moment. Suffice it to say that the job was
executed with extreme wisdom and sensitivity, qualities
which have long distinguished the characters of the two
members of your committee, madam!

MARY [*grabs* JIMMY *by the shoulders*]. Damn it, this is no
joke! What's the matter with you two?

JIMMY. Do that again, you bitch, and I'll slap your big
mouth for you!

MARY *makes to strike him.* GAMA *moves swiftly between
them.*

GAMA. Aw! Aw! No hostilities! Very unwise. Now, what
seems to be the matter?

MARY [*yelling*]. Goddammit! I just want to know what
happened. After all, we're all up to our necks in this
thing!

GAMA. Up to the neck! [*He makes a hanging sign.*] You
heard that, Mr. MacBride? Up to the neck!

JIMMY. Isn't that a bit unpleasant? I think we should weigh
our actions a little carefully before we——

MARY [*yelling again*]. Will somebody tell me what happened? Damn it! And stop this inconsequential mumbling!

GAMA [*mocking*]. In-con-se-quen-tial mumbling!

JIMMY. Once again scholarship conspires against us!

MARY [*soft, very feminine and appealing*]. Please, Gama,
will you tell me? Did everything go according to plan?

GAMA. Everything according to plan! Isn't that right, Mr.
MacBride?

JIMMY. That's right! I dare say I'm extremely gratified with
the way the job was carried out. Extremely gratified!

GAMA. We're all extremely gratified, Mr. MacBride.

MARY. So the stage is set? [*Moving away nervously.*]

GAMA [*laughs hysterically*]. That's right! The stage is set! At twelve midnight, when those fools wind up the conference . . . [*Imitating a Government speaker.*] "This Government stands firm and will not give in to threats from Native agitators and Communist trouble-makers! We have enough resources to handle any mischief from these trouble-makers. . . . Long live the Prime Minister. . . ." And then, BOOM! BOOM! BOOM! The BOMB will go off! Twelve o'clock midnight! I'd like to be there when the City Hall goes up in flames!

MARY. Jimmy, did you clear up all the papers I told you to? Just in case they come around?

GAMA. They won't! Anyway they know enough about the club already, but nothing we've done yet makes us responsible for planting a bomb under the Johannesburg City Hall while the Boers are having their rally. [*Moving to the edge of the stage.*] The very idea! Such an irresponsible idea! Isn't that an irresponsible idea, Mr. MacBride?

JIMMY. Extremely irresponsible! Nobody but an exceedingly inconsiderate person would ever think of it.

GAMA. That's right! And we are very responsible young people.

JIMMY. We believe in negotiations of the kind where a spirit of give and take exists!

GAMA [*laughs hysterically*]. A-ha-haa! That's right, my boy, a spirit of give and take! [*He punches JIMMY on the shoulder, and JIMMY punches him back in a sort of reflex action.*] That's it! Give and take!

MARY [*agitated*]. You two stop behaving as if this was a popular joke! We can all hang for this!

GAMA *laughs hysterically and makes as though he were throwing a noose around JIMMY's neck. He proceeds to tighten the noose, and JIMMY's eyes bulge.*

GAMA. Did you hear that, Jimmy MacBride, me boy? You can hang for this!

JIMMY [to MARY]. Don't worry, pussycat! Everything worked according to plan.

GAMA. Everything according to plan! . . . Boom! . . . Boom! . . . And this is only the beginning!

MARY. Suppose it doesn't go off?

JIMMY. It shall go off!

GAMA. It must go off! It's got to go off! We used an expert.

JIMMY. Knows everything about bombs and dynamite!

MARY. And if it doesn't go off?

GAMA. There will always be another night! The white supremacists will not get away so easily! Oh, no!

JIMMY [contemplating]. At a minute slightly before twelve o'clock midnight, a man will walk down to the basement and set off the detonator!

GAMA. And boom! There'll be a mighty explosion such as Johannesburg has never heard in a long time. There will be huge flames enveloping the city. The wounded and dying and the dead—God rest their souls in peace—will be taken away by ambulances! [He pauses. We hear the jogging rhythm of jazz and the long whine of a plaintive trumpet.] That will only be the start of the rhythm!

MARY [suddenly, absentmindedly]. What rhythm?

GAMA. The rhythm of violence, lovey!

MARY. Gama, I wish you would be serious just for a minute. To hear you talk, you'd think this is a picnic!

GAMA. Who said it was a picnic? We are liberating Africa. What can be more serious? [Pompously.] Africa shall be free!

MARY. He is never serious about anything.

JIMMY. He's never serious about love, which is unforgivable.

GAMA [comes from the direction of the kitchen, drinking beer from a bottle]. That's slander, Mr. MacBride, me boy! I'm serious about love . . . deadly in earnest!

MARY [snatching the bottle away from him]. All you're serious about is sex as far as I can tell!

GAMA. That's academic. What's the difference? You wouldn't want me if I wasn't good at it!

MARY. Pig! You think I'd risk all the laws of this country just for that. If I want to sleep with any man, I can find a white man tomorrow!

JIMMY. Tell him, love! He doesn't know anything about love! All these Natives think it's just getting into bed!

MARY. Why don't you ever shut up? Gama, you mustn't say what you said just now. Because it hurts! Damn it, you know I didn't ask to fall in love with a buffoon like you!

GAMA. So? Fall out of love!

MARY. Gama, you're going to make me very violent in a moment.

GAMA. Threats! Blackmail! [*Moving toward the left of the stage.*] What do you want from me? Soon you'll be asking me to marry you right here in Dr. Verwoerd's country. Mary, you have shoddy dreams!

MARY. I want to hear you say, once in a while, Mary, I love you. I need you. I just want to hear you say it.

GAMA. Mary, dear, I love you! What can I do without you? [*He laughs mockingly.*]

MARY. You think it's funny? A girl wants to hear that.

GAMA. When the struggle is over, I'll tell you that over and over again. It's business first!

MARY [*drinking from the bottle she seized from* GAMA]. Men are monsters!

JIMMY. Especially black men, honey. The dark and lascivious Moors!

GAMA. Black men are kind and generous beyond measure!

MARY. Not when they become pale imitations of Western men. When they become like Jimmy here!

JIMMY. That's a very unfortunate remark, my girl! You might need my shoulder to cry on when your "dark and lascivious Moor" abandons you to a cold world!

MARY. Oh, shut up! You're getting on my nerves!

GAMA. I warned you, Jimmy, never to tangle with a woman when she is in love! Especially with a black man!

JIMMY. Damn conceit!

MARY. I hate white men! My God, I hate them!

*Both* JIMMY *and* GAMA *laugh.*

JIMMY. You want them strong and virile and dark as the night!

MARY. Jimmy, you're such an idiot! What day were you born on?

JIMMY. On the sixth day, when the Lord was lonely!

GAMA [*sitting down next to* MARY *and pushing her hair away from her face in order to kiss her*]. Don't mind him, my love. [*Strokes her behind vulgarly.*] There, does that make you feel better?

MARY [*breaking loose*]. Animal!

GAMA. Women! I'll never understand them. They never make up their minds which they want most: to be stroked or sung poetry to!

MARY. We want both at its proper time. . . . Jimmy, where's Kitty? You look miserable.

JIMMY. African women! They are thoroughly unreliable. She was supposed to come early. And here I am twiddling my fingers!

*Phone rings and* GAMA *takes it.*

GAMA [*mockingly*]. The Students' Club, sir! Well, no, sir! This is a friend speaking. I can call him for you if you want. [*To* JIMMY.] Jimmy, call!

JIMMY. Ask who is it.

GAMA [*into the phone*]. Who's calling, sir? Mr. Philip Bonslow. I'll tell him, sir. Just a moment. [*To* JIMMY.] Some creep by the name of Philip Bonslow.

JIMMY [*crosses to left to take the phone*]. Hello, Philip, my boy. . . . Fine! How are you? [*Alarmed.*] What? You're going where? To the MacPhersons' roulette party? Philip! Philip! When will you learn that life isn't just roulette parties? All right! All right, I'm not interfering with your life! What? No, what I mean is you should dirty your fingers every once in a while . . . while there's still a bit of blood in you. . . . God knows, it won't kill you! No, no, no! I had a girl lined up for you. Very nice girl. She went to Oxford. She's a bit of a leftist, but I thought you wouldn't mind. She's quite harmless really. Of course, she doesn't believe in British control and all that, but she's really nice. Very pretty! Your who? Your wife? What you mean, what about your wife? I thought Sylvia was in London. Has she come back? So, what are you worried about? Oh, Philip, I give up! Call me when you come back from the roulette party!

*He replaces the phone and all three of them immediately break into guffaws of laughter.*

*Blackout.*

## SCENE II

*Same as before. As the lights come on, the three young people are behind the panel door, where they are laying on the food. GAMA comes out through the panel door; jiving his way toward the left, he chooses a record from a stack on the floor and puts it on the phonograph. Immediately, swinging jazz pulsates, and GAMA moves sinuously to its sensuous rhythm.*

GAMA. Mary, is Jojozi coming?

MARY [*from the back room*]. Members of the Committee are supposed to be present tonight. Jojozi may or may not come. He's under no obligation.

GAMA. And Ruth?

MARY [*coming out to the front room*]. Why do you ask? She's not on the Committee.

GAMA. She may come for the party.

JIMMY [*entering*]. Ruth is coming. I met Ruth and Chris at the University, and they're both coming.

GAMA. Good!

MARY. Tonight you're not to flirt with Ruth! Not with any-body!

GAMA. Woman, you forget yourself.

MARY. I mean it! I'm not going to be one of the concubines in the Zulu stable!

GAMA. When did we say the marriage vows?

MARY. If you do, I'll simply disappear with Jojozi!

GAMA [smiling]. The old lech! He would love that!

MARY. That's right!

GAMA. But you wouldn't!

MARY. Don't be so damn conceited! You're not the only man around. . . . What happened to your brother? He was supposed to come early.

GAMA. My chubby little brother! Perhaps he's having a "crisis of conscience"! He should have been a priest in-stead of a revolutionary!

MARY. Some priests can be pretty militant. A damn sight more militant than some fuddy-duddies who pass as politicians!

JIMMY [who is sitting on a chair on left, throwing away a beer can from which he has been drinking]. That's right! Have you ever heard of a man called Trevor Hud-dleston?

GAMA [religiously]. God bless him! He should have been here to give his benediction to this night of violence!

JIMMY. He was a tough priest!

GAMA. Would he have turned the other cheek?

JIMMY. He would have turned his eyes away.

MARY. He was such a saint! And so handsome! [Dreamy.] Such a handsome man.

JIMMY. Which one do you prefer?

GAMA. The saint or the handsome man?

MARY. Both.

GAMA. Jimmy, what's happened to Kitty?

JIMMY. The old bitch! She was supposed to be here at seven! It's now half-past eight! [There is a violent knock *on the door.]* Here she is! [*He moves swiftly and expectantly toward the door on the right.*] You can't talk about her! [*He opens the door, and a sensuous-looking African girl, small and petite, dances through it. JIMMY yells with joy and embraces her.*] Kitty, you dark Jewel of Africa!

KITTY. Hands off, you fool! I heard you calling me a bitch!

JIMMY. That's because I love you! I can't think of anything better to call you!

KITTY [*to MARY*]. Mary, darling, how are you? [*JIMMY interrupts by kissing her.*] Men are such beasts!

JIMMY. Ah, I feel revivified already! There's something mysterious about the African woman. Something mysterious and splendid!

KITTY. A myth for sex-starved white men! [*Moving to kiss MARY, who is seated on the couch.*] How're you, honey?

MARY. I'm fine, Kitty; how're you?

KITTY. All right! Couldn't concentrate on a thing today. In all the lectures I kept thinking about tonight!

MARY. Same here. Somebody dropped a bottle of ink, and I jumped as if a bomb had gone off!

KITTY [*pointing to JIMMY and GAMA, who are having a conversation by themselves on the left*]. Are they drunk already?

MARY. It doesn't make any difference whether they are drunk or not. They always behave like idiots!

KITTY. Gama!

GAMA. Yes, lovey!

KITTY. How did it go?

GAMA. Oh, not that again!

KITTY. I want to know, idiot!

GAMA. At twelve midnight God will speak!

KITTY [*to MARY*]. Did everything go according to plan?

JIMMY. Took a bit of doing, but with talent and extremely good sense on our part, we pulled it off!

KITTY [*to MARY*]. Do you think everything is all right?

MARY. Gama says they planted it in the basement.

KITTY. Will they be hurt? I mean will many people be hurt?

GAMA. What do you think we are trying to do? Tickle them!

MARY [*betraying her own nervousness*]. She's nervous! We're all nervous! Everybody is nervous! Why should we pretend we are not?

GAMA [*shouting and also betraying his own nervousness*]. I am not nervous!

JIMMY. Everybody stop shouting. What's done is done. *They* started the violence! The Government started violence against unarmed people!

GAMA. Did you see the bodies at Sharpeville? Did you see the shoulders of children ripped off by machine-gun fire? Did you see anything? Ask Jojozi to show you the pictures he and the press boys took of the whole show! A butchery, I tell you!

JIMMY [*seriously*]. South Africa is poised between freedom and slavery! Between action and indecision. Only a readiness to act will free this country!

MARY. We just want to be sure everything is all right. After all, this is drastic action.

GAMA. Of course! . . . And this is what this action was intended to be—drastic!

KITTY. If there's a general uprising, is there a follow-up plan?

GAMA. It's for politicians to formulate plans! What we want is action.

JIMMY. To relieve the politicians of their deadly boredom!

MARY. We didn't plan this to relieve politicians of their boredom. If I had known this was the level of your political thinking, I wouldn't have had anything to do with this.

KITTY. Look at the Congo! There can be no success without a clearly thought-out programme. There can only be prolonged butchery!

GAMA. Butchery! . . . Ah, how I hate the sight of blood! May the Lord take pity on us for doing this!

JIMMY. Amen!

MARY. Stalinists!

JIMMY. That's libellous!

GAMA. Jimmy and I don't believe in ideologies!

MARY. You ought to talk! Who was shouting nationalist slogans this afternoon?

GAMA. We believe in political necessities! When society gets this flabby, morally and politically, change is a necessity and violence can only let in a bit of air.

JIMMY. What I fear most in life is boredom! A bomb explosion! Anything but this deadly lull. The clouds keep on gathering, but the storm never breaks!

GAMA. I agree with Jimmy!

KITTY [*sarcastically*]. Isn't that unusual?

GAMA [*ignores her sarcasm*]. Everybody in this country speaks about imminent violence! They've talked about it for so long, nobody believes it will ever come!

JIMMY. Look at people at political meetings! Look at their faces! They are so bored with politicians and their talk of violence, they almost wish it'd break out. People want a change of pace. That doesn't mean they want to give up privilege. They only want sport once in a while!

KITTY. Father Sitwell believes a change in Governmental policies is imminent.

GAMA [*ferociously*]. We don't care what Father Sitwell believes! We're giving Jesus a last chance to choose sides in South Africa.

JIMMY. Gama, my boy, you forget what a powerful name that is. That is the man who once climbed a blood-spattered cross!

GAMA. And once bitten, twice shy, eh!

KITTY. He thinks he's funny! [*To* MARY.] I'm bored with their smart-aleck talk! I'll get myself something to drink.

GAMA. African women begin to drink and that's the beginning of the disintegration of African society.

MARY. For Christ's sake, can't you shut up for a moment!
[*Moving toward the phonograph.*] My God, I'm going
crazy just listening to him.

GAMA *grins. He walks toward* MARY, *who is now inspecting
records. He throws his arms affectionately around* MARY
*and kisses her neck. At the same time the record begins to
play, and a slow hypnotic rhythm begins to fill the room.*
MARY *turns toward* GAMA. *As though involuntarily, they
begin to move their bodies in response to the rhythm,
slowly as though in a daze, their knees touching, moving
backwards, away from each other only to come back again,
as though pulled by a magnetic force, moving, moving
toward each other. Always she throws her head back, a
gesture to which she has become accustomed because of
wearing her hair long; the hair always seems to fall over her
face.* JIMMY *and* KITTY *come in from the back room to
watch, almost entranced, the dancing of the young couple.
Just at this time the door opens and a seventeen-year-old
quiet-faced African student walks in.*

GAMA [*sardonically*]. Tula! My own kid brother! Behold
the Lamb of the Lord come to slaughter!

JIMMY. Tula, my boy, I hear you had a nasty encounter
with the Law this afternoon.

TULA. They had great fun at my expense. Then they
wouldn't let me deliver the petitions to the Mayor's office.

KITTY. What did they do with them?

TULA. Scattered them on the floor.

GAMA. We can expect that from these brutes! Anyway,
we'll show them a thing or two tonight!

MARY. Did you go to the morning lectures today? I didn't
see you.

TULA. No, I didn't go. I was too nervous! I sat at home and
thought about tonight.

MARY. Honey, we're all nervous! I've prepared myself for a
long stretch in jail.

GAMA. My brother even had second thoughts about it. My
little brother doesn't like violence. Blood makes him sick.

JIMMY [*affecting an aloofness*]. Aren't we all being rather inordinately concerned about tonight? I'm not so sure there will be a great deal of damage done. This action will merely injure the Government's pride rather than anything else. Maybe a wall or two will blow off and interrupt a minister's oratory, but that's about all.

GAMA. It's only a start! There will be more violence if this Government clings insanely to its apartheid policies!

TULA. The City Hall is crawling with cops tonight.

MARY. Oh, sure! They were mobilized to watch the Congress meeting this afternoon.

KITTY. Did Gama speak at the meeting?

MARY [*proudly*]. Did he speak? At one time I thought the people would get out of hand! I was thinking, my God, they're going to start rioting and give these monsters an excuse for shooting.

JIMMY. They dare not! Not so soon after Sharpeville anyway. They'll take it easy for a while until the Johannesburg Stock Exchange picks up again.

GAMA. Jimmy, you always underestimate the stupidity of the South African police! We'll see how easy they'll take it after tonight!

TULA [*musing*]. This will be the first time ever that a bomb explodes in public. They're going to comb the entire country for suspects!

GAMA. Let them and see if that helps them any!

TULA. The Liberal Party issued another statement tonight condemning violence.

JIMMY. Gama and I were talking about it this afternoon. We heard they were going to issue a statement. Somebody has to go and see the Liberal Party!

GAMA. Nobody will go and see the Liberal Party. They have a right to their opinion. Since 1912 Liberals in this country have been expressing opinion. They have yet to *influence* public opinion!

JIMMY. The whole history of this country is written in

blood. That's what many people forget. Should be nice to see how the Afrikaners take their own medicine.

MARY. Jimmy, I never knew you could be so bloodthirsty!

JIMMY. It's my cannibalistic tendencies! That's what comes out of associating with Africans just emerging from barbarism!

GAMA. That's right! I come from a long line of missionary eaters! Ever see the beads the Africans wear around their necks? Every one is to celebrate a missionary who was devoured in the good old days when meat was scarce!

KITTY [nauseated]. Gama! Honestly!

GAMA. What's the matter, honey? Can't you stand the smell of flesh?

JIMMY. I bet they wouldn't have eaten Huddleston!

GAMA [grinning]. His skin is too tough! Damn it, that Anglican priest is tough! [Admiringly.] No, Huddleston would have lived, God bless his fighting claws! But some of these priests wouldn't have escaped! They would have made good corn-beef. Hey, Tula, you remember the Sundays we used to go to that church in Sophiatown? What did that African priest used to say?

TULA *smiles shyly.*

TULA [imitating the priest]. You don't have to worry about no white folks! You don't have to worry about nuthin' 'cause when you get to heaven, the Lord Jesus is goin' to put a gleamin' robe around you and you goin' to walk on gold-paved streets! And don't let nobody push you off!

*He smiles shyly after this as a round of applause breaks out. Quite spontaneously, the group's mood shifts into a theatrical satire of a gospel meeting.*

GAMA. Okay, brothers and sisters, if you don't get on to this train, there isn't another one to get you home in time! Come on now! [He claps his hands, then chants.] Come on! What's the matter with ma Jesus!

ALL [chanting back]. He's all right!

GAMA. What's the matter with ma Jesus!

ALL. He's all right!

GAMA. I said, what's the matter with ma Jesus?

ALL. He's all right!

GAMA. Oh, ya, I'm goin' to stand right in front of this bush!

ALL. That's all right!

GAMA. He tole me to stand right in front of this bush!

ALL. That's all right!

GAMA. Oh, ya, He's all right! [*Like a high priest.*] Come on, brothers and sisters! Don't let this train leave you behind now!

*Presently we get the feeling that* GAMA—*like the Afrikaner policemen in a previous scene, who assumed roles of pro- and anti-white—starts off by ridiculing worship, but slips into the genuine mood of African religious feeling as he chants the Gospel songs. While the young people are at it, more push in through the door on the right. First, the bearded Jewish student called* CHRIS *and a girl friend called* JULIE; *followed by a shy baby-faced Afrikaner girl called* SARIE MARAIS, *a new recruit to the New Left Student Group; an Indian girl called* LILI; *an African reporter,* JOJOZI; *and bringing up the rear, a fat, clownish African called* SLOW-FOOT. *All the young people, except the young Afrikaner girl, join in the clapping. She stands out from the group because she looks gawkily shy in this new company. In spite of her earthy Boer body, there is something touchingly ethereal about her, something virginly innocent and fragile about her. She walks gingerly, rather uncertainly, into the room. And she stands apart. All the young people come in laughing raucously or horsing around, but once inside they good-naturedly join in the clapping and Gospel chanting.*

ALL. He's all right!

GAMA. Did I hear you say——

ALL. He's all right!

GAMA. What's the matter with ma Jesus?

ALL. Oh, He's all right!

GAMA. Just what's the matter with ma Jesus?

ALL. He's all right! Oh, He's all right!

GAMA. I said, I'm goin' to stand right in front of this bush!

ALL. That's all right!

GAMA. I'm goin' to stand right here till I hear Him speak!

ALL. He's all right!

GAMA. Stand right here till this bush is set on fire!

ALL. He's all right!

GAMA. Did I hear you say——

ALL. Oh, ya, He's all right! [GAMA *joins in.*] That's right, He's all right! Amen! Amen!

CHRIS. Brothers and sisters, may I have the honour of introducing a new recruit to God's own Tabernacle!

KITTY. Amen!

CHRIS. Miss Sarie Marais. She has been campaigning among Afrikaner students for our S.R.C. candidate at the university. Sarie is a social science major!

KITTY. Alleluyah! Welcome, sister! Let's have the libation!

*The other young people have mingled completely with the group except the shy, gawky* SARIE. GAMA *steps forward and tries to kiss her. The girl steps back, almost involuntarily, and trips over something.* GAMA *laughs.*

GAMA. Watch it, sister! That's no good. [*Contritely.*] I'm sorry; I have an incurable desire to kiss young girls with shy bodies!

MARY [*growing jealous*]. Don't let him, Sarie! He's helplessly corrupt! An awful drooling lech! Stay out of his way if you want to be safe!

SLOWFOOT [*already lifting a glass of brandy*]. He's a fiend with young girls!

JOJOZI. If you want your virginity to remain intact, don't stay too long with him in the shadows!

JULIE. Really, Jojozi, all of you are just making Sarie uneasy! Nobody will harm you, Sarie! Just make yourself at home! Everybody is mad around here!

SLOWFOOT [*sombrely*]. Don't say I didn't warn you!

JOJOZI *slaps the hand of* SLOWFOOT, *who has tried to manoeuvre a glass from his hand.*

JOJOZI. That's right! Your life is totally, irreversibly, and hopelessly in your own hands while you're here, Sarie!

*All this time the girl stands shyly, smiling uneasily and getting out of the way every time a boy comes toward her. TULA advances from the confusion of the crowd; they come face to face with each other. Momentarily, their eyes meet and the girl's eyes fall to her feet. TULA puts out his hand. The girl takes it, and they hold on to each other a bit longer than is necessary, as if they've struck quick sympathy with each other.*

TULA. Hello!

SARIE. Hello!

TULA. May I get you anything to drink?

SARIE [*shyly*]. If you have gin, I'll have a gin and tonic.

TULA. Gin and tonic! [*Laughs.*] Girls seem to drink nothing but gin and tonic!

*They both laugh, and TULA goes to the back room to get her the drink. As he walks through the crowd, GAMA, JIMMY, JOJOZI, and SLOWFOOT make murmuring noises, peering at the boy behind hand-shielded eyes. They are obviously ribbing him for his kind attention to SARIE.*

*Blackout.*

## SCENE III

*Same as before. The signal jazz score which began playing in the very beginning of the play is playing again in a more pulsatingly insistent manner. When the lights come on, we see all the young people behind the panel door, eating and drinking—generally raising hell. GAMA comes out of the back door holding a huge alarm clock in his hands, which he deposits on a table on the far left to face partly the audience and partly the group of actors on stage. While he tries to put it up, the alarm suddenly goes off loudly, attracting most of the young people from the back room. GAMA places the clock properly and turns to the group.*

GAMA. It's a false alarm! Only ten o'clock; you shouldn't
   have bothered!

CHRIS. History is full of false alarms! Meanwhile, drink and
   be merry while history grinds on its tortuous course!
   [He drinks.] Ah, music!

GAMA *starts the record going again.* JOJOZI *grabs* MARY,
CHRIS *takes* JULIE, *and they begin the favourite crawling
dance, called pata-pa-ta. The rest of the young people follow
suit, taking a partner nearest. Only* SLOWFOOT, *who is watching through the back window,* GAMA, *and* SARIE *are not
dancing.* GAMA *spots* SARIE *standing apart from the dancers
and moves slowly, menacingly, toward her, his claws stretched
out theatrically in front of him. However, before he reaches
the apprehensive girl,* TULA *comes out of the back room
with drinks and gives one to* SARIE. GAMA *shrugs his shoulders exaggeratedly and moves off. The music stops.* TULA
*and* SARIE *move toward the front part of the stage, where
they sit nervously facing each other. The rest of the young
people form the backdrop of couples talking, standing in
corners kissing, or girls sitting on top of boys who happen
to be lying on the floor. There is a general horsing around
and tumbling in a form of undergraduate sexual abandon.
Occasionally, drinks are fetched from the back, things are
hurled against doors, chairs collapse and are fixed again.*

TULA [*nodding toward his brother*]. Don't mind him! He
   barks more than he bites.

SARIE [*shyly, almost hesitatingly*]. And you bite . . . more
   . . . than you bark?

TULA [*laughing at the unexpected quip*]. No, no! I don't
   bite at all. May I get you a cushion to sit on? It's more
   comfortable.

SARIE. No, I'm all right, thank you!

TULA. My name is Tula. Gama is my brother.

SARIE. I'm Sarie Marais. He's your brother?

TULA. Are you surprised?

SARIE. Well . . . a bit . . . You're so unlike him!

TULA. My brother has more dash and charm. . . . He's
   more lively. . . . At school he was always a leader.

SARIE [*tentatively*]. And the girls scratched each other's eyes for him?

TULA. You sound as if you disapprove of my brother.

SARIE. Oh, no, I hardly know him enough to disapprove of him. But somehow he seems spoiled!

TULA. That's why girls fall for him. They think they can straighten him out. He's all right really; he loves to horse around. But he's also serious.

SARIE [*looking around the place*]. How did you get a place like this? I mean, where students of all races can mix.

TULA. It belongs to Mary, the girl with the dark hair.

SARIE *turns in the direction in which* TULA *is pointing.* MARY *and* GAMA *are sharing a studio couch on which they are smooching quietly, oblivious to the crowd around them. There's a shocked expression on the girl's face as she turns to* TULA.

SARIE. The police never raid this place?

TULA. They tried once, but there was nobody around. Next time they came, we were singing Gospel songs. They dispersed in confusion!

SARIE *laughs.*

SARIE. Maybe we better start singing Gospel songs!

TULA. Don't start that again. My brother will keep us going all night. Sometimes I think he should have been a preacher instead of studying to be a lawyer.

SARIE. Really? Is he studying to be a lawyer?

TULA. He's graduating at the end of this year.

SARIE. And what are you majoring in?

TULA. Fine arts! Those are my paintings on the wall—and the photographs.

*They both stand up to inspect the pictures as well as the slogan lettering.*

SARIE. It's beautiful. It's very gentle. Now I understand a lot of things about you.

TULA. My brother says fine arts is a profession for women! He thinks it's unmanly . . . somehow.

SARIE. Oh, I don't think so! I think it's a very commendable profession.

TULA. Thanks for saying so.

SARIE [*again looking around the room*]. This is a very gay party.

TULA [*instinctively*]. Have you ever been to many parties like this? I mean where there's free mixing.

SARIE. Well, no, this is the first time. [*Pause.*] Sometimes I think I don't approve of mixing of races—I don't mean just being friends and talking together. I mean the extreme sort! I mean . . . you know what I mean?

TULA. You mean like falling in love?

SARIE. Yes. Then sometimes I think I'm just confused. All this is so new to me. If you are a Boer girl, it takes time to get used to it.

TULA. I know . . . for black people too.

SARIE. The first time I ever met black people on a social level was last year when I came to the university and I had to sit next to a coloured boy. It was strange. I kept thinking something drastic would happen. But nothing happened. You know, I think that's very important. To get together and know each other. Black and white people. You know, to be friends and know how to respect each other. I think respect between people is the most important thing. Don't you think respect is the most important thing?

TULA [*spontaneously*]. Yes, but I think love is more important. . . . Oh, I don't mean that kind of love! I mean real love . . . like loving your enemy. That's real love because it expects nothing in return.

SARIE. Do you believe you can truly love your enemies? Can your people, for instance, or my people ever love each other? In spite of everything?

TULA. By loving your enemy, I don't mean letting people commit crimes against others without stopping them. I

mean one should never hate them or despise them. Real
love brings us all to the same level.

SARIE. Would you have told the Jews to love the Germans
during the rule of the Nazis?

TULA. I would have told them to hate the crimes! To fight
the Germans if necessary, but I'd have never told them
to despise the German people because they succumbed
to evil. The whole world watched while the Jews were
being roasted in ovens. People went into the war only
when their own safety was being threatened. So the
whole world was an accomplice to the Nazi crimes. It is
only when the Jews as well as the Germans know they
are both capable of those atrocities that love can be
possible between them. Love is the understanding that
all people are bound together in guilt and only individuals
are capable of achieving personal salvation. The duty of
every sensitive individual is to see to it that conditions
are created in which he and others like him can become
a majority. Killing for revenge is just as bad a crime as
that which inspired revenge in the first place.

SARIE. That is the most difficult quality. Most loves, at bottom, are really selfish loves. [*Sitting down together.*] You
know, I'm so glad I've met somebody like you tonight. I
mean, somebody I can talk to. When I came, I was so
shy. May I tell you something?

TULA. Please, tell me.

SARIE. I was scared that all of you wouldn't like me because . . .

TULA. Because you're Afrikaner?

SARIE. Yes. I thought you would want to humiliate me in
all sorts of subtle ways. Then Chris said I should come.
I'd really have a good time.

TULA. Oh, we're glad you came. Lots of people who are
members of the club don't like Afrikaners until they
meet individuals. Then they find they like them. When
they say things against the Afrikaners, they're just thinking of them as a group.

SARIE. I know. But it still hurts if you're Afrikaner yourself. Somehow it makes you feel responsible.

TULA. Oh, don't feel like that at all. For instance, we have an Afrikaner student who comes here every now and again. I guess he tells more cruel jokes about Afrikaners than anybody here. Maybe he feels guilty about Afrikaners too, but it's better to laugh about it than to feel miserable. [*Noticing her empty glass.*] May I get you another one?

SARIE [*hesitantly*]. I don't really drink much . . . [*Smiles.*] All right, I'll have another one.

*Just then* GAMA *springs up from the couch, making ferocious noises and pointing an accusing finger at* TULA *and* SARIE.

GAMA. Well! Well! Look at those two! Just look at them! Aren't they going pretty snugly?

TULA *goes to get drinks.*

JIMMY. Aw, come on, Gama, leave the kids alone! They aren't doing any harm.

GAMA. That's what's so wrong about it! They aren't doing any harm!

JOJOZI. Give them time! They always say that between the Bantu and the Boer there's an unnatural attraction.

MARY. What's so unnatural about it?

JIMMY. It's too concentrated! I mean for people who are political enemies!

JOJOZI. My God! Can you imagine the stories in the paper! A Boer girl and a Bantu boy found in flat under compromising circumstances. [*Intones.*] This is the South African Broadcasting Corporation. A Boer girl and a Bantu boy were found by the police under compromising circumstances last night. They were both taken into custody after making signed statements to the police. Contrary to——

CHRIS.——to previous explanations that the girl had willingly proffered herself to the Bantu male, it is now suspected by the police——

JOJOZI.——that the girl had attended a mixed party in some

dingy Hillbrow flat, a haunt for an inter-racial bohemian set——

GAMA.——given to loose living, to promiscuous sex, and abandoned drinking!

CHRIS. And having gone there, the girl had been exposed to more than the usual amount of drinks——

JIMMY. Anyway, just enough to submit herself to the disgraceful demands of a dagga-crazed Bantu youth.

MARY [*takes* SARIE *by the hand*]. Don't mind them, honey! They're the sickest bunch of people you ever saw.

TULA [*coming with the drinks*]. Here, Sarie. Mary, did you want something to drink?

MARY. No, that's all right, honey. You go ahead and talk to Sarie. I'll get myself something to drink.

JOJOZI *and* GAMA *have their arms around each other's shoulders; they are doing fancy dance steps they have learned. Seeing* TULA *and* SARIE *together again,* GAMA *pauses and yells to the entire group in a somewhat drunken manner.*

GAMA. Everybody look at them! What's the matter with those two?

TULA. Gama, will you please leave us alone for a while!

GAMA. Did you hear that? My own brother—my own kid brother—stands there and says to me, Leave us alone! Has your kid brother ever told you to leave him alone?

JOJOZI. He never lived to tell me that. He died an untimely death, poor brother! The son of a bitch had no business to die such an untimely death.

GAMA. I'm sorry about your brother! Sincerely! Well, there's mine and there's no likelihood he will die young!

JIMMY [*crawling on all fours from some dark corner*]. Don't be too sure of that. We have a very efficient police force in this country, dedicated to the elimination of young life!

LILI *crosses in front of* JOJOZI. *She is a beautiful girl, with delicate Indian features.* JOJOZI *grabs her by the arm.*

LILI. Aw, come on, Jo, let go! . . . Will you, please?

JOJOZI. Not so fast, girlie!

LILI. Aw, come on, you're hurting me! Jo, I don't want to play.

JOJOZI [*tries to kiss her*]. Not even love-play?

LILI. That especially!

JOJOZI. Why don't Indians in this country ever "integrate"?

LILI. I just wouldn't like to integrate with *you*, that's all.

*He lets her go.* GAMA *slaps her on the bottom as she passes him.* LILI *turns and tries to pummel him with her fists, which* GAMA *catches expertly; he pulls her roughly to him. She seems to melt in his arms as he kisses her. The group gathers around in sheer fascination.* JIMMY *starts counting like a referee to calculate how long the kiss is going to last. He counts up to ten, his voice rising to a crazed pitch as he nears ten. Just then* MARY *approaches the two and separates them playfully.*

MARY. That's enough!

*The rest of the group applaud the performance.* KITTY *and* SLOWFOOT *emerge from the back room.* KITTY *has got hold of a red garment which she is waving like a matador in the eyes of the fat* SLOWFOOT, *who stumbles after her, trying to butt her with his head. When they make their entrance, the whole group begin to clap hands. They form a circle. The excitement rises to a pitch as* SLOWFOOT *rushes the girl and finally butts her in the stomach so that she goes down. There is wild cheering. It is then the clock suddenly strikes. There is a dead stillness. As the clock stops, the group goes about carousing again as though nothing had happened. Again attention is centred on* TULA *and* SARIE.

SARIE. What is this party for?

TULA [*lying to her*]. Aw, you know, we always have get-togethers! To promote a spirit of comradeship!

SARIE. Every week!

TULA. Every week! Sometimes we have lectures on things like political leadership! Revolutionary tactics!

SARIE. Are you planning a revolution then?

TULA. Well, we aren't planning one now. [*Lying down.*] But, you know, anything can happen in this country. We as students must be prepared! Students everywhere are in the vanguard of the fight against injustice, corruption, and the status quo.

SARIE. I don't think I'd be much of a revolutionary! I couldn't hurt a fly really.

TULA. It is different when you're in the middle of it. Then you have to act one way or another.

SARIE. I don't honestly know which way I would act.

TULA. Anyway, that's not important. It's enough that you're a friend, that you won't have to act against us.

SARIE. I suppose so. You know, Tula . . . [*She looks desperately at him.*]

TULA. Yes?

SARIE. I've suddenly realized how terrible it would be to have to face you across the battle lines! I mean now I know you.

TULA. I know. I don't like thinking about what would happen to my white friends in this country when it really comes to the worst! That is why it's so important for people who think alike, both black and white, to form a united front against the Government, so that the fight will not be black against white but right against wrong!

SARIE. It's very difficult. Few white people want to join hands with black people against the Government. They fear that a change will mean a loss of privilege.

TULA. The young people can do it! There are more of them, both inside and outside the university, who are prepared to join battle. For instance, I never thought I would one day be in a party with an Afrikaner girl. But here we are! [*They are kneeling down, facing each other in the foreground of the stage.*]

SARIE. You know what I like about you?

TULA. No. What?

SARIE. You seem to be very sincere about everything you're doing.

TULA. Oh, we are all sincere about what we are doing here!

SARIE. No, but I mean, one never knows the motives of people for doing certain things.

TULA. You don't know mine.

SARIE. But I can tell they are honourable. I mean you really —well, you seem to like people. I like people who care what happens to people.

TULA. Well, thanks, but I'm really not much better than anybody else.

SARIE. You know something, too? You're very gentle! I mean, a woman can tell these things very quickly. When a man is gentle, a woman can feel it immediately.

TULA. How's that?

SARIE [laughingly]. Well, you sort of feel safe. In many ways you're like my father. He's the gentlest man I've ever known.

TULA. And your mother?

SARIE. I don't have a mother. My mother died when I was very young. I hardly have any memory of her at all. I've always had my father to look to.

TULA. Does your father know about your associations at the university?

SARIE. Well, he knows my views have changed. He knows I mix freely with non-white students at the university.

TULA. He doesn't care? I mean, does he mind?

SARIE. He says I'm about grown enough to think for myself. Sometimes I can tell he says it just because he wants to be good to me, but he's scared! He's scared that I might get too involved. It's not easy for Afrikaner people to accept a thing like that.

TULA. Your father must be very considerate toward you.

SARIE [suddenly, and a bit sadly]. Oh, I wish you could just talk to him, I mean just as we are talking tonight. I wish it were possible to ask you home sometimes, you know, just to talk about things. He likes that. I think that there are so many things he would learn about you, about Africans. It's just that he's never met any apart from servants. My father is a very kind man . . . [*She gets up quickly.*] Sometimes everything seems so futile!

TULA *gets up too. They stand facing each other. Somebody in the background has started playing a blues record.* TULA *and* SARIE *stand for a few seconds just facing each other. Tears are standing in* SARIE's *eyes, and* TULA *tries to smile reassuringly. The other young people start dancing.*

TULA. Would you like to dance?

SARIE. I don't know how to dance! Africans are such wonderful dancers!

TULA. We'll just shuffle around. Who's watching here?

*They begin to dance, first holding each other loosely at arm's length, and then holding each other closely, tightly finally. Sometimes they seem not to be moving at all, just standing and swaying in one area. All the time* SARIE's *face is raised toward* TULA's *eyes. The record stops, but they keep on shuffling, not realizing that everybody is watching them.* GAMA *is delighted to catch them at it.*

GAMA [*banging something on the floor*]. The music has stopped, lovers! [*They break off self-consciously.*] Going snugly, eh!

JULIE. What is it to you!

GAMA. Something about those two offends my sense of good taste. [TULA *and* SARIE *have drifted off toward far left.*] There's something awfully independent about them. Nobody should be that independent!

JOJOZI. What's the matter? Afraid if those two kids become independent, you'll soon run out of sheep to lead?

GAMA. There'll always be people to lead! What do you know about leadership? You're just a gossip columnist on a scandal sheet! One of the worst!

JOJOZI. There aren't enough good people in the world to write for! There aren't enough good people to write about—except those two kids out there! There's a certain charm about them.

GAMA. You must be smelling a good bit of gossip for your column!

JOJOZI. Although I don't believe in people, I prefer charm
  to squalor! I prefer elegance to shabbiness! Those two
  kids have a certain elegance, however threadbare, that is
  touching.

GAMA. You know, Jo, what really offends me about you is
  your affectation of outraged cynicism about the world's
  problems. At heart you're a disgusting romanticist! A
  romanticist! That's what you are!

JOJOZI. What is a cynic but a romanticist turned sour?
  Still, I love those kids! All night they have been surpris-
  ing each other . . . by small things . . . little gestures!
  . . . I like kids who are astonished by life!

CHRIS [taking a close look at his face]. Hey, what's suddenly
  happened to you tonight?

GAMA. It's the winds of change!

JULIE [walking into the back room in the company of LILI].
  If I hear that Macmillan phrase again, I'm going to pass
  out!

JOJOZI. I'm not like Gama! He is a professional executioner!
  I like to get drunk, I like to pinch bottoms; he wants to
  change the world; such men are dangerous!

JIMMY. Oh, crap! Who let Jo take the floor? I thought he
  was interdicted from making public speeches! Jo, do us
  a favour, will you? Stick to your typewriter.

JOJOZI. That's Gama's deputy-executioner! These boys are
  ambitious, I tell you. When we are rid of Verwoerd,
  these boys will take over, and more heads will roll then
  than at any other time in the history of this country!

JIMMY. That's right. . . . And see that yours doesn't roll
  first!

JOJOZI. I have no illusions about the safety of my neck.
  When people like you and Gama get into power, I'll get
  out of the country.

JIMMY. Oh, bosh! Not that we would miss you.

JOJOZI. You won't. Politicians are anti-life. Me? I say bottoms up both to women and to glasses! [He raises his
  glass and tosses a huge drink down his throat before he
  staggers away.]

JULIE [*talking to* LILI *as they emerge from the back room with glasses*]. . . . So he says to me, you're a nice Jewish girl, Julie; what are you doing here? So I say to him, what business is it of yours what I'm doing here or anywhere! So he says to me——

JIMMY [*interrupting rudely*]. Julie, we've heard that story a thousand times! That story is driving me out of my mind!

JULIE. Nobody is asking you to listen! . . . I wasn't even talking to you!

*The clock strikes eleven thirty. It freezes the motions of those members of the group who know something about the night's plans. After this, the pace of the dialogue moves faster, is more weirdly erratic, with more than a suggestion of self-consuming nervousness.*

KITTY [*emerging from somewhere in the room*]. Did anybody hear the clock strike half-past eleven?

JIMMY. Where have you been, blackie? [*She nestles in his arms as though threatened.*]

KITTY. Did you hear the clock?

GAMA. We heard the clock. We've been hearing the clock strike half-past eleven for as long as we can remember.

KITTY. It was different tonight. [*Pause.*] It's a different night altogether.

GAMA. It's like any other night. Just a change in rhythm. It's like any other night.

JIMMY. Warm and pleasant.

CHRIS. Maybe a bit tense! Maybe a storm is gathering. Maybe not.

GAMA. On the whole it's an ordinary night.

JIMMY. Almost humdrum.

CHRIS. Hell, I've seen better nights. Nights full of thrilling excitement and danger. Nights of blood and passion! I've also seen worse nights.

JIMMY. This one is neither the worst nor the best!

GAMA. And yet——

JIMMY. It may surprise a lot of people——

CHRIS. Just a bit of a change in rhythm. . . . People are easily surprised!

GAMA. All together it may be a different night! A bit jumpy! Maybe somewhat painful.

MARY [*lying on the studio couch face down, her hand holding a bottle of brandy next to her; she seems a bit drunk*]. Ah, pain! I understand pain!

KITTY *goes over to see after* MARY's *condition.*

GAMA. There are many in this country who don't! It's time they too understood pain.

JIMMY [*wandering off*]. What a goddam bitchy night! I wonder if it will make any difference. I'm bored with waiting!

CHRIS. I wish I could be there to see it.

GAMA. What for? You can imagine the whole thing, can't you? A man walks down to the basement of the City Hall——

JIMMY [*approaching*]. And he sets off the detonator!——

CHRIS [*apocalyptically*]. Then there is a wild explosion!——

GAMA. That's right! And the power plant blows up!——

CHRIS. The walls go up like a volcano! . . . The whole Pritchard Street is covered in flames! . . . Man, it's mad! Just mad! One has got to see the whole thing happen!

JULIE *emerges from the shadows with* SLOWFOOT *this time.*

JULIE [*to* SLOWFOOT]. . . . So he says to me, Julie, I love you! You are the first Jewish girl I've really loved! I mean, I could marry you tomorrow if you'd let me, he says, but why must you always be seen in the company of black students? So I say to him, if you love me, Carmine, stop——

JIMMY. Julieeeeeeeeeee!

GAMA. Julie, sweetheart, we know what you told Carmine.

JULIE. Was I talking to you? Why can't you shut up until somebody talks to you? Wise-guys!

CHRIS. [*taking* JULIE *in his arms*]. Don't mind these clowns, love. You go on and tell your story, because it's a nice story.

JIMMY. Sure! I guess we can still listen to it, even though it's the hundredth time we are hearing it!

KITTY [*sees the figure of* JOJOZI *sprawled against the wall*]. My God! Look at Jo!

GAMA [*tartly*]. My God, look at Jo! God doesn't want to look at Jo. Jo stinks!

KITTY. Does anybody want coffee? I'm going to make some coffee. [*There are several responses.*] Anybody wants coffee, come and get it.

*Several young people follow* KITTY *into the back room.* CHRIS *goes over to* JOJOZI.

CHRIS [*shaking him up*]. Hey, Jo! Jo! Do you want coffee? Come on!

JOJOZI [*stirring*]. What's the matter with you? Hey, take yo' hands off me, white son of a bitch!

CHRIS. Come on, Jo; the only time your racialism shows is when you're in the pots!

JULIE'S *voice from the back room can be heard distinctly.*

JULIE. So he says to me, Julie, you're a nice kid . . .

JOJOZI [*getting up*]. A man can't even have some sleep without some son of a bitch coming up to muss him up!

CHRIS. Come on! Coffee will do you some good!

JOJOZI [*staggering toward the kitchen*]. Have the Government forces struck? Have the forces of destruction carried out their . . . their . . . their . . . monstrous purpose?

CHRIS. The Government forces have not struck! They are biding their time.

JOJOZI. Biding their time, eh! Well, you can tell them they stink! Everybody stinks! The whole damn lot of them! I'm the only sane person! I get drunk, maybe get myself a nice soft bottom. So what's so evil about that? Okay, you tell me. You're university, aren't you? Well, tell me what's wrong with a nice bottom? What's wrong with a piece of . . . [CHRIS *shshshs him up.*] You don't

bloody well know? And you are university? What do they
teach you up there at the university if they don't teach
you to get out and get yourself a nice bottom? Eh, what
do they teach you? Teach you to go out and shoot Natives like big game! Whites don't know nothing but to
shoot! Blacks don't know nothing but imitate whites!
Gama and the whole son-of-a-bitchin' lot! Don't know
a thing! They think they're changing the world! They are
making it worse than it is already! Why can't everybody
sit down and drink? Well, I asked you, didn't I? Why
can't nobody just sit down and have himself a nice piece
of bottom? Why can't everybody . . . [CHRIS *half pushes
him into the back room.*]

*Blackout.*

# SCENE IV

*Same as before. This time the young people can be seen
milling around in the back room, drinking coffee. The party
is nearing an end. Before the action begins, there is a harsh
throb of jazz, much more insistent than previously, with
jarring rude phrases constantly being interpolated in the
continuous rhythm. When the music subsides, TULA and
SARIE emerge through the panel door from the back room,
carrying their mugs of coffee. They sit gingerly in the foreground of the stage. There is noticeably more warmth, a
greater ease, between the two. When the light picks out
their faces, they seem to be glowing with an innocent,
youthful gravity and concern for each other.*

SARIE. Now it seems that coming here was the most important thing I have done in a long, long while.
TULA. You can't imagine how glad I am you came.
SARIE. All night we seem to have done nothing but talk and
talk, and yet, somehow, I seem to have discovered something important and vital. I can't explain it to you.
TULA. I know how you feel because this is exactly how I
feel. It's like stumbling upon something precious, some-

thing you want to keep. I suppose the pain of discovery is the fear of losing.

SARIE. We can't be losers, because we care, and caring breeds regard; and now that I know something of your affection, even the political problem seems less heavy, less frightful.

TULA. I'm frightened, though. Precisely because I care. There seems to be no way of preserving the important things when history grinds on its course, and yet one wants to preserve the things that one has affection for.

SARIE. There must be a way of redirecting history to avoid tragedy, provided there is enough love. I am a woman, so my optimism is boundless. I don't feel despondent. I used to, but now that I know there must be many people who feel like you on your side, I think I feel more strengthened.

TULA. You know it's very important that I see you again soon; I'm even ashamed to admit it.

SARIE. Oh, please don't . . . because you make me feel important. I just wish that it were not so difficult with all the laws controlling our lives.

TULA. Maybe we can meet for lunch at the university canteen from time to time and talk.

SARIE. Maybe we can too!

TULA. You don't mind if we do have lunch together sometimes?

SARIE. Why I would love to. I don't care what they think.

TULA. It doesn't have to be often.

SARIE. We can meet as often as it is reasonable. Anyway, I always have lunch mostly with people who don't interest me in the least. I'd love to have lunch with you. There's so much to talk about! May I take your cup?

TULA. No, no. I'll take them in for you. [*They both get up.*]

SARIE. That's all right! I'll take them in. [*She goes away with the cups.*] I'll be right back.

TULA *paces the floor. Although his face still retains something of its usual gravity, it is now touched by a dreamy quality. We hear a few bars of soft, fragile melody. The music is interrupted by* JULIE'*s voice from the back room.*

JULIE. So I say to him, Carmine, if there's one thing I can't stand, it's a boy who remains uncommitted in this country, in spite of the grave problems. There's absolutely no excuse for cowardice or indifference!

SARIE *makes her appearance again immediately after this short speech. She and* TULA *move quickly toward each other, and spontaneously* TULA *takes* SARIE'*s hand.*

TULA. Won't your father be wondering where you are tonight?

SARIE. He won't be back until very late. He's gone to the Party rally.

TULA. Oh, I see . . . [*Too abruptly.*] Where did you say?

SARIE. At the National Party rally.

TULA [*manifestly agitated*]. You mean at the City Hall?

SARIE. Yes . . . [*Looking at his face, which he is trying to keep averted.*] What's the matter, Tula? I hope you don't hold that against me. Do you?

TULA. Oh, no. No! You can't understand! You can't know what it means!

SARIE [*alarmed*]. What do you mean? It can't be that important to us, what my father does!

TULA. No. I don't mean that at all. [*He makes to move away.*]

SARIE. Wait! And you know what, Tula? He's gone to tender his resignation to the Party. It's a great night for him! That is something, Tula. He may be no Liberal, but at least he is making a break with the Government régime. You can't imagine what a great step it is for him. He's been nervous all day long. I could see it the way he walked about the house! I could see it the way he stared absent-mindedly at things! Twice I asked him something, and he kept saying, yes, yes, although he wasn't listening to anything I was saying. [TULA *is more agitated and wants to break away from her.*] Tula, the way your face has changed suddenly frightens me. Something must be wrong. It's not my father? [TULA *shakes his head vigorously*.] No, then what is it? You must tell me! It's very important to me!

*Rapidly he walks away into the back room, followed closely behind by* SARIE. *Immediately, he comes out from the back room followed by* GAMA, JIMMY, *and* CHRIS.

GAMA. What's the matter with you? [*He looks at the clock and back to* TULA.] What is it?

JIMMY. What is it, Tula?

GAMA [*shakes him roughly by the shoulders*]. What is it? Can't you talk?

TULA [*wiping his face with the back of his hand*]. Her father! Her father! The only parent she's got too!

CHRIS. What do you mean, Tula?

JIMMY. Whose father?

GAMA. What are you talking about?

TULA. The Afrikaner girl who's here tonight! Sarie Marais!

JIMMY. What happened to her father? Just tell us slowly what the matter is.

TULA. Her father is at the City Hall right now! At the National Party rally! If anything happens tonight, he will be there too! He'll get hurt with the lot!

*The group is stunned. They all turn to the clock; it is eleven forty-five.*

GAMA [*in distress*]. How stupid! How damn stupid! What a damn stupid thing!

TULA. We've got to put the bomb off! We can't go on with it! There's still time to run down to the City Hall and put the whole thing off!

GAMA [*recovering from shock*]. No! Nothing's to be put off!

TULA [*close to hysteria*]. Are you crazy? He's the only parent she's got! That girl has nobody but her father! We can't let him get hurt.

JIMMY. Damn it! Why did we have to get mixed up with her? Why did she have to come sniffing here?

TULA. We can't let the bomb go off!

GAMA. Shut up, will you! You're not giving orders to anybody here! The bomb shall go off as planned! We can't help it if her father is a National Party supporter! He's just as guilty as any other white supremacist! He must perish with the rest!

TULA. He is not a National Party supporter!

CHRIS. What's he doing at the City Hall tonight? Why didn't she tell me about this earlier?

TULA. He's gone there to tender his resignation! He's making a break with the Party! She told me so herself!

*The whole group begins pacing up and down like caged lions without any means of escape from the dilemma. Only* TULA *has made his decision and stands accusingly before them.*

GAMA. Don't just stand there accusingly! It's not our fault her father is at the City Hall tonight!

TULA. We can still do something! Disconnect the whole thing!

GAMA. No, we can't! It's too late!

TULA. It's not too late! If we didn't argue about this, somebody would be running down already!

GAMA [*furiously shaking him and pushing him off*]. Listen, stupid! We've worked hard preparing for this! We've run grave risks! We can't just put it off for one white supremacist who's suddenly suffered a "crisis of conscience." What's the matter with you anyway! Are you in love with her? That's right! You want us to risk our necks rushing down to the City Hall because of your sentimental reasons!

TULA. Don't people mean anything to you? She's alone! She has no relatives! Her father is the only one she's got in the world!

GAMA. People mean something to me. That's why I am involved in this. Because I care about people! Hundreds of black people have been shot down mercilessly by these brutes! You don't remember that. No! And you talk about caring for people! For one white man you want to put off something that's important! Something that

might mean the beginning of a change in this country!
You call that caring about people?

JIMMY [*trying to be reasonable about it*]. Have you told
her about the plans to blow up the City Hall?

TULA. No. She doesn't know it! She thinks me a friend and
here am I, murdering her father in cold blood!

JIMMY. Calm down, Tula! We are all in this! We both
feel sympathy for her! But we must keep our heads!

TULA. Keep our heads and her father is just about losing
his!

CHRIS. Isn't there a way of removing the father from the
City Hall without telling him the reason?

GAMA. When the news breaks, her father will suspect
something and she will suspect us! We can't even explain this to her! We don't know her well enough to
tell her we are behind the blowing up of the City Hall!

TULA [*desperately*]. You can go on arguing about it! I'm
going down to cut the wire off!

*He rushes toward the door. GAMA runs after him and grabs
him by the shoulders. There is a struggle and GAMA hits
his younger brother with a fist repeatedly in the stomach
until he sags down.*

GAMA. You're not running to any City Hall! Damn fool!
You asked for this!

*The girls and the boys pile out of the back room during
the struggle. They are all asking what's happened. CHRIS,
JIMMY, and GAMA are mute. Neither does TULA explain
what it is all about. SARIE rushes to TULA, who is still
on the floor and is groaning. She lifts his face between
her hands and tries to find out what the matter is, but
TULA keeps shaking his head.*

MARY. Gama, did you hit him?

GAMA. Yes, I hit him!

MARY. You really hit him? Your own brother? And for
what?

GAMA. He was going to do something stupid! And don't
ask me what!

MARY [*furiously*]. Gama, I don't want to see you again! And don't ever touch me again! You're a cruel, heartless bully, and I can't stand bullies!

GAMA. Wait a minute! You don't even know what he was going to do! You don't know a thing! Why do you always have to rush to conclusions?

MARY. What conclusions are you talking about? You hit him, didn't you? Jimmy, what was the quarrel about this time?

KITTY. Jimmy, what happened?

JIMMY [*evading the questions*]. Look, this is not the time to talk about it.

*The girls help* SARIE *move* TULA *to the back room to look after his condition.*

CHRIS. What are we going to do about it?

JIMMY. There's nothing we can do about it.

GAMA. It's none of our fault!

CHRIS. Maybe we can telephone anonymously and give him the message that his daughter has been seriously hurt! Anything to get him out of there.

JIMMY. That's a good idea, Chris! That's a splendid idea! Gama, what do you think?

GAMA [*agitated*]. Ya, maybe it will work! What's the City Hall phone number?

JIMMY. We can telephone the lobby, and somebody will send the message into the conference hall.

GAMA. Okay, Jimmy, you call!

GAMA, CHRIS, *and* JIMMY *move toward the telephone, where* JIMMY *dials the number of the City Hall. There is a long quiet, with only the purring of the telephone and the vague voices from the back room. The three young people stand tensely around the telephone. There is no answer.*

JIMMY [*slamming the telephone back to the cradle*]. Not a damn answer! Too busy dreaming up crazy apartheid schemes to even answer the telephone! [*He paces up and down.*]

GAMA. Why do we have to bother? We can't help it if he is there! [*The others nod half-heartedly.*] I mean, I care and all that, but what can we do about it?

CHRIS. There's danger that anybody who goes down to the City Hall might be intercepted by the police. The whole City Hall is ringed by the police.

JIMMY. You're absolutely right, Chris! We might be caught in the act of cutting off wires! There's nothing more distressing than being punished for an aborted plan.

*Every pause now is marked by increased tension.*

GAMA. Goddammit! It's not as if we asked him to be there!

*Pause.*

CHRIS. Thank heavens she doesn't know yet!

JIMMY. She'll soon know! Chris, how the hell did you get mixed up with her?

CHRIS. Wait a minute, Jimmy! Don't try and start pushing the blame onto me now! This group is non-racial! So, we meet a Boer girl at the university who's interested in joining, and we ask her to come along! How could I have known her father was to be at the City Hall tonight?

GAMA. Okay! Okay! Nobody's blaming you! This is nobody's fault! Besides, it's almost time for the bomb to go off! [*With a deliberate attempt at levity.*] Ah, who cares? One Boer gets blown up because he happens to be in the wrong place at the wrong time! It's not the first time it's happened. Hundreds of black people have been killed by Boers! It's a pity if one good Boer gets on the rails of history and gets ground up with the rest. [*Pause. Suddenly.*] Jimmy, what do you think? You think I am right or wrong? Tell me.

JIMMY [*uncertainly*]. Right. Maybe ...

GAMA. Maybe what? Jimmy, do you think I'm right or wrong? Why do you say maybe?

JIMMY. I mean, maybe we should try that number again.

GAMA. Okay, maybe we will get an answer this time.

*They move off toward the telephone, where* JIMMY *tries*

*again. There is complete stillness, during which we can
almost hear the breathing of the three young men. After a
while* JIMMY *replaces the receiver with an irritated bang.*

JIMMY. They're about to be blown off the face of the earth,
and they can't even answer a telephone! Too busy with
the damned apartheid policies to bother!

CHRIS [*slowly, dejectedly*]. I suppose that's it! There's
nothing more to be done!

GAMA [*agitated*]. Suppose that's it? What else is there to
do? We can't destroy everything we've planned for
months because of one crazy Boer bastard! Why did he
have to be there! Why did she have to come here!

CHRIS. Stop putting the blame on her! That girl was invited
to join this group! When all of you started a non-racial
organization, nobody bothered to think about Boers
joining!

JIMMY. Nobody's saying Boers shouldn't join this organization! We are not racialists!

CHRIS. Well, both of you talk as if you're blaming me for
having brought this girl to the party.

GAMA. No, no! We're not blaming you! It's just that she's
made everything that was right seem wrong suddenly.
[*The other young people who have been in the back
room come out. Everybody is remarkably tense. Occasionally their eyes are riveted to the clock.*] Is there anything
left to drink? Mary, is there anything left to drink?

*She doesn't answer him.*

JULIE. Everybody's been guzzling drinks all night! Now you
want a drink!

GAMA. Jimmy, give me a cigarette, will you?

JIMMY [*to* KITTY, *after searching his pockets unsuccessfully*].
Blackie, what did I do with my cigarettes?

KITTY. How should I know? Did you give them to me?

GAMA. What's the matter with everybody suddenly?

MARY [*exploding*]. What's the matter with you? You're
stalking the room like a lion. Look at you!

GAMA. Well, what of it! Maybe I am a lion!

MARY. Stop shouting! You're going to bring all the neighbours running here! Are you all shot up or something?

GAMA. Who's shot up? I don't get shot up that easily! I'll see this through!

SARIE *and* TULA *come in from the back room. There is suddenly a dead quiet again. They stand separately. Tension mounts and is only broken by the drunken entrance of* SLOWFOOT, *who stumbles and falls but manages to save the bottle of brandy he has been hiding from everybody. He looks around searchingly at the group, then takes a sip from the bottle.* TULA *slips out unnoticed.*

SLOWFOOT [*grinning sardonically*]. Ah, I can see a sombre quiet rests heavily upon this illogical conglomeration of the flotsam and jetsam of society! [*Nobody responds to him. He sizes up the group and tries again.*] A dead stillness! I see. Only drunks are not impressed by the sober solemnity of history!

JIMMY. And history is not impressed by the solemn sogginess of a drunkard's mind!

SLOWFOOT. Ah, Jimmy, my boy! I knew you would rise up to the occasion!

GAMA. Will that clot shut up! He's getting on my nerves!

SLOWFOOT [*whistles drunkenly and stumbles forward*]. Hey, waita minute! Listen who's talking now! The tough cool boy! The wonderboy who's in truck with history! And for the first time he's unsure like the rest of us mortals! Gama, rise and shine; immortality is passing you by!

GAMA. If somebody doesn't stop that drunk, I swear I'm going to punch him on his blabbering mouth!

SLOWFOOT. Ah, it "was the best of times, it was the worst of times . . . it was the time of wisdom, it was the time of foolishness!" [*He stumbles forward.*] A time of extreme stupidity! You see, Gama, my boy, you're not the original thing! There've been revolutions before!

GAMA *rushes to punch him one, but he is intercepted by* JIMMY's *swift action.*

GAMA. Damn him! Somebody get this drunk out of here before he gets hurt!

JIMMY. Gama, calm down, for God's sake! Everybody's flying off the handle. What's the matter with everybody?

SLOWFOOT. Nothing's the matter with me. [*Pause.*] Okay, what did I say wrong? Did I say anything wrong? If I did, I heartily apologize—like a gentleman. [GAMA *snatches the bottle from him.*] Now, waita minute, Gama! That's a very arbitrary measure! Even a drunk has a democratic right to retain his bottle—I mean—for all practical purposes. I deman' an explanation why my bottle is being impounded. [GAMA *takes a swig from the bottle. He raises it against the light and discovers there is pretty little left in it. He empties down his throat the rest of the contents and throws the bottle away.*] Ah, the maestro needed a shot in the arm too!

GAMA. And you need a shot in the head!

JIMMY [*suddenly*]. Where's Tula? What's happened to Tula?

SARIE. He said he was going to get some fresh air.

JIMMY. What? Oh, my God!

GAMA. What? When did he leave? What happened? Where did he say he was going? Talk, can't you? Goddammit! [*He shakes the bewildered girl.*]

SARIE. Don't! You're hurting me! [MARY *pulls* GAMA *away.*] What's the matter with all of you? What's the matter with everybody here? What are you planning? What's going on? [JIMMY *and* GAMA *have rushed outside to search for* TULA.] Something is going on here that I don't know about!

LILI. Mary, what's the matter? Do you know what the excitement's all about?

MARY. How should I know? Why ask me? I was in there drinking coffee, and I come out here and there's a general commotion. I don't know what it's all about! [GAMA *and* JIMMY *come in again.*] Gama, is there something wrong?

GAMA [*moving toward the centre of the stage. A note of hysteria*]. You bet something is wrong! Sweet brother of mine has run down there to watch the whole thing happen! He's goin' to be the major witness! Who knows, maybe he's even goin' to sing to the police! Warn them! I bet he's goin' to do that! He's goin' to rush into the hall and tell all those people to get out before it happens! [GAMA *begins to shout in a deranged fashion*.] Get out all you good people! Get out before we blow you up! Can you hear me? Get out of the damned City Hall! You only have five minutes to do it! Get out now or be blown off, goddammit! Can anybody hear me? No, nobody can hear me! Not a damn single person can hear me! You're all too damn busy cooking up your crazy apartheid policies to listen, to care! Well you can damn well perish! All of you perish, and see if I care! I tell you it's your damn fault if you——

*We begin to hear the clock strike the hour of midnight. Suddenly there are rumblings at a distance. Loud explosions, detonations, can be heard within two miles. Then sirens begin to scream, ambulance and police cars. The lights on stage are shaken as though by an explosion; they falter as though a power plant has been affected. A wild jazz rhythm can be heard blending with the rhythmic detonations offstage. The explosions stop suddenly. The whole group rushes for the door. The lights falter and die out suddenly.*

*Curtain.*

## ACT THREE

*The charred ruins of what had been the City Hall. It is*
*about an hour later, but the blown-up building is still*
*smoking. There is a lot of debris over the background area*
*of the stage. Near the ruins lies the still figure of* TULA,
*over which* SARIE *is kneeling, convulsed with sobbing. In*
*the foreground area the two policemen,* JAN *and* PIET, *are*
*conversing in a psychopathic fashion, their backs turned on*
SARIE. *It is hard to tell from the way they are talking whether*
*they are still mentally capable of drawing the line between*
*the dream and the reality.*

PIET. A damn good it's going to do them trying to bluff
    us into thinking there's something they can do!

JAN. Natives need to be taught a lesson.

PIET. Talk about taking action! Who do they think they're
    fooling?

JAN. Natives love talking! I tell you, it's their habit!

*They walk into the lighted area so that we can see their*
*faces, which are covered by the dust from the debris.*

PIET. We can handle any number of Natives! Any blinkin'
    number of Natives!

JAN [*nervously, perhaps reclaimed by reality*]. Hey, Piet,
    you think this was the start tonight?

PIET. What start? What do you mean, the start?

JAN. Well, this is the first time a bomb has exploded in a
    public place in this country! Goddammit, this is the first
    time they've killed our people! I don't like this, Piet! We
    could've been killed if we were in there! I tell you, man,
    they should let us hunt those bastards down and shoot
    them like dogs!

PIET. This is nothing! We'll get them all right!

JAN. So you think this *is* a start?

PIET. What start? Man, talk straight when you talk to me!
    What start? We're in control of the situation here!

JAN. I know.

PIET. Well, don't talk about no start, because there isn't goin' to be any damn start of anything here!

JAN. I was just asking for your opinion!

PIET. I'm giving you my opinion! There isn't goin' to be any damn start for the Natives now or tomorrow!

JAN. Okay, man, you mad at me or something? I just asked.

PIET. I'm not mad at you. I'm mad at *them*!

*A pause.*

JAN. What a night!

PIET. Anyway, we got the situation under control! Completely under control!

JAN *hears the moaning of the girl,* SARIE.

JAN. There's somebody moaning! [*He looks around.*] They took everybody hurt?

PIET. Yah, they did.

JAN *walks toward backstage and sees* SARIE *kneeling over a body.*

JAN. Piet, come and look at this! Man, a white girl too! Kneeling . . . over . . . a bloody kaffir! What's this! [*He yanks her off the body.*] What are you doing with the body of a damn stinking kaffir?

*The girl is convulsed with grief. She doesn't answer.*

PIET. Shit, man, kneeling over a kaffir! Who is she? A Communist or something? Bitch! What is your name?

SARIE [*a sudden senseless explosion*]. Don't you call me a bitch! Don't you call me anything dirty! [*She throws herself at the policeman, who slaps her down.*]

PIET. Do that again, you bitch, I'll teach you a lesson! Get up!

*She gets up.*

SARIE. Brutes! All of you! A whole pack of murderers! All of you! Black and white and yellow! It doesn't make a damn bit of difference! You're all killers! Murderers!

JAN. And what are you? A goddam prostitute! Kneeling over a bloody kaffir!

*She tries to tear at them.* PIET *hits her again. She holds her mouth and begins sobbing.*

PIET. Shut up! You'll get inside for this! Janie, get the handcuffs on her! She must know more about this business here tonight! You're going to talk, you damn slut! Crying over your lover, heh! One of the bomb-throwers!

SARIE [*torn by grief, is no longer arguing with them; it's a sort of soliloquy*]. No, no, no! . . . Not that! . . . He was not a bomb-thrower.

PIET. How do you know? What was he doing here anyway when he got blown up?

SARIE [*sobbing*]. He was so good! So very, very good! One of the very few who could have saved us all.

JAN. How do you know all this? You goin' with kaffirs? I can't stand a white woman who goes with Natives!

PIET. Wait a minute. What's your name?

SARIE. Sarie! Sarie Marais!

*Both* PIET *and* JAN *stand in shocked amazement that she is Afrikaner.*

PIET. You mean you're an Afrikaner and you go with Natives!

SARIE. I wish I had. I wish I had known him better.

JAN. Wait until your parents hear about this, you little slut! My God, wait until your father hears about this!

SARIE. He won't. My father won't hear anything. [*Pointing at the ruins.*] He was at this meeting, and they picked him away already dead.

*Again another long pause.* JAN *and* PIET *are shocked at the mystery developing here.*

JAN. What's this? Am I crazy or is she crazy? You mean your father's just been blown to pieces by a bomb and you have the nerve to weep over a Native?

SARIE. Tula, you were so good! Such a big heart and you needn't have died.

PIET. Good, she calls him! A dirty bomb-thrower!

SARIE [*again throwing herself at the surprised policeman*]. Will you stop calling him names! He tried to save my father! This boy here tried to save my father! You stand here running your mouths, and you think you know something! [*She talks calmly.*] This boy here . . . this boy who lies in the dust here . . . his only crime . . . his one crime . . . is that he tried to stop time . . . he tried to block history . . . for me . . . for my father . . . for you and for all of us! . . . so that we might have . . . time to think . . . to reconsider. . . . He never knew how late it was . . . so he tried, and trying got ground to pieces. . . . He might just as well have stayed home. . . . Look at him now. . . . They wouldn't even take him away in their whites-only ambulances. . . . I feel now a sombre darkness upon life itself.

PIET [*uneasily*]. Ah, let her go, Jan.

JAN. Wait a minute, Piet! [*To* SARIE.] What did you say his name was?

SARIE. Tula.

JAN. This is getting more complicated. Remember, Piet, this afternoon? The Native boy with the petitions?

PIET. Hey, no joke? What's his second name?

SARIE. Why do you ask?

PIET. Could it be? [*He kneels down by the body and searches the pockets, from which he gets out the identity card.*] Look at his identity papers! Tula Zulu! Exactly the same Native from the photograph. Gama's own brother! So, Gama and the lot must know something about this! And you! How did you get involved with the political gangsters?

SARIE [*apprehensively*]. No, it's got nothing to do with Gama!

PIET. Aha, so you know that too! You're going to do a lot of explaining, young lady! I wouldn't like to be in your

shoes! This is sedition! You know that? Jan, get the
handcuffs onto her. She nearly fooled us, too!

*They push* SARIE *out through the right side of the stage. A
slow blues number can be heard gradually mounting into a
harsh, violent, discordant melody. The lights go out slowly.*

### Curtain.

# SONG OF A GOAT

*by*

## JOHN PEPPER CLARK

© Jonn Pepper Clark 1961, 1964

# CHARACTERS

ZIFA, *a fisherman and part-time ship pilot at one of the Niger estuaries*

TONYÁ, *his younger brother and assistant*

MASSEUR, *crippled and itinerant; he is to many the family doctor, the confessor, and the oracle*

EBIERE, *Zifa's wife*

ORUKORERE, *his half-possessed aunt*

DODE, *his child*

NEIGHBORS *as chorus*

# SONG OF A GOAT

## FIRST MOVEMENT

MASSEUR.
  Your womb
  Is open and warm as a room.
  It ought to accommodate many.

EBIERE.
  Well, it seems like staying empty.

MASSEUR.
  An empty house, my daughter, is a thing
  Of danger. If men will not live in it
  Bats or grass will, and that is enough
  Signal for worse things to come in.

EBIERE.
  It is not my fault. I keep my house
  Open by night and day
  But my lord will not come in.

MASSEUR.
  Why? Who bars him?

EBIERE.
  I do not hinder him.

MASSEUR.
  My feet drag, but not so my wits;
  They are nimble as the lamb.

EBIERE.
  My house has its door open, I said.

MASSEUR.
  I can see that. Too open I rather
  Fear. Draught may set in any time
  Now. Let the man enter and bring in his warmth.

EBIERE.
  Of course, I want his warmth.

MASSEUR.
  Then it is his fault?

EBIERE.
  Ask him, please, perhaps he will tell.

MASSEUR.
Has he a house elsewhere?

EBIERE.
No.

MASSEUR.
Well, he is not crippled in any way?
So you turn your face to the wall. That is
The sign of death, my daughter.

EBIERE.
Oh, how I wish I'd die, to end all
This shame, all this showing of neighbours my
Fatness when my flesh is famished!

MASSEUR.
This is terrible, my daughter, nobody
Must hear of it. To think that a stout staff
Is there for you to hold to for support.

EBIERE.
It isn't there, it isn't there at all
For all its stoutness and size.
There just isn't a pith to the stout staff.

MASSEUR.
When did you discover it lacked the
Miracle to bring forth green leaves and fruits?

EBIERE.
After my first and only issue in his house.

MASSEUR.
And since then you have done nothing?

EBIERE.
What could I? I thought it was all in
Consideration for me. You see I had a
Difficult time bringing forth my son.

MASSEUR.
I see. Well, your gates are intact
As their keeper cannot even touch them.
Someone has to go in or they will take rust.

EBIERE.
Oh, no, no, not that!

MASSEUR.
> Well, yes, so I fear. Do your parents know
> About this?

EBIERE.
> No,
> I do not want to hurt him, he is very
> Good to me, besides how will both his people and
> Mine take it?

MASSEUR.
> That is true, my child, but
> All the same you ought to have let your people know.
> There's no shame in that. Worse things
> Have been seen before. Why, even leopards go lame.
> And let me tell you, my child, for
> Every ailment in man there is
> A leaf in the forest. If both families
> Cherish each other so much, a good proposition
> Would be for your husband to make you over
> To another in his family.

EBIERE.
> How can you say a thing like that?

MASSEUR.
> I know
> Such a prospect did not open out to you.
> It is understandable.
> After all, you are just stepping out
> On the morning dew of life with mist all prostrate
> On the ground before you. But when the sun is up
> You'll see better. He should make you over
> To his younger brother. That'll be a retying
> Of knots, not a breaking or loosening
> Of them.

EBIERE.
> That will be an act of death,
> It is what the dead forbid you speak of.

MASSEUR.
> I understand
> Your feelings, understand them very well. But

You are young still, as I say, and do not
Know the ways of our land. Blood of goat
So large a cowrie may pass thro' its nose,
A big gourd of palm wine and three heads of
Kola-nut split before the dead of
The land, and the deed is done.

EBIERE.

Leave me, I say,
Take your crooked hands off me. I'll not
Stay here any longer to hear this kind of talk.
If you see me at your threshold again, call me
As big a fool as Zifa who sent me to you
For a cure he knew was unnecessary.
Here is
Your one and sixpence. Now let me pass.

MASSEUR.

Do not take it so ill, child, I mean my
Proposition, you may do worse.

[*She goes out and another comes in in haste.*]

ZIFA.

Ebiere,
She was here just now. I heard her skirt flutter
In the wind as I came in but even as I called
Her footsteps died out on the grass.

MASSEUR.

My son, are you the husband of her who ran
Out now? You have allowed the piece of fertile
Ground made over to you to run fallow
With elephant grass.

ZIFA.

What do you mean?

MASSEUR.

Anyone can see the ears and tassels of
The grass from afar off.

ZIFA.

Has she told you something?

MASSEUR.

Here, son, the woman has told nothing.

    Don't you see the entire grass is gone
    Overlush, and with the harmattan may
    Catch fire though you spread over it
    Your cloak of dew?

ZIFA.

    I am not such a child as to set fire
    To my land for fowls of the air to scratch
    And pick up grubs.

MASSEUR.

    You have, for no fault of your own,
    But you ought to have called for help.

ZIFA.

    You talk of help. What help can one expect
    That is placed where I stand? People
    Will only be too pleased to pick at me
    As birds at worm squirming in the mud. What,
    Shall I show myself a pond drained dry
    Of water so their laughter will crack up the floor
    Of my being?

MASSEUR.

    All this is folly, Zifa. No
    Man ever built a house or cleared
    A piece of ground all by himself. You ought to have
    Asked for help in your plight.

ZIFA.

    This is a plight
    That allows for no help.
    And I will not be the man
    To open myself for others to trample on.

MASSEUR.

    So it is the woman who must suffer
    Neglect and waste?

ZIFA.

    The woman must wait. The thing
    May come back any day, who knows? The rains
    Come when they will.

MASSEUR.

    She has waited too long already,

Too long in harmattan. The rains
Are here once more and the forest getting
Moist. Soon the earth will put on her green
Skirt, the wind fanning her cheeks flushed
From the new dawn. Will you let the woman
Wait still when all the world is astir
With seed and heady from flow of sap?

ZIFA.

I know
All that. And because of that I try to sharpen
My cutlass on flint to clear the land. Is it my
Fault I cannot lift up my lifeless hand?

MASSEUR.

This is the third flood of your hoping.

ZIFA.

Yes, yes, that is very true,
I admit it's been so these several falls
Of the flood though as another rose my heart has risen
With it only to be left aground once more.

MASSEUR.

How much longer will hope hold out?

ZIFA.

I will not give up my piece of land!

MASSEUR.

One learns to do without the masks he can
No longer wear. They pass on to those behind.

ZIFA.

What is your meaning? I cannot
Follow the drift of your talk.

MASSEUR.

In a situation
Like yours one may be content to drift as do
The weeds of the stream. But that carries very
Little, because the tide always turns
Back on one.

ZIFA.

What have you been telling my

Wife, man? I sent her on to you to
Rub, not to turn against her man.

MASSEUR.

So you beat your ears, young man. If your wife has
Been faithful to the point of folly, that
Is your business and hers. But why must you
Send her on to me to take the birth cure
When the fault is not with her? Others
May have taken your fees and agreed to help
You keep up appearances. I will not be
One of them. What, are people to understand she failed
To respond even to the touch of my fingers?
Think,
Man, it is three floods now as you yourself said.

ZIFA.

Others have had to wait more, Why, Ogun's
Wife has been known to wait seven years
To bring forth fruit. Meanwhile I may
Regain my power.

MASSEUR.

No, it is there I fear
You do wrong by her. Ogun was consistent
With his cultivation of the land which
Was his. Only in his case the land would not
Yield of its own. Why, I remember the case
Very well as I had to be called in
To break the curse upon it. This
I traced to the foot of a tree on
The other side of the evil grove and there
The burden was voided and buried
In the crook of twin buttress roots.

ZIFA.

Don't I remember it!
All the town followed as she danced her way
To the root of her trouble. She kept us men
On the drums all day, she did. But in the end
She brought forth a child.

MASSEUR.

> And a very healthy seed
> It turned out to be. It was worth waiting
> Many moons for. Every season, they still
> Bring me gifts of yam and fish.

ZIFA.

> Oh, why is such a cure not open to us
> Men? I'd give the gods and my fathers
> The fattest bull in the land to retrace
> My course and cast off this curse.
> I want my son to have brothers and
> Sisters. It isn't that I do not care.

MASSEUR.

> I can see you care very much. Everyone
> Can see that. You buy your wife the truest
> Madras, beat for her the best gold and
> Anyone can see she is very well-fed.
> But we fatten our maidens to prepare for fruition,
> Not to thwart them.

ZIFA.

> I do not thwart her;
> It is I who am thwarted.

MASSEUR.

> What then do you propose to do?

ZIFA.

> I have been to all experts between swamp and
> Sand. What has any of the lot been able
> To do but suggest I adjust myself to my curse?
> Curse! My father who they dared
> Not spit at when he lived is dead
> And lying in the evil grove. Was that
> Not enough penalty?
> Of course, I have recalled
> Him into town so at times of festival he can
> Have sacrifice.

MASSEUR.

> I think of the man's start, his end,
> And my head fills out. I knew him well.
> Why, if ever there was a killer of

    Fish and another of crabs, we were
    That pair. Ask anybody in all
    The seven rivers.

ZIFA.

    And am I to blame
    If all was fish that came to his net?

MASSEUR.

    Of course not. You did what every
    Dutiful son would do when you brought
    Him back home among his people.
    It may have been a little bit early
    For one who died of the white taint.

ZIFA.

    And for that they have picked my flesh
    To the bones like fish a floating corpse.
    Others grumble it was in time
    Of flood. They will all be too ready now
    To smirk if they hear I am become
    Drained of my manhood.

MASSEUR.

    God made the tree
    Apah straight and erect.

ZIFA.

    I have heard
    All that talk before. What I want is
    A way out, a way to lead me
    Out of this burnt patch of earth.

MASSEUR.

    There is a way out I spoke to your wife
    About only a little while ago.
    But you yourself saw even now how the hen
    All but blew down the house with the flutter
    Of her wings. With the cock himself, the walls
    May well give in and I am too old
    To start raising green thatch for my grey hair.

ZIFA.

    Let me hear it.

MASSEUR.

    No, better go in

To her first and do not rear too high
Your crest. The poor woman is in a state for brooding.

ZIFA.

I cannot look her in the face now our
Secret is out.

MASSEUR.

Your secret is not
Out and will remain safe.

ZIFA.

Next everybody would be saying, there
Goes the cock with the flaming-red crest
But touch the thing and you'll find it
Colder than a dog's nose.

MASSEUR.

There is no need
To whip yourself into this frenzy, Zifa.
Now I know you, I may as well tell you
I massaged your own father when we were
Both supple and strong together and could
Throw any challenger on the wrestling
Ground. In all that time I have not shared
A man's secret with another. Why should I
With you whom I helped to bring into this world
And whose fortunes I should love to watch
As a father his son's?

ZIFA.

Forgive me, Father,
It is the thought of so many things makes
Me mad. I will not be separated from
My wife. She herself will not agree to it.

MASSEUR.

How do you know that?
Have you ever considered another should
Take over the tilling of the fertile
Soil, and had wet mud flung back at you?

ZIFA.

You lame thing, you crawling piece
Of withered flesh with the soul of a serpent,
Shall I crush you between my palms and wipe

Your face on the ground? you weaker
Than a fowl of the earth that wipes
His beak in dust after meal. Shall I wring
Your neck of fibre? How dare you suggest
A thing like that to me? I am strong and
Alive still and dare you open your filthy
Mouth to suggest I pawn my land?

MASSEUR.

You are eaten up with anger but although
You crush me, a cripple, between your strong
Hands, it will not solve your problem. What I
Suggest our fathers did not forbid even in days
Of old. Why, when the hippopotamus wants
A canoe, it also wants paddles.

ZIFA.

Dirt, dung, and drippings at dark! I am
That hippopotamus. I spit but it falls
On my head.

MASSEUR.

No, the gods forbid. I know
You are overwrought, my son, but that is
Because you have this curse upon your head.
Really, you must go now and sit
On what I suggest. The soil is sacred
And no one man may dispose of it. Both
Your families will have to sit together and
Talk the matter over.

ZIFA.

And is that all
The help you can offer? They say the crooked
Wood tells the expert carver.

MASSEUR.

Not when the tree
Is blasted, my son.

ZIFA.

Oh, Ebiere,
My wife, my wife, has it come to this?
And what is to become of me?
Of course, they will have to kill me first.

MASSEUR.

Do not
Think it that way, my son. Some till, but others
Must catch bird or fish. Each is a lot
With its own song.

ZIFA.

I will die first.

MASSEUR.

No, that is a child's talk. Even I,
That am cripple in more ways than one, live
And hope to some purpose for my people.
Why should you talk then of dying? One must
First lay out all things to talk of going
Home. So go home now and to your wife
And act on these things.

ZIFA.

For her and for everything I salute
You. Now I go.

MASSEUR.

Go well then, son, and the gods
And dead protect you.

ZIFA.

Stay well, Father, and do not forget me as
You make them offerings of sacrifice.

MASSEUR.

I'll surely not forget you in my prayers.
Well, there goes a man deep and furious as
A river underground. I hope he keeps
The lid down on his wife, for I fear
She is fretting already. Oh you dead
And gone, take your fat and flesh
But leave us our skin and bones.

## SECOND MOVEMENT

ORUKORERE.
    Woo-oo-oo-oo-oo-oo-oo-oo-oo-oo-oo
    Woo-oo-oo-oo-oo-oo-oo-oo-oo-oo-oo-oo-oo
    All you people run this way! !

ZIFA.
    Who is that crying for help?

TONYÁ.
    It's she, our father's sister.

ORUKORERE.
    I say come out here, all you people.
    A goat, a goat, I hear the cry of a goat.

ZIFA.
    Will you keep quiet!

TONYÁ.
    Somebody's been giving her drinks again.

ORUKORERE.
    A goat, a he-goat, don't you hear
    Him crying? Wo—oo—oo—oo! !
    Will you come out, all you people?

1ST NEIGHBOUR.
    What's the matter now?

2ND NEIGHBOUR.
    Is anyone dying?

3RD NEIGHBOUR.
    Has your house caught fire? In this
    Weather of high wind, the fish wrack
    Must be well above fire.

ZIFA.
    There, will you keep quiet, Mother!

TONYÁ.
    Now she's roused the whole town again.

ZIFA.
    Oh, keep quiet, Mother!

ORUKORERE.

I won't, I won't, I hear a goat crying
Out for help and you say I should keep quiet.

1ST NEIGHBOUR.

Oh, it is the woman again!

3RD NEIGHBOUR.

What does she say?

2ND NEIGHBOUR.

There is so much snuff in her mouth it
Is impossible to hear what she says.

ORUKORERE.

I must find him, the he-goat;
His cry is everywhere, don't you hear it?
It is all over the house; I say, can't
You hear the poor billy bleating?
It's bleeding to death.

1ST NEIGHBOUR.

I don't hear anything.

3RD NEIGHBOUR.

This is strange.

2ND NEIGHBOUR.

Well, how are the goats around here?

ZIFA.

They are all turned in for the night.

TONYÁ.

All are squatting behind chewing the cud
Till the moon is up.

ORUKORERE.

There goes the cry again! I am sure
A leopard has the poor thing in his grip.
We must save the poor brute.

2ND NEIGHBOUR.

What is this she is saying?

3RD NEIGHBOUR.

If there is a leopard here, then this is
No place to stay.

1ST NEIGHBOUR.

Did she say a leopard? Get a lantern then.

ZIFA.

Will you stop that nonsense!

TONYÁ.

Please, you know how it is with her;
How then can you take her serious?

1ST NEIGHBOUR.

It should be easy to see a leopard
If he were here. His eyes should be
Blazing forth in the dark.

3RD NEIGHBOUR.

So I hear. I have heard them likened
To the lighthouse out on the bar.

2ND NEIGHBOUR.

And its motion is silent as that big house.
We must be careful.

ORUKORERE.

Of course,
You do not hear him bleating, the goat,
How could you? The ram does not cry
Out for help although led into captivity.

ZIFA.

Orukorere, will you stop this nonsense?

ORUKORERE.

There goes the cry again.

[*She makes off.*]

1ST NEIGHBOUR.

Stop her, we must stop her.

2ND NEIGHBOUR.

She will do herself harm if she goes on like this.

3RD NEIGHBOUR.

She may have seen something for
All we know.

ORUKORERE.

Don't you hear it?

Don't you, deaf of this world?
Are your ears so sealed and congealed
With pulp of plantain, you do not hear him?

ZIFA.

I told you people none must pour
Her wine any longer. Must I beat it
On calabash back before you take me serious?

1ST NEIGHBOUR.

Surely no one has given her drinks.

2ND NEIGHBOUR.

Orukorere doesn't need anybody's drink.

3RD NEIGHBOUR.

It's hard getting a bottle even for
Sacrifice these days.

ORUKORERE.

Do not hold me!

ZIFA.

Leave her alone there, Tonyá.

TONYÁ.

People will say now she is mad.

ORUKORERE.

I must find him, the leopard
That will devour my goat, I must
Find him. Surely his footsteps will show
Upon the mud? Surely, those claws bloody
From hunt of antelopes in the forest
Will show in the sand? Or has the wind
Swept them off before housewives come
Upon them with brooms at break of day?
Or sports him no spoors?

1ST NEIGHBOUR.

Follow her, let's follow her.

3RD NEIGHBOUR.

The woman may have double vision after all.

2ND NEIGHBOUR.

There she is again. She has torn through
The plantains behind.

ORUKORERE.

> A true leopard flings out his specks even
> At dark, they will spark forth to tell
> The king of the forest is out stalking. And
> He throws his catch up over the roof
> Thatch, however high, to catch it on
> The lee before the quarry falls;
> Else he is no true hunter. We must halt
> Him, put a stop to this fault.

TONYÁ.

> She has fallen, she has fallen!

3RD NEIGHBOUR.

> This is strange.

1ST NEIGHBOUR.

> More than strange.

2ND NEIGHBOUR.

> Zifa, you really must do something.

ZIFA.

> Do what? Put her in a room with goats
> And tie her to a log? Isn't
> That what you will have me do?

2ND NEIGHBOUR.

> Nobody said you should shut her up.

3RD NEIGHBOUR.

> No, not with goats among their slime and
> Dung.

1ST NEIGHBOUR.

> Nor tethered to a log with chains.

ZIFA.

> Then what will you have me do, you sane souls
> Of Deinogbo? Or do you think I have
> Not heard your laughter cackle in the play house when
> She passed all smeared with ash and dust?

TONYÁ.

> Leave them, they are not worth your anger. I
> Should take them up myself if
> I thought it worthwhile.

1st Neighbour.

   We did not come to make trouble.

2nd Neighbour.

   It was her cry brought me out of my house.

3rd Neighbour.

   If eyes do not see, lips will not cry.

Zifa.

   Go away to your houses then
   And tomorrow if any of you finds
   Nothing to cry about in his house
   Let him come to me and I'll dance
   With him even to the market place.

3rd Neighbour.

   We are sorry to see you so.

2nd Neighbour.

   See to her, the woman, your aunt.

1st Neighbour.

   She is foaming in the mouth.

Zifa.

   Go away, I said. Tonyá, let's take her in.

Tonyá.

   Yes; oh, see how she shudders.

2nd Neighbour.

   That's a queer family.

3rd Neighbour.

   A curse lies heavy on it.

1st Neighbour.

   Of the woman there can be little doubt.

2nd Neighbour.

   And to think she was one time
   The sweetest maid in all the creeks.

3rd Neighbour.

   She will have no man for husband.
   Why, young men came from all over the land
   To ask her hand of her father.

2nd Neighbour.

   They all got it from him, you cannot

Doubt that. He would as easy kill inside the
Clan as outside it.

1ST NEIGHBOUR.

Remember how the people of the sea
Chose her for their handmaiden.

2ND NEIGHBOUR.

Sure, but then she was so proud she would
Not listen to what the oracle said.

3RD NEIGHBOUR.

As a result, they have put this spell on
Her. But although she has this double vision
Nobody believes a word she says, even
Outside of the gourd.

1ST NEIGHBOUR.

Then, you think there is something
To this her raving?

3RD NEIGHBOUR.

Do not ask me. In
A family like that there always will spring
Up leopards. But that they have goats
In their midst one may as well go
And seek eggs among cocks.

2ND NEIGHBOUR.

Yet she cried a goat. I really can
Not understand them of that family.

1ST NEIGHBOUR.

There, let us be off. I can see
His wife is coming.

2ND NEIGHBOUR.

She is grown very queer of late too.
See how she carries her wood?

3RD NEIGHBOUR.

Bring up a chicken among hawks
And if she is not eaten she will eat.

1ST NEIGHBOUR.

She certainly looks stiff for all her fatness.

3RD NEIGHBOUR.

    It is the wrong type what with that
    Her clay colour.

2ND NEIGHBOUR.

    They say he doesn't go in
    To her anymore, but I wouldn't discuss that.

EBIERE.

    Who can those be skulking away
    Like goats before ants?

DODE.

    Mother, Mother!

EBIERE.

    Here's a dragonfly I caught you on the way.

DODE.

    O oo! how bright his colours! But, Ebiere,
    Mother, Mother, she's been——

EBIERE.

    All right, all right, Dode, I quite follow.
    Your aunt's been drunk again and
    Seeing visions of houses burning.

DODE.

    No, it was a goat this time. It was crying
    Because a leopard had it in its claws.

EBIERE.

    And so your father and Tonyá have taken
    Her in to sleep it out.

DODE.

    Yes, they have. But what is a leopard? Is it
    Big as a cow?

EBIERE.

    Leave leopards alone to the elders
    Of the family. Your father is honoured
    For collecting their scalps but everybody
    Discredits your aunt, who only sees
    Them in visions. Well, was everybody
    Waiting for me to come back and put
    On the lamp?

TONYÁ.

Careful, Ebiere, she has vomited all
Over the floor.

EBIERE.

Thank you, but I can find my way.

ZIFA.

You are back from the bush, I am
Glad of that. We were about coming out
To you when she started seeing
Things once more.

TONYÁ.

It is so embarrassing,
Everybody has been here to see her.

EBIERE.

I saw them going out as I came in.
They didn't even stop to greet me.

TONYÁ.

Zifa drove them off the place.

ZIFA.

I had to. Now, do you think you could clean
This up?

EBIERE.

Of course, I will. Let me get some
Piece of cloth to mop it up. The woman
Is almost a child once more.

TONYÁ.

A child?

EBIERE.

Why, yes. Anyone can see that from how
She behaves. And for that alone I get
Rather fond of her.

TONYÁ.

That is a foolish thing to say.

ZIFA.

No, Tonyá, no.
She knows what she is talking.

EBIERE.

Really, I wasn't trying to be awkward. Of that

You will agree we have enough
Already. Well, I thought you said you put
Her to bed to sleep it off?

TONYÁ.

So we did.

ZIFA.

Yes, we did.

DODE.

She is singing, she is up and singing.

EBIERE.

You hear her, too, Dode, don't you? Listen!

TONYÁ.

She is coming out.

ORUKORERE.

The leopard, I have missed the leopard
That will despoil the prime goat of our yard
But I do not hear the victor's cry.

DODE.

Nor I, Mother.

EBIERE.

Keep quiet, Dode; will you?

ZIFA.

There is nothing like that here.

TONYÁ.

We looked everywhere while you slept.

ORUKORERE.

So I slept? And you didn't find
Him? I knew it was no proper leopard.
There, I see it sports the long slide
Of the earth one. You know it is the dumbest
Of all beasts whether in town or bush, yes,
Even as the beast strikes you dead on the sand.

ZIFA.

So from leopard it is become a snake?

ORUKORERE.

How should I tell? I must go out first
And find him.

ZIFA.

No, you must not.

TONYÁ.

She is going to start all over again.

ORUKORERE.

I feel so dry. Zifa, will you give
Me some coins out of the pot you buried
Under your bedstead?

TONYÁ.

Give her if that will make her quiet.

ZIFA.

I gave you some yesterday, didn't I?
It's what you have spent drinking all day?

ORUKORERE.

Money is sweet yet it doesn't bubble fat.

DODE.

Please, give it her, Father.

ORUKORERE.

No, he won't, my son; although he ate
Yesterday. Therefore he will not eat today!
Well, let us sing, boy, oh let's
Sing of souls tied down with ropes
Of piassava so strong they break!
"Bailing out to Accra! It's
To Accra I must bail,
This cooking of gin, it's
Killed me, oh, it has!"

EBIERE.

Now you two, do leave her alone;
I'll go and get food for each one.

## THIRD MOVEMENT

EBIERE.
  A grown-up fellow like you, strappling as
  A banana sucker, you still do not
  Know how to wash your body properly.
  There, steady! Let me bathe you. You have all
  The time only been rubbing the water on
  Your belly, and a big pot you have. Of course
  You call for farina before the cock calls
  Forth the day. When dawn breaks, mouth opens, and
  With you it stays so till dusk closes in.
  Now what are you yelling for? Anybody
  Would think you were being circumcised all
  Over again or that you have yaws on
  You. Take that! And that! Now you can holla
  All day just as you please. I suppose your
  Race can boast of that.

TONYÁ.
  What are you
  Smacking the boy for, Ebiere?

EBIERE.
  Better be
  About what you are doing. Don't splash
  Me with water, I told you, you scamp!

TONYÁ.
  That's enough; we don't allow our children
  To be knocked on the head like that.

EBIERE.
  Don't you lecture me on how to beat my child.
  What do you know of child-rearing anyway?

TONYÁ.
  Enough to know that knocking a child on
  The head like that makes him prone
  To attacks from smallpox. We simply forbid
  It in the family. You may smack

Him on the backside if you please
But do not beat the boy on the head.

EBIERE.

I can well see you people care for children
A great deal.

TONYÁ.

Yes, we do. Here, Dode, come
This way and I will carve you a fine canoe out
Of this corkwood and bamboo. I have enough
Floats already to fence off the bar.

DODE.

Will I be able to go to sea like you
And Father?

TONYÁ.

Even so. Witches sail
In groundnut husks; and this boat I shall carve
You is many, many times fitter than any

[EBIERE *hisses.*]

Witch's craft. Why, what do you make that sound for?

EBIERE.

Does it give you pain?

TONYÁ.

From a snake such a sound is only to be
Expected; it is the signal of spite and
Sinister motives. But coming out of a woman
Like you with all the things a wife would want
In the world, I do not know what to make of it.

EBIERE.

Poor, poor, father-of-my-marriage, what
Can you or anybody in this house do
About anything? At least, one has first to know
The roots to be able to gather the leaves.

TONYÁ.

Ebiere, yes, I confess I do not know
Much. Both of you, you and Zifa, say very little.
But I do know that you have gradually
Become bitter over the months. Why, look
At how you cuffed the little boy just now.

Anybody seeing you would think you were his
Stepmother.

EBIERE.

And he not my only child.

TONYÁ.

I wasn't thinking of that.

EBIERE.

You ought to have
Been, yes, long before now, since you are
So solicitous about my well-being.

TONYÁ.

Everybody wants children of course.

EBIERE.

Thus the elders pray: Only one seed
The elephant brings forth at a time until
The house is full, yes, until the house be
Full even if this takes ten falls of the flood.

TONYÁ.

Ebiere, you are bitter as bile. Lots
Of people there are who want children but
Have not been blessed with a fine one as you have.

EBIERE.

That is bad, isn't it? Especially
As custom dictates those who die childless
Be cast out of the company of the fruitful whose
Special grace is interment in the township.

TONYÁ.

The Witch of Nine Plumes has your stomach
For her cauldron.

EBIERE.

She is a good cook, she
Must be, to have boiled me dry of all content.

TONYÁ.

I do not mean that, I mean you ought
To be contented and not be so short
Of temper with everyone. You cuff the child
On the skull, and have taken to scolding and nagging
All day. Have you cooked in time today for my

Brother's home coming? Many times
These past market days it has been so.
Why, what is become of you? A man
After long stay at sea deserves a proper and
Regular dish when he arrives home. I wonder
Zifa is so given to your new
Irregular ways.

EBIERE.

Don't talk to me about
Your brother or about my irregular ways,
I tell you, don't talk to me of them.
Irregular ways! What do you know about
Irregularities, anyway? If food was
Not ready by noontide, that would be
Irregular, wouldn't it? If I saw
My period and stayed indoors and cooked
For you and your big brother, that would
Be irregular by all standards
And practice, wouldn't it? You that are so correct
And proper you know all these things.

TONYÁ.

Don't you clap your hands in my face, woman!
If my brother takes all this from you, I
Certainly won't, do you hear me? I will
Not have it.

EBIERE.

You talk of your brother
And of his patience as if patience were
His alone and he alone has suffered.

TONYÁ.

Surely, he has suffered much abuse
From you lately.
Why, the whole village is talking.

EBIERE.

Talking, are they? Like you are doing now
About his forbearance and his
Sufferings. What do they know about suffering and
Patience? And you, what do you know about them?
Of course, it is the woman who is in the wrong

Always—I who have suffered neglect and
Gathered mould like a thing of sacrifice
Left out in sun and rain at the crossroads.
You talk to me of my short temper; what
Short temper have I when it is pulled and
Tugged at daily like a hook-line?

TONYÁ.

You certainly are showing it today,
And nobody has baited you.

DODE.

Mother, Mother, don't!

EBIERE.

Stand aside, child. Flesh with thorn
In it must bud pus.

TONYÁ.

Nobody stuck
Thorns in your flesh; why should you smart so?

EBIERE.

You are a greater fool than the idiot
In the market place to ask a question like that.

TONYÁ.

I said, Ebiere, I'm not your husband.

EBIERE.

Well, aren't you? Since you know his duties better
Than he does, why don't you take them up? If you
Don't, I should laugh your whole race to scorn.

TONYÁ.

What you want is a good cry. Now will
You take your hands off me?

EBIERE.

Do it, do it now
And show you are strong.

TONYÁ.

I do not have to
With you to show I have one bone. Many who
Doubted have felt its weight in the wrestling pit.

EBIERE.

Well, fell me down then; it would be so much
Easy for you to do, I being no cow.

TONYÁ.

I say take your hands off me. Ebiere,
You certainly are desperate for danger.
See how like waters whipped by the wind you
Have run amok. Take your hands off.

EBIERE.

No, no, show your powers, I say,
Floor me, march on me, strike me down as
You did Benikpanra the Bull to show
You are the strong man of the family.

TONYÁ.

Why, Ebiere, you are mad, so gone far
Leaves-gathering, and you are hot all
Over, oh so shuddering, shuddering
So, you want to pull me down, which is
A thing forbidden; now take that then, and that—Oh my
    father!

EBIERE.

So I am crazed, completely gone leaves-plucking,
And you? Aren't you shuddering too, oh,
So shuddering in your heat of manhood you
Have thrown me? Now, hold me, do hold on and
Fight, for it is a thing not forbidden!

                [*Cock crows beyond.*]

DODE.

Help, help! My mother, my mother! Tonyá
Is wrestling on
The floor with my mother!

ORUKORERE.

What is it, child, what is the matter? Can't
I have a little sleep but one
Of you in this house must kick me up?

DODE.

There, there, look there, they have rolled

And dragged each other over the doorstep,
And now the door is slammed behind them.

ORUKORERE.

Why, boy, these are no leopard and goat
Interlocked between life and death, but
Two dogs at play. Poor child, let me close the door.

DODE.

Will you leave them to fight there? My
Uncle is the strongest man in all
The creeks. He will kill my mother.

ORUKORERE.

He will not, my son, rather it is she
Who may kill your uncle. Oh, my son,
My son, I have seen a sight this dusk to make
The eagle blind. I heard the cock crow
As I woke up from sleep. That was sign
Of omen enough but little did I know
It was this great betrayal of our race.

DODE.

You won't separate them then?

ORUKORERE.

Only the gods and the dead may separate
Them now, child. And what is your poor father
To do should he hear that the liana has
Entwined his tree of life? I said there was
A serpent in the house but nobody as usual
Will take me serious. Yet the hiss of the creature
Was up among the eaves, down under the
Stool. Last night I cried it had coiled itself
Into a pad to pillow my head but the house
Was full of snoring sound and as usual
Everybody snorted. Well, come on,
Son, and I'll get you some snuff.

# FINAL MOVEMENT

ZIFA.

I cannot believe it, I just cannot;
Eyes may as well be ears and night, day. My
Own brother, whom I have looked after
As a son; if it is true, I'll cut off his
Neck with my cutlass. Yet there he was sprawled on
My bed when I thought he was still out
Inspecting hooks in the bush.
And when I would call up the boy,
She comes between us holding my hand
With the injunction, oh let the man sleep,
He is tired and mustn't be woken up at
This dead of night. The man!
When did he become man to her?
With her he was always the bad boy to
Be bullied and scolded: "No sense in Tonyá,"
"Tonyá has ruined this again," from cock's
Crow till the cuckoo's song. Now she stands
Guard over him in my bed against me.
I'll kill them both if it is true.
It cannot be true; only last night they
Had one of their fights but my aunt, she was so
Much in grip of drink she could not separate
Them
Nor call in help. So they struggled like
Two iguanas till outspent, they stopped
Of their own. Her account was too garbled for
Anyone to gather anything.

ORUKORERE.

It is market day
Again, awake all of you!
Hello, my son who delights me, who never
Lets me touch mud, is that you?

ZIFA.

I kneel to you, Mother, although the
Sun has gone to sea.

ORUKORERE.

Has it? Well, has it? I thought it all night.
But rise, my son. You were not made
For mud. But you are up early, which is
A thing very good, for that means you
Are offering the gods sacrifice today.
One cannot tell how always watchful they
Stand warding evil spirits away from
The gates until misfortune enters the house.

ZIFA.

Misfortune has been my guest these many floods.

ORUKORERE.

My son, are they still at the gate, the
Housewives who deserted the hearth?

ZIFA.

A guest after being fed looks up
At the sun. But these many years I have been host
To a guest that will not return.

ORUKORERE.

Oh, he must! He will sometime, but shall we
Pass today, a day dedicated to the dead
And to all gods, is it to be spoilt
With such bitterness of heart?

ZIFA.

It is others who have spoilt my day.

ORUKORERE.

You must not say a thing like that.

ZIFA.

Why shouldn't I when my bed is barred from me
For my brother to sleep on?

ORUKORERE.

Is it even so? The world must not hear of it.

ZIFA.

The world will, even today. Yesterday you
Said they had a fight, is that true?

ORUKORERE.

A goat and a leopard may as well wrestle.

ZIFA.

Now, look here, Mother, I am tired of
Being in the toil of parables.

ORUKORERE.

No, not so strong, these hands you seek
To break have held you to my breast.

ZIFA.

God knows I will not be violent
With you. But why will you not tell
All that you know? The very trees in my
Grove are being
Felled level with the ground; you yourself say
You hear them crashing one upon another,
And yet you do nothing to stop them.

ORUKORERE.

Indeed, I am doing all I can to arrest
Their fall, but which of you has shown a
Heart to give me a helping hand?

ZIFA.

Save me, Mother, save me from this
Disaster I fear has befallen me.

ORUKORERE.

Of course, I will. There, my child, rest
Your head on my shoulders shrunken up
With age. But they still can give my son support.
Who knows how milk enters the coconut?
Now, don't sob, oh, my son, my son, do
Not cry! Only the goat may cry
When the leopard has him in his toils,
And I'm sure my son is no goat.

ZIFA.

It is, it is so degrading.

ORUKORERE.

I know. But there, I think your brother is
Coming this way.

ZIFA.

He must not see my tears.

ORUKORERE.

That's my boy. The strong weep only at dead
Of night.

TONYÁ.

So the adder
Has risen, Mother? I did
Not see you, Zifa.

ORUKORERE.

The puff-adder may
Rise late, but it must not be caught asleep
Else it will stir in the pot.

ZIFA.

Where is Ebiere?

TONYÁ.

At the waterside to fetch water. Tonight
You very well know is the start of market
Tide and she's hurrying to cross over
With your last night's catch, which by the way
Was no larger than a kite's haul.

ZIFA.

She is not going to market this tide.

TONYÁ.

Well, is anything the matter here?
She's all set to go.

ZIFA.

Shut your mouth, will you? I say
She will not go to market today.

TONYÁ.

There is little starch or farina left
In the house; she has to go
And barter the fish for these.

ORUKORERE.

Now, Tonyá, do not cross your elder
Brother. Go in and look for the he-goat,
The one that is for sacrifice.

TONYÁ.

I go, Mother. The poor thing cried, all
Night and all thro' today; perhaps it knows
Its day is near night.

ZIFA.

You see how things are
Between the two? Ebiere now consults him
Even in matters of household. What further
Proof do I want now?

ORUKORERE.

Proofs are
A thing for the blind. Here, you see this
Calabash? I have laid fern fronds
Over it, and the white soil of Edo
Has turned to mere in it already.

ZIFA.

I do not need cleansing; perhaps others do.

ORUKORERE.

You will stand where you are and let me
Begin with you, being head of this house.

ZIFA.

Indeed, am I head still?

ORUKORERE.

Of course. Only one elder there is to a house
And the young are water. One head and a
Long tail, that is our one prayer in life.
How many times do I have to tell you that?

ZIFA.

All right, Mother, cut the circles under your
Heel. I am going in for a little while
But will be back before the seven are
Complete in front of the shrine.

ORUKORERE.

I shall be waiting for you. My poor poor
Child, he has blundered upon the beast that
Is preying upon him. But what is to become
Of us in this house?
We have slept with wives who should

Be outdoors, have eaten of the meals they prepared
In their corruption, and passed under lines on which
They hung their underclothes. In such
Circumstances, what help, what quest
But to look up to the dead? Ah, my brother, it
Was good you were called home early to our fathers
Else you would now see your sons like bad
Fish eating one another. That goat
Again! I cannot bear its cry. I must go
And find me a live chicken to carry
Out this ritual.

[EBIERE *sings.*]

EBIERE.

What do you want with the goat?
One would
Think you were a boy still, and not man.

TONYÁ.

We must be careful, Ebiere. My
Brother and aunt, they were here
Together just now.

EBIERE.

What about that? They know nothing.

TONYÁ.

We cannot be too sure. They asked of me
To fetch the goat for sacrifice and
Should be back here any time. Ts, ts,
The goat is drinking the water.

EBIERE.

Let it be. I am so happy today. I think what I
Told you is true. Come and feel it.

TONYÁ.

No, no, we must not do that here under
Light of day.

EBIERE.

It is there,
All right, I know it, and it is for you. Oh,
I am so happy. Tonyá, let's fly
And set up house in another creek. You'll

Cast your net and I'll hold the stern until
We have our child.

TONYÁ.

You are mad, Ebiere,
Here, step back and pick up your pot. My
Brother
Is querulous as things are.
He says you must not
Go to market today.

EBIERE.

Then we shall be
Together this night. Another of his ships
Comes in tonight, doesn't it? What shall I cook
For you? You know we must fly before
He comes back at dawn.

TONYÁ.

Oh, I think you are gone crazy too,
Everybody in this house. I'll tell him,
Yes I will. Now, pick up the pot and
Go in, Ebiere.

ZIFA.

Let the pot be.

TONYÁ.

Oh, I can hardly stay on my feet.

EBIERE.

It is as well. The thorn in the flesh
Will draw pus.

ZIFA.

I said let the pot be.
Mother, come out here quick.

ORUKORERE.

Here I am. Now, what does this mean?

EBIERE.

Ask him, he should be able to tell,
Being in such frenzy.

TONYÁ.

Keep quiet, Ebiere. You must not speak
Like that of my brother.

ZIFA.

> Thank you, my good brother, but I
> Think I can well fend for myself.

ORUKORERE.

> Will someone tell an old woman what is
> Happening in this house?

ZIFA.

> I'll tell you, Mother, soon enough; you
> Said I should make sacrifice to the gods.
> These past several years we have none of us
> Followed your word. Being the elder,
> I agree, I am to blame for this. But now
> I obey you and will make instant
> Sacrifice to the gods.

ORUKORERE.

> But you are
> As yet not cleansed, and for that matter all
> The concession is reeking with rot and
> Corruption.

ZIFA.

> In that case, it needs drastic
> Cleansing, which is what we shall now all perform.

ORUKORERE.

> Be careful, son, and do nothing that is
> Rash. When the gods ask for blood it is
> Foolish to offer them oil.

ZIFA.

> You shall
> Be satisfied with all that I do today,
> Mother. Here, Tonyá, hold the goat by
> The feet and I will by the horns. And you,
> My wife, see how with one stroke of my knife
> I sever the head from the trunk.

ORUKORERE.

> A brave stroke, my boy, a brave stroke!
> There was only one man in all the creeks
> Who could do it like that, but he died many
> Years ago.

ZIFA.

  See how erect
  The blood spurts! It should cleanse the compound
  Of all corruption today. But hold on,
  One little detail more and we shall begin
  In real earnest.

TONYÁ.

  What is that?

EBIERE.

  The blood, it has soiled my clothes.

ZIFA.

  Well, never mind that. A little soap soon
  Washes that off. Here, Tonyá, hold forth
  The head with all its horns.

TONYÁ.

  There!

ZIFA.

  Good. Now, put it inside the pot.

ORUKORERE.

  What is that you ask of the boy?

EBIERE.

  The man is mad!

TONYÁ.

  Why, the thing is impossible.

ZIFA.

  It is not. I said put the head in the pot.

TONYÁ.

  I will if you so desire.

ZIFA.

  Yes, I not only desire it, I demand
  It. That's right, just like that.

TONYÁ.

  It won't go in any further.

ZIFA.

  Who told you? There, push, brother, push,
  Oh push with all your might!

TONYÁ.

The pot will break if I push harder.

ZIFA.

So you know that? But never mind. Push,
I say, till the head enters in, horns
And ears, all of them.

ORUKORERE.

The woman has fainted!

ZIFA.

Has she? Let her then, and you, my
Brother, you see how the pot is broken!

TONYÁ.

This was a trap, a trap, and you think
You have caught some grass cutters.

ZIFA.

Haven't I? You just wait and see.

ORUKORERE.

I said the woman has fainted and nobody
Listens! Why, what are you about?
Run, Tonyá, run, your brother has picked up
His cutlass and will kill you!

ZIFA.

He is running, the coward, he is
Running and will save his neck.

ORUKORERE.

Kill me first then.

ZIFA.

No, do not cross me. It is none of your
Fault but I'll get at him, I say
Do not cross me. Don't you see they admit
Their guilt? One collapses and the other
Flees. Now, he's fled in and barred the door.
I shall not let him escape me. I will
Break open the door, break it and get at
This monster. Now, will you come out, thief,
Noonday thief.

TONYÁ.

I am no noonday thief!

If you leave your piece of cloth in the open
At night, what becomes of it?

ORUKORERE.

Help, oh help,
You people, my sons, my sons, they have both
Turned beasts and will devour each other.

ZIFA.

So that is your answer, thief? Well, open
And I'll tell you the sun, although
It dries the cloth, never assumes it. But
You have, you have, and left me naked
Before our enemies.

1ST NEIGHBOUR.

Why, what is the matter here?

2ND NEIGHBOUR.

Has anyone fainted?

3RD NEIGHBOUR.

Is it fire upon the fish wrack?

ORUKORERE.

Oh, no, it is no common fire has
Consumed us. There, go to him before
He breaks down the door and does his brother
Harm. And this woman here, she is dying.

3RD NEIGHBOUR.

What can be happening here?

1ST NEIGHBOUR.

There, bring some water. Some of you, go
And hold the man.

2ND NEIGHBOUR.

Thrust hand in her mouth
Till she retches. No, not so, take hold
Of her jaws and keep them open else they'll lock.

ZIFA.

Keep clear, all of you if you like the taste
Of soup. Now, open up, I say!
Or must I break down the door?

2ND NEIGHBOUR.

He has a cutlass!

3RD NEIGHBOUR.
  He'll kill everybody!

1ST NEIGHBOUR.
  What may have caused this madness?

ORUKORERE.
  Do not ask, do not, but each will eat
  Each although the soup be sour in the mouth.
  Will no one go to him? Then I will. But
  Good people take away the woman and
  Bring her back to life.

3RD NEIGHBOUR.
  Yes. We will
  Do that, we will do that. What a day!

2ND NEIGHBOUR.
  So the thing is true,
  That Tonyá sleeps with the woman, his brother's wife?

1ST NEIGHBOUR.
  That is bad.

2ND NEIGHBOUR.
  This is no place to talk. Take her up!

1ST NEIGHBOUR.
  Yes, better remove her quick. He will
  Surely kill her also if he comes back.

3RD NEIGHBOUR.
  You cannot store up fire in the pot;
  It will blow up and fill the place with rot.

ORUKORERE.
  There he has broken in, he has broken
  Down the door while we babble here
  Like hens among corn.
  I'll not let him
  Damn his soul, I'll not.
  Zifa, Zifa,
  Listen to a poor woman, listen, Zifa!
  He is gone in, gone in, and now
  We shall see what is not seen.

ZIFA.
  Tonyá, Tonyá, where will you run now?

I have got you caged in—even like
A fish in a trap.
Ah! What have we here?
He is gone and hanged himself on the loft!

ORUKORERE.

Did I hear the man right?

[*She falls down.*]

3RD NEIGHBOUR.

Too well, I fear, too well.

1ST NEIGHBOUR.

There the boy hangs dangling in the air.

2ND NEIGHBOUR.

He did it with his loincloth, standing
On the mortar upturned.

ZIFA.

Do not run, oh do not run away, you
People. I said the wretch has gone and
Hanged himself on the loft. But it is I
Indeed have killed the boy—my brother.
Poor, poor brother, do you hang aloft
There smiling in my face? I sought to kill
You but in that office you have again
Performed my part.
You veer away from me; why should you
Not avoid me as one with smallpox when
I have taken my brother's life? For though
You see me bloodless it is this arm
Did this deed and this cutlass you see dry
Is flowing even now with the red blood
Of my brother, the brother, the boy born after me
To look after but who now has twice taught me
My duty. Here I break my matchet upon
My head and may everything fly apart
Even as I throw these iron bits asunder.
The poor, brave boy has truly done for me.
Good people, I hope you understand. It
Is not that I desired to drink out
Of his scalp, which is unnatural, but that boy,
He went in to my wife, my wife whom

Although under my roof for five years
I could not possess, for you see
I am powerless between my thighs. Was
That not a brotherly act? He sought to keep
What his brother was powerless to keep
In the house. My house, it has collapsed
In season that is calm to others. My fathers
Built it before my time that my children
And theirs to come may find a roof above
Their heads. And now what have I done
With it? In my hands it falls into a state
Of disrepair and now is fallen,
Fallen. Nothing stands; I will go
And find a new place of rest.

3RD NEIGHBOUR.
Where is the man going has brought this ruin
On his head?

2ND NEIGHBOUR.
There follow him quick,
He is making for the beach as one in sleep.

1ST NEIGHBOUR.
And what is to happen to this poor woman
Now a bundle of rags on the ground?

ORUKORERE.
Let me be, oh, do not try to lift me
Up but let me lie in the ruins they have
Wrought between them.

2ND NEIGHBOUR.
Let us follow the man.

1ST NEIGHBOUR.
Shut the door, keep it shut. There comes his son.

3RD NEIGHBOUR.
Indeed, that is no sight for women or
Children to see.

DODE.
Mother, where is Ebiere?
I heard my father's voice—who is he
Angry with? Not with Tonyá or Ebiere?

ORUKORERE.

    Cast your catch aside there and come over
    Here and sit between my knees.

DODE.

    I'll put them in first. Isn't there a lamp
    In this house?

ORUKORERE.

    There will never be light again in this
    House, child; this is the night of our race,
    The fall of all that ever reared up head
    Or crest.

DODE.

    Mother, what are you saying?

ORUKORERE.

    How should I know, son? I looked for a staff
    Long enough to kill a serpent I knew
    Was strangling my goat. In my search is my defeat.

DODE.

    So you had a sacrifice! Why, you didn't
    Tell me; I could have brought along
    My playmates, I wanted so much to hold
    The hind legs while Father struck.

4TH NEIGHBOUR.

    Is anyone here in this house? Ebiere—
    She is coming to, but I fear
    The woman has had miscarriage.

DODE.

    What's that she says about my mother?
    Oh where is she?

ORUKORERE.

    There, another blow
    Has been dealt the tree of our house, and see
    How the sap pours out to spread our death. I
    Believe it, now I believe it. White ants
    Have passed their dung on our roof-top.
    Like a tree rotten in the rain, it
    Topples. What totem is there left now
    For the tribe to hold on to for support?

DODE.
  My mother, I want my mother!

ORUKORERE.
  Do not seek to stop him. Let the antelope
  Run before the hunters arrive.

3RD NEIGHBOUR.
  Madam, madam, why should it be my lot
  To bring you this?

ORUKORERE.
  Speak up, man, what effect
  Can the words you bring have now? Don't you
  See it is raining over the sea tonight?
  On the sands sprawling out to dazzle
  Point till eyes are scales
  This outpouring should be impression
  Indeed. Here only waves pour out
  On waves, only dunes upon dunes.

3RD NEIGHBOUR.
  Then you give me great relief where there
  Is little relief. The sea has submerged
  Us; because we are all thereunder I can
  Deliver my burden with little cry.

ORUKORERE.
  What is the drift of your tongue? Say, has
  Lightning struck him down that walked
  Into the storm, his head covered with basin?
  I heard the roll of thunder out to sea.

2ND NEIGHBOUR.
  That was no roll of thunder you heard, madam,
  But the lowing of a ship coming in.

ORUKORERE.
  Oh, I see. So they have come and taken
  Him to the other shore before me?

1ST NEIGHBOUR.
  Even so, madam. How did you know?

ORUKORERE.
  Never mind, tell the manner of my son's
  Going forth.

3RD NEIGHBOUR.

Well, you saw how he
Went out of here as one in sleep. He said
Nothing more and so, silent, we followed
On his heels. It was a heavy walk, the fishing
Baskets scattered all about, the new canoes
Carving on the shore. And the grass was wet
On our feet. Presently, fording the sands,
We saw him reach the water's edge. Just then
That noise you said you heard as distant
Thunder rolled out to where we stood. It was
A steamer calling out for a pilot
To pass beyond the bar. At the sound of it,
Zifa seemed to start out of his sleep: "Blow,
Blow, sirens, blow," he bellowed as in reply,
"And blow till your hooting drown
The moaning of the sea. No blow
Will be stronger." The owls, he said, that should
Hoot at night have this afternoon blown down
His house as they have the ancestral hall
Open in the market place. And the stalls there
That should crowd with voices are filled now
Not even with the buzz of houseflies. All
Are fled, fled, and left behind
Bats to show their beards by day.

ORUKORERE.

And what did you, you men of Deinogbo?

3RD NEIGHBOUR.

What could we? The thing was so like
A dream at flood time it was
Impossible to hold at anything.

ORUKORERE.

Go on, who am I to question you? I heard
The goat crying all the while and thought
It a leopard stalking.

2ND NEIGHBOUR.

Just then,
Madam, the ship blew its siren
A second time. "You may blow and hoot," Zifa

Answered back, "from here to the other shore
But I will not come to you tonight.
Your throat may be iron, your flesh
Iron. But that is not it," he said,
And with that waded into the deep
As one again in sleep.

ORUKORERE.

Umaloku, Umaloku, three times
I call upon you, look to my boy! But
What boy? Oh, what boy? Inside there
One hangs dangling like a fruit full
Before its time. Who will pluck it?
And out there you have brought tidings
Of another who walked of his
Own will into the night. On whom then
Should I call? Houseflies are not
Known to answer a call at night,
So on whom then shall I call?

3RD NEIGHBOUR.

Do not cry, do not cry!

1ST NEIGHBOUR.

Come in out of the night dew.

2ND NEIGHBOUR.

Here is lamp to light you in.

ORUKORERE.

Take away
The light. Will you take away your lamp?
What, am I become so like a statue
That discovered among ruins in
The sun-set day, you wonder at
Yet will not bow down to? I know
I have lost both my face and limbs.
Recognition therefore is become a thing
For houseflies and bats, is it? I say,
Let there be no light again in this house,

[*She snatches the oil lamp and dashes it to the ground.*]

Let there be none! But good people,
Bear with me, you will bear with me, won't

You? You see, black birds whose immortal
Knot both my sons have tied and slung
Have gathered the loot, all the loot,
And left behind not one seed of my fruit.

1ST NEIGHBOUR.

Come away, we understand.

3RD NEIGHBOUR.

It is late, come away.

2ND NEIGHBOUR.

Come away, tomorrow is a heavier day.

*The End.*

# ALTERNATIVE CLOSE

[*in place of the last three lines, for those who want the*
MASSEUR *back!*]

A VOICE FROM WITHOUT.
   Who is that crying in the dark?

NEIGHBOURS.
   He comes, oh, he comes!

ORUKORERE.
   Who comes? So it is you, manipulator
   Of broken bones and flesh torn out of joint.

MASSEUR.
   Daughter of Umaloku, the delight
   Of God and pride of unguents,
   Whom the merpeople desire, I come
   Ahead of the snail and tortoise.

ORUKORERE.
   Then you come with your house
   Entire above your head. Yet I see
   No plumes of smoke.

MASSEUR.
   Rain made a pond
   Of my hearth several floods ago.
   But need we recall that?

ORUKORERE.
   I recall nothing. Why,
   In my head there breeds a consort
   Of frogs, and they sing so many
   Songs I cannot in the market murmur
   Tell one season from the other.

MASSEUR.
   True, true; one might as well number
   Rain drops on roof thatch.

ORUKORERE.
   Oh, thatch! Everywhere
   They either spring leak or catch fire.

MASSEUR.

    It is their way. But although
    The iroko is our burden, we have
    For staff the silk cotton tree.

ORUKORERE.

    Have they left us any
    To hold on to for support or cover?
    All around, I smell only grass
    Running to flames, sand to water.

MASSEUR.

    Naked then we stand as before. But if
    We shiver, what will children out
    In their first rain?

ORUKORERE.

    Dode, now the rain
    Has caught him too. Elder mine,
    I thought at first to rebuke
    You for coming when the market
    Is over. Others have made off
    With the wares you put a price
    On. But now all that is over and
    Only the laughter of wind fills out
    In my ears. I will go and see
    To the chickens wet in the rain.

MASSEUR.

    Go, good woman. And you people
    Of Deinogbo, let me tell you, rain
    Or sun, it has been a clean fire. No doubt
    There are some, as she said, among you
    Who will say it is I started it all.

2ND NEIGHBOUR.

    You started it?

1ST NEIGHBOUR.

    How? Do tell us that, old man.

3RD NEIGHBOUR.

    What of the young woman
    Taken from another clan?

MASSEUR.

This was no fire begun
By ordinary hand. All fire comes
From God, else why the thunder?
The young woman, being tinder,
Caught it first, consuming farmer
And helpmate in the process. I sought
To bring them water but all
I had was a basket. Now, see
How burnt to charcoal the land
Lies, even to the shrubs on the hedge.

3RD NEIGHBOUR.

I said you cannot contain fire
In a pot. It will blow forth.

1ST NEIGHBOUR.

Before we knew it, the blaze was beyond
Control, its wild multiple tongues
Licking raw heaven's hooded face.

2ND NEIGHBOUR.

And although we fought
With all breath and brine, the noise
From those bamboo rafts aloft
Smothered us in the face.

MASSEUR.

You may well cry. But this is nothing
To beat your breast. It was how
We all began and will end. A child,
Once out of the womb, will shout,
Even like the chick or seedling
Out of its shell. And whether
For pain, for laugh, who can tell? But now you
Have lived to this day, perhaps you are ripe
To hazard a crack at life's nut. Still,
Do not, my people, venture overmuch
Else in unravelling the knot, you
Entangle yourselves. It is enough
You know now that each day we live
Hints at why we cried out at birth.

1ST NEIGHBOUR.
Come away, now we understand.

3RD NEIGHBOUR.
My heart cuts, and it is dark all over the land.

2ND NEIGHBOUR.
So dark, we must be away.

MASSEUR.
Home or on the strand,
Tomorrow for you spells another day
And the strain, the strength of the band.

*The End.*

# THE RAIN-KILLERS

*A Play in Four Acts*

*by*

ALFRED HUTCHINSON

*To Hazel*

# CHARACTERS

GRAN SHONGWE
MAPULE
MFUNDISI
MA-NKOSI
ZWANE
MA-ZWANE
HLOPE
MA-HLOPE
MA-GWAGWA
MAZIYA
SERGEANT MABIKA
CONSTABLE DLADLA
CONSTABLE NGWENYA
MA-NGWENYA
CONSTABLE NKOSI
BUS DRIVER
MA-SIBEKO
SIBANDE
MA-KUMALO
MA-MATSEBULA
MANGENYEZA
PAUL
SAMUEL
JOHN
MARK
ELIJAH
MOSES
GIDEON
MTSAKASI

SCENE: The action of the play takes place in Mzindi Village in a Native Reserve in the Eastern Transvaal, South Africa.

# THE RAIN-KILLERS

## ACT ONE

*At the bus terminus outside the village store in Mzindi.
The time is early afternoon. Beside a road which leads off to
the left, GRAN SHONGWE stands in the shade of a tree and
waits for the arrival of the bus. Enter MA-NKOSI from the
right.*

MA-NKOSI. Good day, Gran Shongwe. Whew, it's hot!
The sun is digging up the earth. What brings you so
far today?

GRAN. Good day, Ma-Nkosi. How are the children?

MA-NKOSI. They are alive. We see the sun and the drought.

GRAN. The sun and the drought. Don't talk about that,
Ma-Nkosi. Come out of the sun into this good-for-
nothing shade.

MA-NKOSI. The sun and the drought. Yesterday there was
a speck of cloud on the Mpakeni mountain and I
thought perhaps——

GRAN. Aw, I saw it too. Where is it today? Gone. We're
troubling ourselves hoping. This is no land. I'm waiting
for the bus. Mapule's coming back today. I'm just from
Bhai's store and I nearly died of shock. Things are so
dear.

MA-NKOSI. You can say it again, Gran Shongwe.

GRAN. Bhai's charging his own prices.

MA-NKOSI. Times are bad. No money. Bhai helps, though.
Where would we be without the credit he gives us?

GRAN. You're right, Ma-Nkosi, Bhai is an Indian-of-God
even if Zwane talks of getting the government to drive
him out. Says the store must be run by an African—
himself.

MA-NKOSI. Aw, Gran Shongwe, Zwane's things don't end.
Zwane thinks of nothing but his own stomach.

GRAN. This bus of drunkards. It's late again. Come out of

131

the sun, Ma-Nkosi; you're just like these children of today who won't listen.

MA-NKOSI. All right, Gran Shongwe.

GRAN. Drive a bus and drink. Where did you hear of such a thing?

MA-NKOSI. You can ask again, Gran Shongwe. It's a disease. One would think we weaned our children on beer. It's hot. The water holes are drying up.

GRAN. Yes. This could be like the great drought in the time of Chief Sogasa—this Chief Sidlamafa's grandfather. The world rotted with dead people and dead beasts. And the vultures took over the land. That was before you were born, just before the big war between the Boers and the English.

MA-NKOSI. Let's hope it's not like that.

GRAN. Have you heard from your husband, Ma-Nkosi? When is his contract on the mine finishing?

MA-NKOSI. He's still got three months. It's just like being a widow. No difference. They come home, stay a month, two months, make a child, and they're off. We're left struggling with children and soil which gives nothing.

GRAN. It's hard. But what can be done?

MA-NKOSI. Now this drought. [Claps hands.] I'm even afraid to go to the lands. Last time I went there, I nearly wept.

GRAN. I know. It kills the eyes.

MA-NKOSI. Have you heard that they're collecting money to go and ask Maziya for rain?

GRAN. Don't make me laugh in this terrible sun! What does that senile fraud of a witch doctor know about making rain?

MA-NKOSI. That's what I heard, Gran Shongwe.

GRAN. Maziya. Who is Maziya? Rain belonged to the old chiefs—the kings: Sogasa and Maguba. These chiefs of today, what do *they* know? When they try to lift their tails, the white man throws them into jail. Maziya. Who is Maziya? Since when is Maziya a king? If they have money to waste, let them go to Maziya. Not a penny from me.

MA-NKOSI. The things of Mzindi don't end. There's Mfundisi praying for rain. And now Maziya may be sacrificing for rain. Which one is God to listen to? These are the rain-killers. All of us.

GRAN. And who are those with money to waste?

MA-NKOSI. I hear Zwane is behind it.

GRAN. The leading member of the church! Mfundisi's right-hand man!

MA-NKOSI. It surprises me too.

GRAN. Well, he's all right. He's rolling in money. Zwane! That disgracer of law and custom. Don't talk about Zwane to me. He should remember his brother's children before he runs to Maziya to waste money. He should remember the children he has robbed of their inheritance so that today they roam the earth like a bird that has lost its nest. . . . Ma-Nkosi, don't talk to me about Zwane if you don't want to make me angry. I'm angry as it is with this bus which won't come.

MA-NKOSI. It's coming, Gran Shongwe.

GRAN. When? When this sun has killed us! You, too, talk like that Zwane!

MA-NKOSI. What have I done now, Gran Shongwe?

GRAN. It's this sun, my girl. And people like Zwane. Zwane is a chameleon which doesn't know its own colour. On one side he's a believer; on the other he holds on to the old ways—and he breaks the laws of both. Zwane! Zwane! I hear he's angry with Mfundisi.

MA-NKOSI. Angry with Mfundisi?

GRAN. It's something about a vote. Don't you go to the church meetings?

MA-NKOSI. That! You mean the church council meetings. Yes. Zwane wanted to be made keeper of the council's purse, but the vote went to Magagula.

GRAN. I'd sooner trust a skunk with eggs than Zwane with money. Zwane, that breaker, that disgracer, of the law. Zwane, who robbed his dead brother's children of their things.

MA-NKOSI. Shhh . . . Not so loud, Gran. Zwane has many ears.

GRAN. What "Shhh"? I will talk. I told Zwane to his face. I'm not one of you people who are afraid of Zwane and his money. The trouble with you people of today is that you keep quiet about so many wrong things. The pillar of the church. Goes about the village wearing holy airs. Mfundisi is too trusting. He's a good man, but he knows nothing about people. You wait. If it's the same Zwane I know, he'll open his eyes. I swear by my daughter who married a Musutu and died in a foreign land, I'd sooner trust a puff-adder than Zwane. There! I've spoken! Go and tell him! I'll tell him to his face. In the old days he wouldn't have got away with it.

MA-NKOSI. Aw, the land now belongs to the white man, Gran Shongwe.

GRAN. And does the white man allow things like this?

MA-NKOSI. Well, there it is. Do you hear it?

GRAN. Hear what?

MA-NKOSI. The bus. It's coming up the rise.

GRAN. Call these things ears! I'm getting deaf.

MA-NKOSI. There it is. Can you see it?

*Sound of approaching bus.*

GRAN. Yes. It's coming to us as if the world was on fire! The bus of drunkards! And my granddaughter in it.

BUS DRIVER [*offstage*]. Mzindi. All change. Women under; men on top.

GRAN. He's sober today. I don't see Mapule.

MA-NKOSI. It's full today.

*Several passengers enter from left. Some go into the store.*

GRAN. Ah, there she is. Mapule! Here I am!

MAPULE. Gran!

GRAN. My granddaughter. Welcome back. Come let me

kiss you. There [*Kiss.*] and there! [*Kiss.*] Aw, you're
beautiful. Let me look at you. You're just like your
mother, who left me to die under foreign skies. You're
back, Mapule?

MAPULE. I'm back, Gran. Good day, Ma-Nkosi. How are
you?

MA-NKOSI. Welcome back, Mapule. I'm alive, my girl.
Just the drought and the sun——

MAPULE. Did you miss me, Gran?

GRAN. Miss you! Ma-Nkosi, help me to listen to this. Do
you hear what this child is saying? Miss you? I didn't
know what to do without you. I didn't know how to
push the days forward so that you would come back to
me. If you talk like that again, I'll put you across my
knee, big beautiful young woman that you are!

MAPULE. Aw, Gran. What have I done? [*Laughs.*]

GRAN. Yes, big beautiful young woman that you are. Ah,
my girl, it's so nice to see you. But what have you come
back to? Not a drop of rain since you left. Is it raining in
Lusutu?

MAPULE. I left in rain. They are already eating green
mealies there.

GRAN. We're dying here, Mapule. I struggled when you
were away. Your gran's not young, you know. The
driver's sober today. Hello, driver. What's happened
today?

*Enter* BUS DRIVER.

DRIVER. What do you mean, Gran Shongwe?

GRAN. You're sober.

DRIVER. Aw, Gran, you make me out to be a drunk . . . in
front of this girl of Lusutu. Aw, aw. She's beautiful, that
girl of yours, Gran. Bavu! Girl of Lusutu. Bavu! Girls
reject men and go to men. There's no girl went to an
animal! You should marry me, girl of Lusutu. Aaron has
no cattle for *lobola*.

MAPULE. Go away, driver. What about all your girl friends
who wait for you at the bus stops?

DRIVER. I'd throw them all away and keep only you. You're Number One. The way you are beautiful, one could even think of buying medicines to make you love him.

GRAN. Do you forget that her father is a bull of a police sergeant? He'd come here, put the handcuffs on you, and march you off to prison.

DRIVER. Small matters those, Gran Shongwe. I could even die for a girl like yours.

GRAN [laughing]. The boys of today. They woo a girl in front of her grandmother.

DRIVER. It's the new look, Gran.

GRAN. You can say it again, my child. You are so handsome when you haven't been drinking. Why don't you stay like this?

DRIVER. Aw, Gran Shongwe, you disgrace me! And in front of this young lady! I've seen you, Gran Shongwe. [Exit DRIVER through store.]

GRAN. All right, my boy. Keep away from beer. [To MAPULE.] Mapule, Aaron Ngwane is not back.

MAPULE. I know, Gran.

GRAN. How stupid of me. Of course, you young people can write. How is he finding his work?

Enter ZWANE, MA-ZWANE, and MA-HLOPE. They stand to the right of the store.

MAPULE. Here comes that man Zwane. He's left his wife and that fat Ma-Hlope. I hope he hasn't come to greet me.

GRAN. Greet him back if he does.

MA-NKOSI. Yes, do.

ZWANE approaches them.

ZWANE. Ha! Ha! Welcome back from Lusutu. You return with the sun. How are you, Mapule?

MAPULE. I'm well, Father Zwane.

ZWANE. And you, Gran Shongwe?

GRAN. Alive, Zwane.

ZWANE. And Ma-Nkosi?

MA-NKOSI. Alive, Zwane. We see the drought.

ZWANE. Ha! Ha! We'll soon smell out the girl of Lusutu for bringing drought to us. Ha! Ha! Ha! I'm going to the store. See you again. [*Exit into store.*]

MAPULE. I don't like that man.

MA-NKOSI. You're not the only one. Zwane is a jackal. He's vengeful and vindictive. His ways are not straight. You should see the depression in my husband's skull. Just like a shallow clay pot. Zwane did it. When they were young and Zwane was trying to court me, they had a fight. When it was over, they shook hands and my husband thought no more about it. He was sitting at ease one day when Zwane stole up to him and dealt him a terrible blow with his knobkerrie. That's Zwane for you. Ah, here comes Mfundisi on his old bicycle. Zwane must have seen him and got out of the way.

MAPULE. But why should Zwane want to get out of Muruti's way? They've always got on well.

MA-NKOSI. I don't think they will anymore. Zwane wanted to be treasurer of the church council, but the votes went against him. But look at those two women— Ma-Zwane and Ma-Hlope—staring at us. Don't they have the decency to greet——

MAPULE. They're like that. They don't talk to me. Here's Muruti.

*Enter* MFUNDISI *on his bicycle.*

MFUNDISI. Welcome back to Mzindi, Sister Mapule. I hope you bring rain, like your name.

MAPULE. Good day, Muruti. How is Ma-Muruti?

MFUNDISI. Don't you know? She has gone to her mother in Natal. Her mother is very ill.

MAPULE. I didn't know, Muruti. I hope she gets better.

MFUNDISI. Thank you, Sister Mapule. How's Lusutu?

MAPULE. All right, Muruti.

MFUNDISI. And your father?

MAPULE. He's well, Muruti.

MFUNDISI. That's nice. Is it raining there?

MAPULE. Yes, Muruti.

MFUNDISI. Not here. Not here. We are having prayer services for rain. Another this evening. But I suppose you're tired after your journey?

MAPULE. I'll come, Muruti.

MFUNDISI. Good. See you at church then. How are you, Gran Shongwe and Ma-Nkosi?

GRAN. We're well, my child. Just the sun and the drought.

MFUNDISI. The sun and the drought, Gran Shongwe. Sister Mapule, can you help with the washing? Gideon and I are hopeless.

MAPULE. Yes, Muruti. I'll come on Wednesday.

MFUNDISI. Thank you. I must be off. Ma-Hlongwane's child is sick. Stay well. See you tonight, Sister Mapule. [*Exit on cycle.*]

MA-NKOSI. There goes a good man. Working in this heat.

DRIVER *comes out of store and sits down.*

GRAN. Yes, Ma-Nkosi. A good man. Look what he's doing for Gideon—the Sibiya orphan boy. Feeds, clothes, and sends him to school just as if he were his own son. It's a pity they don't have children of their own.

MA-NKOSI. They're still young, Gran Shongwe. They may still get children. Where there's suffering, illness—there you'll find Mfundisi.

GRAN. He's a good boy, Ma-Nkosi. Tell us the news, Mapule. Is your father well?

MAPULE. He's well and sends his greetings. Let's go home, Gran. Are you coming with us, Ma-Nkosi?

MA-NKOSI. Yes.

GRAN. When does he say he is coming to see me?

MAPULE. He said, "one of these days," Gran.

GRAN. Ah, your mother. My poor daughter. Married a Musutu and died under foreign skies. But your father is a good man.

MAPULE. Those women are staring at us!

GRAN. Never mind them, Mapule. Tell us the news.

MAPULE. Tomorrow I'm going to see the lands.

GRAN. It will break your heart . . . the mealies . . . the pumpkin . . .

GRAN SHONGWE, MA-NKOSI, *and* MAPULE *exeunt right.* MA-ZWANE *and* MA-HLOPE *come forward.*

MA-ZWANE. There goes that bitch of a Musutu girl.

MA-HLOPE. Coming to teach our children bad ways. [*Spits.*]

ZWANE *comes out of the store.*

MA-ZWANE. Ah, here's Ebenezer's father from the store. See how he follows that bitch with his eyes. [*To* ZWANE.] Why must you go running after that bitch of a Musutu girl? Disgracing yourself! Stop looking at her. I'm talking to you!

ZWANE. Who said I was looking at her? She's a nice girl. She works a damned sight harder than some women I know.

MA-ZWANE. Nice girl! Which side of her do you mean? She's come to trouble other women's husbands and show the children bad ways.

ZWANE. The children in this village don't need showing.

MA-ZWANE. Did you see how she'd painted her mouth and was wearing high-heeled shoes?

MA-HLOPE. She fancies herself, she does. The bitch.

ZWANE. She looks very nice. She's very pretty.

MA-ZWANE. Pretty! Her morals stink. A bloody foreigner come from Lusutu to spoil our country.

ZWANE. Since when do you own this place?

MA-ZWANE. I don't own it but I do have a duty to protect my children. She's here to corrupt them.

MA-HLOPE. Yes. She stole my daughter's boy friend.

ZWANE. It's not her fault if she's prettier than Tryphina.

MA-ZWANE. Ebenezer's father, if you don't want to make me angry, stop talking about that little bitch.

ZWANE. Who started?

MA-ZWANE. As if it was not enough to go running to greet her—with all your teeth showing like a hyena's. Left me standing here like a bloody fool. Made me a laughing-stock. It's you men who spoil the Musutu bitch. You make her think she's wonderful. You and Mfundisi. Talking to her as if she was a real person.

ZWANE. What is she then?

MA-ZWANE. A flirt. A man-crazy bitch—that's what she is. I don't know what you see in her.

ZWANE. Don't you? Ask us men——

MA-ZWANE. You a man? Don't make me laugh!

ZWANE. What do you mean?

MA-ZWANE. I mean what I say. There are men and there are men.

ZWANE. Woman, are you swearing at me?

MA-SWANE. I'm just telling you. You're an old man, but you behave like a randy goat.

ZWANE. Woman, are you saying I'm impotent? Who made your children then? Tell me!

MA-ZWANE. They're yours. But you're grown up now. Be-have like that instead of running after that little bitch.

ZWANE. Who says I want her?

MA-ZWANE. You men are all the same—Mfundisi too. The whole village wants to sleep with her. You'd think she was a bitch in heat! She behaves like one.

ZWANE. Did you say Mfundisi?

MA-ZWANE. Why not? He's still a young man, and his wife's away. That dog-collar means nothing.

ZWANE. You're mad. Mfundisi wouldn't look at another woman.

MA-ZWANE. You're as blind as a bat. All this "Sister Ma-pule" doesn't fool me. But let me tell you this: If you want a spare wheel, don't get mixed up with that rub-bish. There are better women in this village.

Zwane. Mfundisi, eh? Come, let's go home. You're nothing but an old cow—a jealous old cow.

Ma-Zwane. I may be an old cow. I've borne you six children. But I'm not a bitch.

Zwane. Don't shout! Those people are listening.

# ACT TWO

## SCENE I

*Two days later at* GRAN SHONGEWE's *kraal.*

*To the left of the stage a cluster of three huts, partially en-
closed by a semi-circular reed fence, is set against a back-
cloth of thorn bush and scrub. The front of the main hut
is exposed to the audience. Outside the hut are a fireplace
and an assortment of cooking utensils: tins, pots, and a
wooden pestle and mortar for pounding maize. It is early
morning; there is an intermittent crowing of cocks and lowing of cattle.* MAPULE *sits outside the main hut cooking
breakfast.* GRAN SHONGWE *comes out and joins her.*

MAPULE. Good morning, Gran. How did you sleep?

GRAN. Morning, Mapule. Sleep? I didn't sleep a wink. I
tossed about all night. I had dreams of old times. My
father—Mahlosi—and Chief Sogasa. All the people my
father had killed were pointing at me. . . . Aw, it was
terrible. I feel as tired as if I'd not been to bed. Aw, another blistering day. Not a rag of a cloud in sight. What
are you doing today?

MAPULE. I'll do a few things round this house and then go
to tackle Mfundisi's washing.

GRAN. It must be hard for the poor boy. That Gideon
knows nothing. When is his wife coming back?

MAPULE. I don't know, Gran. Here's water to wash.

GRAN. Thank you, Mapule. You spoil me. Aaron Ngwane
is a lucky man to get such a hard-working wife.

MAPULE. Others work too, Gran.

GRAN. I must dodder to the lands. Old age is a nuisance. I
never thought I'd be like this one day.

MAPULE. Gran's not old. Now if you were as old as
Maziya——

GRAN. I wouldn't like to be old like that. I'd rather die.
I don't want to be a burden to people.

MAPULE. I'd look after you, Gran.

GRAN. No, no. You have your own life to live. I've had
mine. It wouldn't be fair. Maziya clings to life as an old
bark clings to a tree. Let me think. What would he be
now? His regiment—his age group . . . The Governor?
No. Older than that. The Buffalo or the Locust . . . I
don't remember. But he's very old. All his children have
died, but he still remains. No, I wouldn't like to live
that long.

MAPULE. Eating corn is nice, Gran. It's good to be alive.

GRAN. When you're young, yes. But when you haven't the
teeth to chew the corn, what's the use? And then a
drought like this. Just an extra mouth to feed.

MAPULE. No, Gran. How can you talk like that? How's the
sour porridge?

GRAN. Nice, Mapule. Very nice. That Aaron Ngwane's a
lucky boy. Have you told your father about him?

MAPULE. Yes.

GRAN. What does he say?

MAPULE. I've told you about it, Gran.

GRAN. I've forgotten. This old head! Things enter in one
ear and go out of the other.

MAPULE. He says it's all right.

GRAN. And the *lobola*? Did you tell him Aaron was poor?

MAPULE. I did. He says everybody's poor. Aaron will pay
*lobola* whenever he can—as time goes on.

GRAN. Your father is a good Musutu-of-God. And Aaron
had better look out or else he'll have the handcuffs on
him! He must know he's marrying a police sergeant's
daughter!

MAPULE. Aw, Gran.

GRAN. He must understand he's not marrying a stray, a
pauper's daughter. He must know he's very lucky. What
are the Ngwanes? Dogs! Dogs! In the olden days we
wouldn't even look at them.

MAPULE. Aaron's a good man.

GRAN. He is. Or I wouldn't let his shadow fall on my door.

*Enter left* MA-NKOSI, *calling.*

MA-NKOSI. I ask for shelter, Gran Shongwe. May I enter the enclosure?

GRAN. Enter, Ma-Nkosi. You're very early.

MA-NKOSI. I thought I'd take advantage of the morning. But it's hot already.

GRAN. Another scorching day, Ma-Nkosi. There's no rain going to come.

MA-NKOSI. Aw, Gran Shongwe. How the weeds flourish is beyond me. I sometimes feel I'm just wasting my time.

GRAN. If it doesn't rain by next week, I'm giving up. I tell you we're finished. A few more days of this and I don't know what we're going to do. . . . We'll have to trek to the cities——

MA-NKOSI. The white people don't want us there.

GRAN. And what are we going to do then?

MA-NKOSI. I don't know. . . . Sit here and die.

GRAN. It's going to be like the great famine in Chief So-gasa's reign——

MAPULE. It will rain.

GRAN. Rain, Mapule? What are you talking about? All the prayers, and now Maziya fooling the people. No, God has turned his back on us.

MAPULE. It will rain.

GRAN. You just say, "It will rain; it will rain"! Where's the rain, Mapule?

MA-NKOSI. Did you hear the Zwane child is very ill again?

GRAN. Again? I thought he was better. Why don't they take him to hospital?

MA-NKOSI. I don't know. Zwane has something against hospitals. You can't understand Zwane's things.

GRAN. Come, let's dodder along to the lands. Although why I should be bothering about weeds when there'll soon be nothing left, I don't know.

MAPULE. I wish I could come too, Gran.

GRAN. You go and help Mfundisi with his washing.

MAPULE. Go well, Gran. Go well, Ma-Nkosi.

*Drumming.*

GRAN. What's that? Drums in the morning? And coming from the veld too.

MA-NKOSI. It's Maziya. He says he's removing the witches' pegs, which prevent rain.

GRAN. The senile old fool! What does he know about making rain? Drumming! Making a noise! Just making the sun worse for us. Let's go, Ma-Nkosi. Carry my hoe for me, my girl. Thank you. That's a good girl.

*Exeunt GRAN and MA-NKOSI.*

## SCENE II

*The village. The back-cloth shows a number of huts, and in the centre of the stage is a well, equipped with a rope and bucket, etc. MA-SIBEKO is pounding corn outside her hut on the extreme left of the stage. SIBANDE sits on a stone, whittling a stick. MA-KUMALO is washing clothes beside the well. MANGENYEZA enters and drinks water from the well. MA-MATSEBULA begins sweeping outside her hut to the right of centre. Children's voices are heard, and MFUNDISI enters left with several children.*

CHILDREN. Mfundisi. Mfundisi.
    Here comes Mfundisi.
    Good morning, Mfundisi.
    Good day, Mfundisi.

MFUNDISI. Good morning, my children.

MA-SIBEKO. Don't cling to Mfundisi with your dirty hands!

MFUNDISI. It's all right, Sister Sibeko. Good morning. How's the sick cow?

MA-SIBEKO. It's better, Mfundisi. Only the people are
drying up.

MFUNDISI. This drought, Sister Sibeko. We are having another prayer for rain this evening. Are you coming?

MA-SIBEKO. I'll see, Mfundisi.

MFUNDISI. Good morning, Brother Sibande. How's the leg
today?

SIBANDE. As usual, Mfundisi. Thank you. I'll limp along to
the prayer-meeting tonight.

MFUNDISI. I'll see you there. Good-bye.
    Good morning, Sister Kumalo. Busy with the washing
so early? How's Jacob? Does he write from college?

MA-KUMALO. He writes, Mfundisi. He's well and likes
college.

MFUNDISI. Good. Have you heard about the prayer-meeting
for rain tonight?

MA-KUMALO. Yes, Mfundisi. I shall be coming.

MFUNDISI. And you, Brother Mangenyeza?

MANGENYEZA. What prayer-meeting, Mfundisi? I want to
know where they're drinking beer today—that's all. I'm
not going to pray for something done on purpose. Drive
out the witches, and you'll have rain.

MA-KUMALO. Don't worry about him, Mfundisi. He sleeps
and wakes up at the beer pots.

MFUNDISI. Come, Brother Mangenyeza. Come and help us
with your prayer.

MANGENYEZA. No, no. Thank you very much.

PAUL [a child]. Mfundisi, can I join the football club?

MFUNDISI. Next year, Paul, when you're bigger.

SAMUEL. Mfundisi, can I join the choir?

MFUNDISI. Yes, if you mother allows you.

JOHN. Mfundisi, my mother said I can come to Sunday
school. She's bought me a pair of trousers.

MFUNDISI. Good. I'll expect you on Sunday then.

MARK. Mfundisi?

MFUNDISI. Yes, Mark?

MARK. Er—I forgot. I forgot what I was going to say.

PAUL. Forgot! Stupid!

MFUNDISI. Never mind, Mark. You tell me when you remember.

SAMUEL. My father's gone to work in Jo'burg. He's going to bring me a present, Mfundisi.

MFUNDISI. That's nice, Samuel.

JOHN. My father's an *ilijoyini*. He works in the mines. Deep in the ground, digging out money. He's far away.

MARK. My father works on the railway line. Chuff, chuff, chuff . . . P-e-e-e-p!

JOHN. That's not the sound a train makes, stupid! Like this! [*He imitates a train whistle.*]

PAUL. My father's a waiter in a hotel where white people stay. A big hotel with lots of white people. Eh, Elijah, your father's a stay-at-home . . . a woman's man!

ELIJAH. You know he broke his leg. You're talking rubbish.

MFUNDISI. Now, now, young men. None of that.

PAUL. A funny sort of broken leg that doesn't heal. He's afraid of work.

MFUNDISI. Paul, don't talk like that.

MOSES. My father says he'll never work for a white man, Mfundisi.

PAUL. That's why he's a crocodile. He doesn't pay his tax, and every time he sees a policeman——

MFUNDISI. Paul, that mouth of yours. You're chasing me away.

PAUL. It's true, Mfundisi. I saw him. He ran away to the bush. He slept in the veld for a whole week.

MOSES. You're a liar. He came back the same night. You're lying.

MA-MATSEBULA. Paul, what are you saying? Come home this very moment. You think it's a joking matter! The rest of you, go and play. You're bothering Mfundisi. Off with you!

MFUNDISI. Yes. Run and tell your parents there's a prayer-meeting for rain in the church tonight.

CHILDREN. Yes, Mfundisi. [*Exeunt running.*]

MA-MATSEBULA. The children talk, Mfundisi.

MFUNDISI. Yes, they don't know.

MA-MATSEBULA. This place of old men, women, and small children. It's hard to bring up the children with their fathers away, Mfundisi. It's hard without the menfolk. Struggling with the oxen and plough . . . scratching the sterile earth. The men only return to make children and then go off to work again. Sometimes I don't know where to turn. Children will talk, Mfundisi. I hit Paul, but it doesn't seem to help.

MFUNDISI. It's as you say, Sister Matsebula. We can only pray God to give us strength.

MA-MATSEBULA. And this drought. Not a cloud in the sky —aw! Go well, Mfundisi.

WOMAN [*to* MA-MATSEBULA]. There goes that Man-of-God. He must be going to the Zwanes to see the sick child. You never have to look for him when there's trouble, sickness, or death—he's always there.

MA-MATSEBULA. I always say he's too good for this wicked place. Too good.

*Enter* HLOPE *and* MA-HLOPE.

MFUNDISI. Good morning, Brother and Sister Hlope. Have you heard about the prayer-meeting tonight?

MA-HLOPE. We've heard, Mfundisi. We're a bit stuck, but we'll try——

MFUNDISI. Good. Stay well. [*Exit* MFUNDISI.]

MA-HLOPE. You see what I told you! There's that Musutu bitch again, running out to talk to Mfundisi, pushing herself forward. I tell you there's something between them. Look at them. Ma-Zwane's right.

HLOPE. Aw, Tryphina's mother. Mfundisi wouldn't dream of a thing like that.

MA-HLOPE. What's wrong with him? Even old crocks like

you can't keep your eyes away.

HLOPE [*chuckling*]. The body grows old but the heart remains young.

MA-HLOPE. Aw, what do you see in her? The man-troubling hussy has come back to corrupt our children. Do you forget she stole Aaron Ngwane from our Tryphina? Does that mean nothing to you? Go on, defend her. You're all the same. Look at Mfundisi. If he's not careful, she'll unfrock him. I know her sort.

HLOPE. You're dreaming. He doesn't see the woman in women.

MA-HLOPE. He'll get a cool reception if he's going to the Zwanes.

HLOPE. Why?

MA-HLOPE. Zwane says Mfundisi fixed the votes so that he wouldn't become treasurer of the church committee——

HLOPE. Nonsense.

MA-HLOPE. And Zwane doesn't want to hear about sending the child to the hospital. Aw, Mfundisi surprises me, talking to that scrap of a girl as if she were a person——

HLOPE. What do you think she is? An animal?

MA-HLOPE. You go and find something to do instead of defending her. The egg-eating bitch.

HLOPE. Don't you?

MA-HLOPE. Yes, now that I'm a grown woman. I never ate eggs at her age! And fish—she eats fish!

HLOPE. Many Swazis eat fish nowadays—it's not only the Shangaans and Thongas.

MA-HLOPE. She has no respect for our customs; she laughs at us.

HLOPE. Some of them are silly, I dare say.

MA-HLOPE. And sweeping out the rubbish at night! Forever washing and preening herself. . . . I shouldn't be surprised if she was rotting somewhere!

HLOPE. Rubbish!

MFUNDISI *passes*.

MA-HLOPE. See, there he goes at last. All smiles. Yes, he's going to the Zwanes. They'll fix him up.


## SCENE III

*The Zwanes' house. A square room with whitewashed rough plaster walls on which some photographs and magazine pictures are pinned up. To the far right of the stage a door leading to the outside of the house is open. Near the open door stands a large kitchen dresser which is somewhat cluttered. On the left near a large iron bedstead is a door which leads to the one other room in the house. To the front, left, stands a sofa, while in the centre of the stage is a table with four wooden chairs.*


MFUNDISI [*knocking at the door*]. Good morning, Brother and Sister Zwane. May I come in?

MA-ZWANE. Good morning, Mfundisi.

MFUNDISI. How's the child, Sister Zwane?

MA-ZWANE. He's bad, Mfundisi. It came suddenly.

MFUNDISI. Brother Zwane, I think you should take him to the hospital.

ZWANE. Hospital! There's no hospital! Those doctors and nurses know nothing about healing.

MA-ZWANE. I agree with Ebenezer's father. I don't trust that hospital.

MFUNDISI. What do you mean, you don't trust the doctors and nurses? They spent years training. They know their work.

ZWANE. Well, no child of mine is going to hospital. I've made up my mind.

MFUNDISI. You talk like a child, Brother Zwane. You surprise me.

ZWANE. I've made up my mind. Call it childish if you like. That's your opinion.

MA-ZWANE. Mfundisi, have you forgotten what they did to Mabaso's child? Killed him—that's what the hospital did.

MFUNDISI. People die in the best hospitals. Everything was done to save Mabaso's child. You can't go against the will of God——

ZWANE. No child of mine is going to hospital.

MA-ZWANE. All the terrible things they do to a person in hospital.

ZWANE. Ebenezer's mother, hold your tongue!

MA-ZWANE. Yes, Ebenezer's father.

ZWANE. Don't talk about things you know nothing of.

MA-ZWANE. As you say, Ebenezer's father.

MFUNDISI. Have you sent for the clinic nurse?

ZWANE. No clinic nurse is going to touch a child of mine.

MFUNDISI. But, Brother Zwane, you can't be serious. What's happened to you? You were one of the first to ask for a clinic, and you welcomed it.

ZWANE. I know better now.

MFUNDISI. But, Brother Zwane . . . You a member of the church—a leading member—to talk like this! What's come over you, Brother Zwane? I don't understand.

ZWANE. It's no use, Mfundisi.

MA-ZWANE. All those needles. And those things from baboons and white people.

ZWANE. Woman, I said keep quiet!

MA-ZWANE. Yes, my lord. Your child comes back a different person. You hardly know it——

ZWANE. Woman!

MA-ZWANE. I'm silent. Silent, my lord.

MFUNDISI. Brother and Sister Zwane, this grieves me very much. The Devil is trying you. I'll remember you in my prayers. . . . I suppose you can't come to the prayer-meeting for rain tonight?

ZWANE. We can't.

MFUNDISI. Ah! Brother and Sister Zwane, I hope you'll think again. I hope you'll think again.

ZWANE. It's final. No child of mine is going to the hospital. No child of mine is going to be touched by any clinic nurse. We'll try our own ways. Good morning, Mfundisi.

MFUNDISI. May the Lord show you light. Good morning, Brother and Sister. I pray the child gets better. [*Exit.*]

ZWANE. The fool. The damned hypocrite. Thinks he owns this village. The good man! The holy man! I know him. Stabbed me in the back. Do you think I don't know? He turned people against me so that I couldn't become treasurer. Brother and Sister Zwane! Ha! I'll get even with him. You'll see. He'll be glad to go back where he came from before I've finished. I swear by Almighty God —as my name's Zwane—I'll teach him a lesson. I'll teach him about people. [*Shouts of children outside greeting* MFUNDISI.] Do you hear that? There goes the great man of this village. God Almighty himself!

MA-ZWANE. And that church! That Musutu bitch preening herself. It encourages her, that church does. I tell you, Ebenezer's father, I can't stand the sight of that girl. I can't see myself under the same roof as her. She thinks she owns the church. It's either she goes or . . .

ZWANE. Or what?

MA-ZWANE. I don't know—or I stop going to church. Yes, Mfundisi must choose——

ZWANE. That's it! Ebenezer's mother, this is the one sensible thing you've said in your life. Go. Get Ma-Hlope, Ma-Nkosi—no not that one. Get Ma-Gwagwa and some of the other women. Go to that hypocrite and tell him what you've just said. Tell him to choose between that bitch of a Musutu girl and yourselves. That should put him in a fix. By God, it will give him something to think about instead of biting me by the ankles.

MA-ZWANE. And Maziya? When do we go to ask for the divining bones? I want to know what's wrong with the child.

ZWANE. Tomorrow. Tomorrow. Do this now. By God. By God. This will give him a headache. And I'm not through with him yet. Go now, Ebenezer's mother. What are you waiting for?

MA-ZWANE. I'm going, Ebenezer's father.

## SCENE IV

*At* GRAN SHONGWE's *kraal. It is early afternoon.* MAPULE *is alone. She is busy working and cooking, humming a tune as she works.*

*Enter* ZWANE *from right.*

ZWANE. Good day, Mapule.

MAPULE [*startled*]. Oh, it's you, Father Zwane.

ZWANE. You sound surprised. Don't you expect me to visit you? Where's Gran Shongwe?

MAPULE. At the lands.

ZWANE. Wait a moment. Is this how you treat visitors at Lusutu?

MAPULE. I'm very busy, Father Zwane.

ZWANE. Ha! Ha! Ha! You don't even ask me how I am or what brings me here.

MAPULE. I told you I'm very busy.

ZWANE. You have a heart of stone, girl of Lusutu. Here. Here's a present for you.

MAPULE. Thank you, Father Zwane, but I don't accept presents.

ZWANE. Not even from an old friend?

MAPULE. You're not my friend, Father Zwane. You could be my father.

ZWANE. The more reason why you should. Ha! Ha! Ha! Take it. It's to welcome you back to Mzindi.

MAPULE. Father Zwane, we've been through this before. I've told you I can't take your presents. I mean it.

ZWANE. You take presents from Aaron Ngwane.

MAPULE. That's different. We're betrothed.

ZWANE. So you still want to throw yourself away. What can Aaron do for you? He hasn't even got the cattle to pay *lobola* for you.

MAPULE. Money isn't everything. He'll find the cattle. If he doesn't, it doesn't matter. . . . Father Zwane, I'm busy.

ZWANE. You're cruel. Won't you even give me hope that someday. . . ?

MAPULE. Father Zwane——

ZWANE. Forget the Father.

MAPULE. Why? You're old enough to be my father.

ZWANE. It doesn't matter with a man. Don't you know the saying: Only those who wish, grow old? Ha! Ha! I'd make you happy.

MAPULE. You're wasting your time. I've given you my answer. I don't want you. I don't want to be your spare wheel. You surprise me—a grown-up man trying to make love to girls. It removes your shadow, lowers your dignity. What do you take me for? Do you think I could do such a thing?

ZWANE. You wouldn't be the first.

MAPULE. Then go to those who do it. I'm betrothed. I don't love you. I'm not that sort of girl.

ZWANE. Betrothed to Aaron Ngwane! Well, cattle replace one another, you know! Ha! Ha! Ha!

MAPULE. You—a man of the church! What would Mfundisi say if he heard about this?

ZWANE. Do you think I care? For all I know, he's after you too. He's a man for all his collar. Don't you be bluffed——

MAPULE. Father Zwane, I'm busy.

ZWANE. Busy, eh? We'll see where that will get you!

MAPULE. What do you mean?

ZWANE. You'll see. You with your high and mighty airs. This is Mzindi, and I'm the bull of this village. We'll see.

*Exit ZWANE.*

## SCENE V

*The setting for this scene should be divided into two distinct parts. One part, perhaps a half or two-thirds of the stage, should represent MFUNDISI's living-room. It should be furnished somewhat austerely. There is a desk, a bookcase, two leather armchairs, and a table. Religious pictures and texts decorate the wall. To the right of the stage is a door leading to the kitchen, and approximately in the centre of the stage is a door leading from the living-room to the other part of the stage, which should represent the forecourt to MFUNDISI's house. Part-way through the scene, when the women leave the house, the lights in MFUNDISI's living-room may be dimmed or put out.*

*The time: late afternoon on the same day. MA-ZWANE, MA-HLOPE, and MA-GWAGWA knock at MFUNDISI's door; he opens it.*

MFUNDISI. Ah, come in. Come in, Sister Zwane, Sister Hlope, Sister Gwagwa; it's good to see you. Please take seats. Oh, it's hot.

MA-ZWANE. We'll stand, Mfundisi. We're in a hurry.

MFUNDISI. A woman's life is a busy one—a family to look after. What can I do for you, Sisters?

*Pause.*

MA-HLOPE. Speak, Ma-Zwane.

MA-ZWANE. We have come about a sore matter. A very sore matter.

MA-GWAGWA. Yes, yes.

MA-ZWANE. Mfundisi, you know us. We attend church regularly.

MA-HLOPE. We try.

MA-ZWANE. We pay our church shillings. Even if sometimes we fall behind.

MA-GWAGWA. We do our best.

MA-ZWANE. We do our best for the church, Mfundisi. We don't like to see it spoiled. We have our failings——

MA-HLOPE. Who hasn't? But we try.

MA-ZWANE. We have come about that Musutu girl. She's back.

MFUNDISI. Sister Mapule, you mean?

MA-ZWANE. If you like to call her that. She's no sister of mine.

MA-HLOPE. Nor mine. Nor mine.

MA-ZWANE. Mfundisi must choose between us and that girl——

MA-HLOPE. She's a disgrace. She's spoiling our children. Teaches them bad ways.

MA-GWAGWA. She has no respect. She's proud. Never greets. I even saw her smoking a cigarette. And she paints her mouth——

MA-ZWANE. No, no, Ma-Gwagwa. You're bringing in your own things. We didn't come for that. She has loose morals and is corrupting our children.

MA-HLOPE. We don't want her in our church.

MFUNDISI. And is this what you have come about?

MA-ZWANE. Yes, Mfundisi.

MFUNDISI. Sisters, you know that the church is not yours or mine. It is God's house. Even if Sister Mapule had loose morals or was disrespectful, proud, I could not turn her out. The church would accept, not reject, her. The church is not for the good; they don't need saving. St. Luke, Chapter 15, Verse 7: "I say unto you that likewise joy shall be in heaven over one sinner that repenteth, more than ninety and nine just persons, which need no repentence . . ." I'm afraid, Sisters, you ask for the impossible.

MA-HLOPE. But that girl makes no effort to mend her ways. She revels in sin. We all sin, God knows, but we don't boast about it.

MFUNDISI. This is strange. This doesn't sound like the Sister Mapule I know.

MA-HLOPE. She bluffs you. In church she's all goodness. But in the village . . . You don't know her, Mfundisi.

MA-ZWANE. We live with her. We know her deeds.

MA-GWAGWA. Let her go back where she comes from.

MFUNDISI. Is it because Sister Mapule is a Musutu that you are here?

MA-ZWANE. No, no. A Musutu is a human being. It's not that. It's her morals.

MA-HLOPE. Mfundisi, you don't notice because you always see the best in people.

MFUNDISI. This is a very sad matter. I will speak to Sister Mapule about this and——

MA-ZWANE. No, no, Mfundisi.

MA-HLOPE. This is between us.

MA-GWAGWA. We don't want to spoil our name in the village. No. Rather not say anything to her.

MFUNDISI. I'll talk to her. You have made a complaint against her, and it's only right that she should hear it. Now, let us pray, Sisters. Let us ask for God's grace. [Kneels.] O God, who has said that when two or three of us are gathered in thy name, thou wilt grant them their requests, strengthen and purify us that we may look with love and kindness on our fellows. Protect us from jealousy, envy, and hate; and help us to be patient, tolerant, and humble. I ask you to help these sisters, to show them the path of charity. We ask this through the name of our Lord Jesus Christ. Amen.

CHORUS. Amen. [They rise to their feet.]

MFUNDISI. Go well, Sisters. God be with you.

CHORUS [feebly]. Stay well, Mfundisi. [Exeunt.]

MA-GWAGWA. He's defeated us!

MA-HLOPE. I told you, Ma-Zwane. I told you it was useless going to Mfundisi. I knew he'd take the girl's part.

MA-ZWANE. How was I to know? You agreed, didn't you? I didn't drag you there.

MA-GWAGWA. Now we've made fools of ourselves. Whatever will he think of us? I could kick myself.

MA-ZWANE. Do you care so much what Mfundisi thinks of you?

MA-HLOPE. It doesn't bother me in the least. That Musutu bitch. She took Tryphina's boy friend——

MA-GWAGWA. Forget your own troubles. We're doing this for the church—our church. Oh, but we've made fools of ourselves.

MA-ZWANE. Yes, Ma-Gwagwa, we spoke for the church. But tell me, what sort of church is this? Think! Do you call that a church? No. I can't see myself in it.

MA-GWAGWA. What do you mean, Ma-Zwane?

MA-ZWANE. What I say. If that girl doesn't go, I will.

*Exeunt.*

# ACT THREE

## SCENE I

MAZIYA's *kraal, which is littered and unswept and obviously in a state of ruin. There is a background of thorn bushes.* MAZIYA *sits in the shade of a tree to the left of the stage.* MTSAKASI *sits, gently but insistently drumming, to the right of the two derelict huts which are to the right of centre. It is late afternoon on the next day, and* ZWANE, MA-ZWANE, MA-HLOPE, *and* MA-GWAGWA *have come to ask* MAZIYA *for the divining bones. They enter from the left and stand at the precincts of* MAZIYA's *kraal.*

ZWANE [*calling*]. You are great, Maziya. We ask for shelter. You, the gnarled old tree that withstands the hurricane, the black bull that roars and the sky trembles . . . The witches know and fear you.

MAZIYA. Mtsakasi! Stop drumming. [*Drumming stops.*] Great? Go and tell that to the Mfundisi. What do you want from me, Zwane? Am I not a louse so small that you cannot find me in the seams of Mfundisi's clothing?

ZWANE. We cry, Maziya. Save us.

MAZIYA. Save you?

ZWANE. Protect us. We are crying.

MAZIYA. Go to your church. Go to your Mfundisi. Since when have you stopped being a believer? Aren't you the great man of the church—Mfundisi's right-hand man? Don't you raise your bottom to the sky, shut your eyes, and shout "Hallelujah"?

ZWANE. The church has defeated us, Maziya.

MA-ZWANE. We were bluffing ourselves.

ZWANE. Shut up, woman. I'm talking.

MA-ZWANE. I'm quiet, Ebenezer's father.

MAZIYA. Draw near. Come to this useless shade. [*They walk towards him.*] And you too, Ma-Hlope. The world is turning. What is your cry?

ZWANE. We have come to ask for the divining bones, Maziya.

MA-ZWANE. We are troubled by the witches of this place.

MAZIYA. Witches, eh?

ZWANE. No. Don't listen to the woman, Maziya. Ebenezer's mother, leave this to me. Do you hear?

MA-ZWANE. I have heard, my lord.

MAZIYA. And these other people—what do they want?

ZWANE. They are our ears. They have come to help us hear.

MAZIYA. People of the church wanting bones! How do I know you haven't been sent by Mfundisi?

ZWANE. Aw, Maziya, you think bad of us.

MAZIYA. Yes, yes. Why not? Yesterday you were saying, "I'm a believer. I won't have anything to do with a heathen." You're like a wanton woman, who flits from one man to another. Who will trust her?

ZWANE. We agree we have done wrong. But save us, Maziya. Do not turn your back on us.

MAZIYA. It's you who turned your backs on the customs and traditions of the people. But I knew you'd come back. One day the churches will all die. I say so. I know.

ZWANE. We've come back, Maziya. Help us.

MAZIYA. A man raising his bottom to the sky like a rietbuck! A man crying, weeping tears! Heeeheeeheee! [*Imitates crying.*] What's that? What do you think the women must do when the men now do the crying? [*Sound of church bells ringing.*] You hear? You hear? What's that for now?

ZWANE. They say they're praying for rain.

MAZIYA [*contemptuously*]. Praying for rain! This place is

littered with witches' pegs which chase away the rain.
Yesterday I pulled out a few. This place smells of witches.
From an ant heap I took out the most frightful things.
And from up a tree brought down such things as would
frighten away any rain. . . . Praying for rain, are they?
Let them first get rid of the witches. They'll see no rain.
[*Hooting of owl.*] Do you hear the witches' bird? The
sun has hardly set and they're already about their witch-
ing work. Witches have grown bold. Ah, for the old
days. We would have called for such a witch-hunt that
would have cleaned up this witches' hole. Ah, to have
lived to see this come about! Death is too slow, too cruel
to me. [*Pause.*] Mtsakasi, bring me my snuff-box. So
you've come to ask for the bones, eh?

ZWANE. That's what we've come for, Maziya.

MAZIYA. You've come at a bad time. Some witch has
blackened my bones.

CHORUS [*disappointedly*]. Awww——

MAZIYA. You say "Awww." But isn't it you who coddle the
witches? That church is the home of witches. It smells
of witches. [*Takes snuff.*] Heeee! That's nice snuff for you.

ZWANE. Try, Maziya. Protect us.

MAZIYA. Protect you! Why even Ma-Shongwe, the daughter
of the great hero Mahlosi, is one of these believers! And
Ma-Nkosi, daughter of Magonso, the lion-killer! Why
come and ask me to protect you? Go to your Mfundisi.
He's your protector.

ZWANE. Aw, Maziya. We are your children. Save us.

MAZIYA. I'll try. I'll go to the *Ndume** and ask the spirits
. . . Though why I should do it, I don't know. I'm an old
fool to do it. An old fool.

ZWANE. It's your kindness, your greatness, Maziya. Nothing
else.

CHORUS. It's nothing else.

MAZIYA. Save your flattery for Mfundisi—that traitor who

* House of the Spirits.

brings the white man amongst us. Killer of the people. Help me up, Zwane. Aw, these legs. Witches have long been trying to maim me. And my stick.

ZWANE. Here it is, Maziya.

MAZIYA. This land of witches! Look at it burning up! [*Spits and shuffles off to the right.*]

ZWANE. How old he is. All his old friends are dead. He's an ancestor already. A gust of wind would sweep him off his feet. Yet he lives on. I hope the spirits listen to him.

MA-HLOPE. Have you got the "purse-opener"—a half-crown or something? Otherwise he won't open the pouch of the bones.

ZWANE. I've got it.

MA-HLOPE. And something to wash his hand with?

ZWANE. I'll give him ten shillings. That should be enough. Ah, here he comes.

MA-ZWANE. He's got the bones. Now we'll hear who's bewitching my child.

*Re-enter* MAZIYA.

MAZIYA. Hey, you, Mtsakasi. Son of a witch! Come here this moment. Bring the drum and my goat-skin. Come and play for these bones. Aw, it's hot. Just like the great drought in Chief Sogasa's time, which finished many people. Put down my goat-skin. Help me down, Zwane. Ah, thank you. It's old age. Sit on the mat. [*Pause.*] Ehhmm . . .

ZWANE *and the others sit.*

MA-HLOPE [*whispers*]. The purse-opener.

ZWANE. Here's the purse-opener, Maziya.

MAZIYA. Place it on the goat-skin. Play up, Mtsakasi; drown those church bells. [*Drumming for a while.*] That's enough. *Vumani bo!* Agree, I say! [*Rattles the bones.*]

CHORUS. *Siyavuma!* We agree!

MAZIYA. Agree properly. *Vumani bo!*

CHORUS [*livelier*]. *Siyavuma! Siyavuma!*

    MAZIYA *throws the bones on the goat-skin. A silence.*

MAZIYA. Hau! You have come about a heavy matter. A very heavy matter. *Vumani bo.*

CHORUS. *Siyavuma!*

    MAZIYA *spills the bones again.*

MAZIYA. See that little girl on its side. . . . The paths are dark. Hau, what's this I see? Death! Let me look again. *Vumani bo.*

CHORUS. *Siyavuma!*

    MAZIYA *throws the bones again.*

MAZIYA. A sick child!

CHORUS [*frenziedly*]. *Siyavuma! Siyavuma! Siyavuma!*

MAZIYA. Very sick.

CHORUS. *Siyavuma! Siyavuma! Siyavuma!*

MAZIYA. It came suddenly.

CHORUS. *Siyavuma! Siyavuma!*

MAZIYA. The child is bewitched.

CHORUS. *Siyavuma!*

MAZIYA. *Vumani bo!*

CHORUS [*enthusiastically*]. *Siyavuma!*

    MAZIYA *throws the bones and there is a long silence.*

MAZIYA. What do I see? A woman giving something to the child. And stealing the child's footprints in the sand? [*Excitedly.*] She's eating the child! *Vumani bo!*

CHORUS. *Siyavuma!*

MAZIYA. She wears dresses. The clothes of the whites.

CHORUS. *Siyavuma!*

MAZIYA. Here she is entering the church. What's this! She's a believer! She's a woman of the church! *Vumani bo!*

CHORUS [*frenziedly*]. *Siyavuma! Siyavuma! Siyavuma!*

MAZIYA. I see her laughing with Mfundisi.

CHORUS. *Siyavuma!*

MAZIYA. I see her getting off a train—or is it a bus? She was away!

CHORUS [*at the peak of frenzy*]. *Siyavuma! Siyavuma! Siyavuma! Siyavuma!*

MAZIYA. Aw! Aw! She has bad medicines. Not of this place. She has bad medicines, that woman. She's not of this place.

CHORUS. *Siyavuma! Siyavuma! Siyavuma!*

MAZIYA [*excitedly*]. She's killing the child! She's killing the child. She must be stopped! Stop her! She'll finish the people.

CHORUS. *Siyavuma! Siyavuma! Siyavuma!*

MAZIYA. She must be driven back where she came from.

CHORUS. *Siyavuma! Siyavuma!*

MAZIYA [*in a changed voice*]. You have heard. The bones have spoken.

ZWANE. Hau, we've heard, Maziya.

CHORUS. We have heard.

ZWANE. Maziya, here is something to wash your hands with. Something to thank the bones.

MAZIYA. Put it on the skin, Zwane.

MA-ZWANE. A witch on top of it!

MA-HLOPE. She came all the way from Lusutu. I always said so. Why didn't she burn when she rescued Ma-Tabete's little girl from the burning hut? And people thought she was so brave! And she took my Tryphina's man——

MA-ZWANE. I want my child. I want it well. I'll teach that witch. She'll go flying back where she comes from!

MA-HLOPE. Laughing with all the men in the village. She knows what she's doing!

ZWANE. I should have known. That woman was never out of my dreams.

MA-ZWANE. And you, you are always laughing and joking with her. As if there are no real people to laugh with! But my child. I want it. I want it well.

MA-HLOPE. She must go!

CHORUS. She must go!

ZWANE. About the child, Maziya. Can you help us?

MAZIYA. Aw, her medicines are strong. They are bull medicines. She's Number One witch. I don't know, Zwane. I can try.

ZWANE. Her medicines can't beat yours, Maziya.

MAZIYA. What are you talking about! They are of other lands. You don't know what you are talking about. Don't you hear she has bull medicines? I'll have to tie mine—mix them so that they'll clash. There'll be such a clash as you've never seen. They'll fight. They'll wrestle . . . Aw, I don't know. A witch will smell. Oh, yes. I have a few things in my medicine horn. She must look out. It will cost you a beast—you know that?

ZWANE. It's all right, Maziya. What is a cow to a child's life?

MA-ZWANE. To the witch! I want my child well! Let's go to the witch.

MAZIYA. Go carefully. This is now the world of the white man. Don't blunder. Remember what the whites did to Chief Sidlamafa. [*Hooting of owl.*] Do you hear her servant? Come to spy on us. Oh, that owls should now brazen the day, doing their nefarious work before the eyes of man. Away, vile bird. Shoo, bird of the night!

ZWANE. The world rots with witches. The white man protects them.

MAZIYA. And that church of yours.

ZWANE. And the rain will not come because of them. I was a fool to become a believer once. Now, all of you, do nothing rash. Leave this to me. Do you hear?

CHORUS. We hear, Zwane.

ZWANE. Ebenezer's mother, do you hear what I say?

MA-ZWANE. I do, Ebenezer's father. But that witch!

ZWANE. Maziya, we thank you. You'll hear from me about the child. I'll bring him. [*To his party.*] Let's go. You've heard. Stay well, Maziya.

MAZIYA. Go well. Mtsakasi, play the drum and chase away the witches and their owls.

*Drumming.*

## SCENE II

*The Zwanes' house. The next morning. A knocking is heard.*

ZWANE. Who's there?

MFUNDISI. Brother and Sister Zwane, it's me.

MA-ZWANE. It's Mfundisi.

ZWANE. What does he want? Can't he leave us alone? All right, let him in.

MA-ZWANE *opens the door.*

MFUNDISI. Good morning, Brother and Sister Zwane. How did you sleep? [*Pause.*] Er . . . I've come to look at the child.

ZWANE. There's nothing to look at. Go and ask those . . .

MFUNDISI. Ask who, Brother Zwane?

ZWANE. No. Nobody.

MFUNDISI. Brother Zwane, is anything wrong?

ZWANE. Stop the "Brother" and "Sister" talk.

MFUNDISI. What's the matter with you, Brother Zwane?

ZWANE. I said forget about the "Brother" and "Sister." We're not Brother and Sister anymore.

MFUNDISI. Why?

ZWANE. Why? Because we don't belong to the church anymore. From now on.

MA-ZWANE. Your church has defeated us. Do you call that a church where . . . where . . .

ZWANE. Woman, leave this to me. I'm the head of this kraal.

MA-ZWANE. Yes, Ebenezer's father. But my child. I want my child.

MFUNDISI. Brother and Sister . . . Er . . . Mr. and Mrs. Zwane——

ZWANE. That's better.

MFUNDISI. What's this? What has happened?

ZWANE. Nothing's happened. We're just leaving the church, that's all.

MFUNDISI. But this is impossible.

ZWANE. Impossible?

MFUNDISI. I don't believe it. You don't mean that you're resigning from the church?

ZWANE. That's what we're doing and what we have done. We and the church have parted ways.

MFUNDISI. But why? Why?

ZWANE. Oh, for many reasons.

MFUNDISI. Such as?

ZWANE. Reasons.

MFUNDISI. But which?

ZWANE. Lots of reasons.

MA-ZWANE. My child. I want my child. I won't have it killed.

ZWANE. Shut up, woman!

MFUNDISI. What's this about the child? I told you to take the child to the hospital.

ZWANE. And I told you that no child of mine was going to any hospital.

MFUNDISI. Has this anything to do with yesterday's delegation, when Sister Zwane, Sister Hlope, and Sister Gwagwa came to see me about Sister Mapule?

MA-ZWANE. Yes.

ZWANE. No. It has nothing to do with it.

MFUNDISI. Has it anything to do with the treasurership of the council?

ZWANE. Don't be silly. Do you think I cared for that? I have enough trouble looking after my own money. Not to——

MFUNDISI. Then what? What is it?

MA-ZWANE. The church is full of——

ZWANE. Woman!

MFUNDISI. You started to say that the church was full of. Full of what, Ma-Zwane? Full of what? I ask you. Surely it's not that thing about Sister Mapule. We settled that.

MA-ZWANE. I'm saying nothing. I just want my—I'm silent, Ebenezer's father.

MFUNDISI. What's this? You begin to say something, then you stop. You leave it hanging in the air. Why aren't you frank with me?

ZWANE. There's nothing to be frank about. Your church——

MFUNDISI. *My* church? I don't own the church!

ZWANE. You behave as if you do.

MFUNDISI. What do you mean?

ZWANE. Never mind. Forget it.

MFUNDISI. Never mind? Of course I mind. I mind very much. Let's talk. Let us not hide anything. I'm sure we can sort out this thing.

MA-ZWANE. I'm not coming to any church.

ZWANE. Just say we're tired, that we've failed.

MFUNDISI. But that's not true. You're a leading member of the church. Why don't you come out with it? If you have any grievances—even against me—voice them. I'll call a general meeting. Is that all right?

ZWANE. What for? I've told you—we've resigned. We're finished with your church.

MFUNDISI. It's not *my* church. It's *your* church. Anyway, God is not finished with you. He never is.

MA-ZWANE. You'll never see me put my foot in that witches' nest—Sorry, Ebenezer's father, sorry.

MFUNDISI. What's this about witches? Witches? What witches? Sister Zwane, what's this?

ZWANE. She's just talking. What she meant was that we are not coming to church anymore. We're through with it. We've decided, and nothing you say will make us change our minds.

MFUNDISI. And the child?

ZWANE. We're taking care of that. The child is being seen to.

MFUNDISI. Oh, what a day! What a day! What is happening? Let us pray. Let us pray.

ZWANE. We're not praying.

MFUNDISI. Not praying?

ZWANE. Not praying. That's what I said.

MFUNDISI. Oh, God! Oh, God! All right, I'll pray for you.

ZWANE. Not here.

MFUNDISI. I'll ask God to show you his light. What a day!
Good-bye Bro—Mr. and Mrs. Zwane. Stay well. What
a day! [*Exit* MFUNDISI.]

ZWANE. Go well, Mfundisi. [*In an undertone.*] Hypocrite.
Ha! Ha! That's hit him hard. Wait till Hlope, Ma-
Hlope, and Ma-Gwagwa tell him they're resigning too.
. . . Ha! Ha! Big man of Mzindi, beware!

### SCENE III

MFUNDISI'*s house. Late afternoon.* MFUNDISI *is pacing up
and down and sighing.*

MFUNDISI. Oh, what a day! What a day! Where have I
gone wrong? Resigned! Why? Why? Why? [*Calls.*]
Gideon! Oh, he's gone to the store. Whew, this heat.

*There is a knock at the door.*

MAPULE [*from outside*]. Gideon, are you there? Hurry up
and open the door.

MFUNDISI. Oh, God. It's Sister Mapule. Preserve me. [*Opens
the door.*] Come in, Sister Mapule.

MAPULE. Muruti! I didn't expect you in. Are you not well,
Muruti?

MFUNDISI. I'm all right, Sister Mapule. It's this heat. It's
so hot. What a day it's been! The heat is getting to our
heads. There's something brewing. If I wasn't a Christian,
I'd say we were bewitched.

MAPULE. It's hot, Muruti. I've just come to finish the
ironing.

MFUNDISI. Poor you, struggling with all that washing.

MAPULE. It's nothing, Muruti. It will soon be finished.

MFUNDISI. You'll find us a hopeless pair—Gideon and me. My wife, Charity, says we're nothing but children.

MAPULE. She's right, Muruti. Men are children—no matter how big or old they are. My father is the biggest baby you ever saw. Where's Gideon? I hope he's put on the irons.

MFUNDISI. He has. I sent him to Bhai's store.

MAPULE. You look ill, Muruti. Why don't you go to bed?

MFUNDISI. It's nothing. It's just the heat. Oh, what a day it's been! What a day!

MAPULE. It will rain soon. Muruti, why do you look at me like that?

MFUNDISI. Did I look at you? I didn't know . . . I was thinking how beautiful you are.

MAPULE. Aw, Muruti.

MFUNDISI. You know it. Don't pretend you don't. You're the loveliest girl I've ever seen.

MAPULE. Please, Muruti. You embarrass me.

MFUNDISI. Mapule!

MAPULE. Yes, Muruti?

MFUNDISI. Never mind. [*Sighs.*] Don't look at me like that.

MAPULE. I must get on with the ironing. Would you like some tea, Muruti?

MFUNDISI. Yes, please. Oh, what a day! Sometimes I hate this place. Sometimes I wish I'd never left my native Natal. Do you ever feel like that?

MAPULE. Yes, Muruti. Many times.

MFUNDISI. We're foreigners—the two of us. You from Lusutu and I from Natal. I'm in good company.

MAPULE. I'll make the tea, Muruti. It's so hot. [*Exit into kitchen.*]

MFUNDISI [*sighs heavily*]. Oh, God. As if I don't have troubles enough. Save me, God, from the stirrings of

the flesh. Let me look on her with innocence. Oh, wretch
that I am. Wretch! Wretch! [*Pounds his chest.*] I don't
know what's happening today. Oh, this heat. The Devil
is abroad. Why do I have these evil thoughts? Is it true,
what they say about her? She seems willing enough . . .
one push, and . . . Oh, no! No! No! No!

*Re-enter* MAPULE.

MAPULE. Muruti, what is it? What's the matter? You are
not well. Go to bed, just for today. Here is the tea,
Muruti.

MFUNDISI. Thank you, Sister Mapule. I'm worried about
something. No, no, nothing to worry about.

MAPULE. I must get on. The irons are hot.

MFUNDISI. Mapule!

MAPULE. Muruti?

MFUNDISI. No. Never mind. Where's Gideon?

MAPULE. You said you'd sent him to the store.

MFUNDISI. Oh, yes. I forgot. Finish your ironing, then I
want to talk to you.

MAPULE. Yes, Muruti. [*Exit.*]

MFUNDISI. Oh, God. What did I nearly do? I must take a
hold on myself. This heat melts the will like butter. Oh,
Charity, why did you have to go away? This sun. This
damnable day. Why does passion throb in me with the
frenzy of a thousand tom-toms? Ah, there's my Bible.
Let me read it. [*He turns the pages.*] Yes, this could have
been written about me. Hebrews 13, Verse 4: "Marriage
is honourable in all, and the bed undefiled; but whore-
mongers and adulterers God will judge . . ." Yes, God
will judge me. I have sinned in my thoughts. I am replete
with adultery. I have been unfaithful to Charity. It's
true! It's true! [*Stands up and speaks with resolve.*] I must
work. Yes, I must work. Work drives away evil thoughts.
Work purifies. But I'm not going to run away from her.
I will look temptation in the face and flush the Devil

from the secret bushes of my soul. [*Aloud.*] Sister
Mapule!

MAPULE. Muruti?

MFUNDISI. Come here a moment, before I go out.

*Re-enter* MAPULE.

MAPULE. Yes, Muruti.

MFUNDISI. There's a serious matter I want to talk to you
about. Sit down, Sister Mapule. It's my . . . er . . . duty
to bring certain things to your notice. [*Coughs.*] Er . . .
well . . . certain allegations have been made about your
morals and . . . er . . . your conduct generally. Are you
listening?

MAPULE. I'm listening, Muruti.

MFUNDISI. The thing is, a delegation of women came to see
me—Sisters Zwane, Hlope, and Gwagwa.

MAPULE. A delegation, Muruti? What for?

MFUNDISI. They came to complain about you.

MAPULE. About me, Muruti?

MFUNDISI. Yes, about you. They say that your morals are
loose, that you are a bad example to the children . . .
I'm not saying this, Sister Mapule. I'm only repeating
what they said.

MAPULE. I realise that. What did they want?

MFUNDISI. They came to ask me to do something about it.

MAPULE. Something? What, Muruti?

MFUNDISI. To exclude you from the church.

MAPULE. Expel me, you mean?

MFUNDISI. Yes, to keep you out.

MAPULE. Well, that's simple enough. I won't go to church.

MFUNDISI. No, no. Don't be hasty. Listen. I told them that
I couldn't do that. That the church was the house of
God and that everyone was welcome—the good and the
bad.

MAPULE. Then what do you want me to do, Muruti?

MFUNDISI. Do? Nothing. Nothing. As it is, Zwane and his wife have resigned from the church.

MAPULE. Resigned? Because of me? I told you——

MFUNDISI. No, no. It had nothing to do with you; I'm sure of that. Zwane wouldn't give any reason. But what I want to know is—is it true what they say about you?

MAPULE. That my morals are loose?

MFUNDISI. Yes.

MAPULE. I don't know, Muruti.

MFUNDISI. What do you mean? You must know.

MAPULE. I don't say I'm not a sinner. I'm not better than other people. I do wrong things.

MFUNDISI. But are your morals loose?

MAPULE. I get tempted . . . I go with Aaron Ngwane. But Muruti, why do you want to know this? I'm a sinner.

MFUNDISI. Ah, we all are. That is why we pray for forgiveness. I am a greater sinner than you, Mapule.

MAPULE. Muruti?

MFUNDISI. It's true. I've sinned against you.

MAPULE. No, no, you've never——

MFUNDISI. You don't know, Mapule. I want you! I desire you! You've tormented me since the first day I saw you.

MAPULE. Muruti! Muruti! What are you saying?

MFUNDISI. It's true. Now don't pretend to be shocked. There, now you know it.

MAPULE. Muruti, this is not you.

MFUNDISI. Who is it then? It's me all right. Muruti, who has eyes only for his wife. [*Laughs hoarsely.*]

MAPULE. I must go now, Muruti.

MFUNDISI. No. You're not going. You can't leave me like this.

MAPULE. No, no, Muruti. Don't come near me. Please, Muruti.

MFUNDISI. You can't run away now. Come, I won't be the first man. [*Catches hold of her.*] Kiss me, Mapule. Come on, kiss me. [MAPULE *struggles.*]

MAPULE. No, no, Muruti. What are you doing? Let me go! Let me go, Muruti!

MFUNDISI. I'm not letting you go now, Mapule. Be kind to me.

MAPULE. No. Let me go! [*Slaps his face. His collar, which has come loose in the struggle, falls to the ground. There is a pause.*] Muruti, your collar—it has fallen. What have I done?

MFUNDISI [*sobered*]. Don't pick it up.

MAPULE. Have I hurt you?

MFUNDISI. No. I deserved it. It's all right. It's all right. Oh, God. What have I done?

MAPULE. It's all right, Muruti. It's the Devil. Here's your collar, Muruti. Take it.

MFUNDISI. What have I done? What have I done?

MAPULE. Here's your collar, Muruti. It's all right. I won't talk about this.

MFUNDISI. You're not angry with me then?

MAPULE. Not angry. Just disappointed. I could cry.

*A cough from the kitchen.*

MFUNDISI. Is that you, Gideon?

GIDEON. Yes, Mfundisi.

MFUNDISI. When did you come back?

GIDEON. Just now, Mfundisi. This moment.

MAPULE. I'll finish the shirt I'm ironing and go home, Muruti. [*Exit.*]

MFUNDISI [*slumps into chair*]. What have I done? What

have I done? Oh, Charity, why did you have to go away and leave me to this?

*Brief Curtain.*

*Later. Evening sounds: lowing cattle, etc. A knock at the door.*

MFUNDISI. Open the door, Gideon.

GIDEON. Yes, Mfundisi.

*Enter* HLOPE, MA-HLOPE, *and* MA-GWAGWA.

MFUNDISI. Good evening, Brother Hlope, Sister Hlope, and Sister Gwagwa. I hope I see you well. Sit down, please.

MA-HLOPE. We're not sitting, Mfundisi. We have come to tell you that we are leaving the church.

MFUNDISI [*wearily*]. Oh, you too. Well, I can't stop you, can I? I have heard. What a day this has been!

HLOPE. You don't look well, Mfundisi.

MFUNDISI. I'm all right. I'm all right. Go well. Good night.

CHORUS. Good night, Mfundisi. [*Exeunt.*]

MFUNDISI. O God! How troubles pile on me—like thunder clouds in a fevered western sky.

*Enter* GIDEON.

GIDEON. Here's supper, Mfundisi.

MFUNDISI. No thanks, Gideon; I'm not hungry.

GIDEON. Mfundisi!

MFUNDISI. Yes, Gideon?

GIDEON. Mfundisi, I heard that Father Zwane and others went to Maziya to ask for the bones yesterday.

MFUNDISI. Gideon, didn't I tell you not to repeat gossip to me?

GIDEON. Yes, Mfundisi.

MFUNDISI. Went to Maziya, eh?

GIDEON. About the sick child, Mfundisi.

MFUNDISI. Bring me my torch, Gideon. I'm going to see Maziya now. [*Door opens. Hooting of owls.*] Good night, Gideon.

GIDEON. Good night, Mfundisi.

## SCENE IV

MAZIYA's *kraal. Hooting of owls, the cry of jackals, and the sounds of night life.* MAZIYA *is warming himself by a small fire.*

MFUNDISI [*calls from the left*]. Oh, Maziya. I ask for shelter. It is night.

MAZIYA. Who are you who walks by night? Draw near, that my old eyes may see you.

MFUNDISI. It's me—Mfundisi.

MAZIYA. Mfundisi! What brings you to my ruins? Come and sit by the fire. There's a log. Watch out for scorpions.

MFUNDISI. It's hot, Maziya.

*Hooting of owl nearby.*

MAZIYA [*excitedly*]. Shoo! Away, bird of witches! To your mother with you! Aw, witches have grown bold. What brings you here, Mfundisi?

MFUNDISI. A heavy matter, Maziya.

MAZIYA. Then let it fall lightly on my old shoulders. Throw some more wood on the fire, that I may see your face. [MFUNDISI *does so and there is a crackling of fire. A pause.*] Your heart is heavy. Why?

MFUNDISI. It's this drought, Maziya.

MAZIYA. I am old and have seen many things. You are sorrowing.

MFUNDISI. I have come about Zwane's sick child.

MAZIYA. Zwane's sick child?

MFUNDISI. Don't pretend you don't know. They were here yesterday to ask for the divining bones, and you are going to heal the child.

MAZIYA. Ha! Ha! Ha! You are not as foolish as you look. You have sharp ears, young man.

MFUNDISI. It's true, isn't it?

MAZIYA. Hee! Hee! Hee! It is. Your spies are sharp!

MFUNDISI. This is no time for levity, Maziya.

MAZIYA. Levity! Am I capable of levity at my age? Levity is for the young.

MFUNDISI. You can save the child if you tell Zwane to take it to the hospital.

MAZIYA. Why don't you?

MFUNDISI. I tried but failed.

MAZIYA. And you expect me to do it for you?

MFUNDISI. I ask you. I beg you for the sake of the child.

MAZIYA. Suppose Zwane and his wife refuse?

MFUNDISI. They'll listen to you. Tell them you can't treat the child.

MAZIYA. But I can. I can. The great man of Mzindi village telling me to lie in my old age! I thought believers never lied! Your paths are not straight. You are the ones who destroy the people.

MFUNDISI. Oh, Maziya, you know that's not true.

MAZIYA. Not true? You are the ones who open us up to the white man. You split the tribe into believers and non-believers. Not true! Then what is true?

MFUNDISI. That we are leading the people out of darkness into light. That——

MAZIYA. Leading the people? Yes, like a mischief-making old cow that leads the herd to the crocodile pool!

MFUNDISI. No. We're taking them out of the darkness of the past into a new light.

MAZIYA. New light! Is it the new light to split the nation? To set brother against brother? No, Mfundisi. You are leading the people into the wilderness.

MFUNDISI. And you are holding them back.

MAZIYA. Yes. Back to their customs and traditions. Back to the ways *Nkulunkulu** showed us from the beginning of time. You want to destroy our roots.

MFUNDISI [*patiently*]. Maziya, listen. The old Africa is gone. No crying will ever bring it back. The ancient clay pots are broken, and we are moulding the new ones—better ones. The old ways are lost and overgrown——

MAZIYA. Because of people like you! But the ancestral spirits will revenge. Why do you think it won't rain? Why is there all this confusion, Mfundisi? You want to be a black white man. Why?

MFUNDISI. No, Maziya. I don't.

MAZIYA. Then why are you turning your back on the ways of our people? Why are you chasing the white man's ways? You are not content to be a black man.

MFUNDISI. Yes, Maziya. But we want to get rid of the poverty and ignorance of the past. We want to create a better life.

MAZIYA. Mfundisi, you talk like a child. Don't we starve now? And why? Because the white man took our country. All the big white farms you see around here were once tribal land. You know the ways of the white man. For all your schooling where has it got you? You are bundled together with raw things like me. Mfundisi, if you want to help the people, go and ask the white man for our ancestral lands.

MFUNDISI. We do ask, Maziya.

* The Creator.

MAZIYA. And does the white man hear? No. Follow the white man and you are heading for the precipice. We are different from the whites, Mfundisi. That's how *Nkulunkulu* made us, and that's how we shall be. You are troubling yourself, Mfundisi—you can't make a donkey into a horse.

MFUNDISI. We are all people—black and white. In the eyes of God there is no difference.

MAZIYA. You believe that?

MFUNDISI. Yes. We are made in God's image. We are equal in his sight. God doesn't say "This man is white; this one black . . ."

MAZIYA. We are all equal, eh? Then what is this? What is this? Why do the whites eat while we go hungry? Why do the whites hate us?

MFUNDISI. It's the sinfulness of man, Maziya. God will show us the way.

MAZIYA. When? Let this God show the white man. Let him show them now. Not tomorrow, when we are all dead. And this heaven of yours—do black and white go there?

MFUNDISI. Yes, everyone, without distinction of race or colour.

MAZIYA. Then there's strife in your heaven. You don't know your white man if you think heaven will change him. They'll be throwing stones in your heaven. I know. They're using you, Mfundisi—using you to do their dirty work. Long ago they came here with their Bibles. Then others came asking for land. And Chief Sogasa gave it to them. Some took our daughters too. And while we were still asleep, came the police asking for taxes. Taxes! What for? We pay our tribute to the Chief. But the police don't listen. They throw us into prison. We cry and cry, but they won't listen. You know nothing, Mfundisi.

MFUNDISI. There are good and bad whites, just like us. You can't say all whites are bad and all blacks are good. People aren't like that.

MAZIYA. You are lost, Mfundisi. You are in a thick bush. What has good and bad to do with it? We're different. We have different ways. And this new God you worship, what makes you so sure he's the true God?

MFUNDISI. I know. I believe. It was revealed to me. God sent his only son to earth to show us the way. He came to preach love between brothers and love between the nations.

MAZIYA. Then he has failed.

MFUNDISI. No, it's coming.

MAZIYA. You'll wait a long time—until your eyes are red. You won't change people, Mfundisi. You're wasting your time.

MFUNDISI. Things do change, Maziya. They will change for the better. We have schools now and hospitals. The doctors in the hospitals have great knowledge, and they know how to cure people. This matter I came about— Zwane's child. Will you tell Zwane to take him to the hospital?

MAZIYA. No, the child is my patient. Your hospital can't cure him.

MFUNDISI. You're taking a risk. If the child dies, the police will want to know why.

MAZIYA. I'm not afraid of your police.

MFUNDISI. Maziya, I beg you. Use the power you have for good.

MAZIYA. I will heal the child. I know what is wrong with it. The child is bewitched. Yes, bewitched by the same people who raise their buttocks to the sky and groan, "Amen, Amen, Amen."

MFUNDISI. You refuse then?

MAZIYA. I can do nothing.

MFUNDISI. Think carefully, Maziya. You're old. Wisdom
is said to live in old people like you.

MAZIYA. I have given you my answer. It is late. I must go
and rest my tired old bones. Give me my stick, Mfundisi.
Thank you. Now lift me to my feet. You are a good boy.
I hope it passes—the thing that is troubling you.
[*Hooting of owl.*] There's that bird again! Shoo! Bird of
witches! Go to your mother! Good night, Mfundisi.
You're a good boy, but you're lost. Remember my words.
[*He shuffles off. Exit.*]

MFUNDISI. Remember, I warned you, Maziya.

*Turns and exit.*

# ACT FOUR

## SCENE I

*At* GRAN SHONGWE'*s kraal. It is morning.* GRAN SHONGWE
*and* MAPULE *sit shelling groundnuts outside a hut to the
left of the stage.* MA-HLOPE, MA-GWAGWA, *and* MA-
NGWENYA *stand talking in a group to the right of the stage.*

GRAN. Mapule, is there something wrong?

MAPULE. Wrong, Gran?

GRAN. You heard me. You look sad.

MAPULE. I'm all right, Gran.

GRAN. I tell you things are not all right in this village. Look
at those women standing there. Do you see them? Why
do they look at us and spit?

MAPULE. People spit, Gran. There's no law against it.

GRAN. That's no ordinary spitting. I swear by my grey hairs.

MAPULE. You're imagining things, Gran. I'm just going to
the well to get some water. [*Picks up can and puts it on
her head.*]

GRAN. Not now, Mapule. It's Ma-Hlope, Ma-Gwagwa, and
Ma-Ngwenya. Don't go. They're pointing at us.

MAPULE. I'm going, Gran. I'm not going to be stopped by
those women—not by that fat dump of a Ma-Hlope. I'm
going——

GRAN. You're just like your mother. Mapule, hold that
tongue of yours.

MAPULE. I won't say a word, Gran.

*As* MAPULE *moves across the stage, a group of children run
on from the far right, playing and shouting. They see* MA-
PULE *coming, stop, and begin to run away.*

CHILD. Here she comes. Run away!

MAPULE. Hey, you, Paul. Why are you running away?

PAUL [*stops and turns round*]. My mother said I must never talk to you, because you're a witch. You ride a baboon at night and eat little children.

MAPULE. Tut-tut, Paul. You must have been naughty and your mother was frightening you.

*Exit* PAUL, *running right.* MA-NKOSI *enters right and joins group of women.*

MA-HLOPE. Here she comes, the Musutu bitch. Come this way. Her shadow mustn't fall on you. Ma-Nkosi, this way.

MA-NKOSI. Rubbish! What child's game is this?

MA-HLOPE. The bones at Maziya's smelt her out.

MA-NKOSI. Rot! You're mad.

MA-GWAGWA. Sh! Not a sound as she passes.

MA-NKOSI. You women are mad.

MA-HLOPE. The bitch! Stole my daughter's man.

MAPULE *passes.*

MA-NKOSI. Good day, Mapule. Don't you know me today?

MAPULE. Good day, Ma-Nkosi. I'll see you later. I'm in a hurry now. [*Exit.*]

MA-HLOPE. The bones smelt her out.

MA-GWAGWA. Without any beating about.

MA-NKOSI. You leave that girl alone. She wasn't a witch when she pulled Tabete's child from the burning hut, was she?

MA-HLOPE. Then why didn't she burn if she's not a witch?

MA-NKOSI. I said, leave that girl alone. You've caused her enough misery as it is! I'm going. I have a husband and children.

MA-HLOPE. Leave the witch alone! Since when have you become the protector of witches?

MA-NKOSI. Ma-Hlope, leave me out of this!

MA-HLOPE. Of course, it's not your child she's bewitched.

MA-NKOSI. Ma-Hlope, do your ears hear properly?

MA-HLOPE. You were always one for pulling in the opposite direction.

MA-NKOSI. You fat mischief-making bitch!

MA-HLOPE. Bitch yourself!

MA-NKOSI. I'll sort you out here and now!

MA-HLOPE. Leave me! Keep your hands off me! Women, tell her to leave me.

MA-GWAGWA. Please. Please, women. Ma-Nkosi, please. We're grown up.

MA-NKOSI. I'll sort you out! You've forgotten me, eh?

MA-HLOPE. Ma-Gwagwa, tell this woman to leave me. I'm not fighting with her.

MA-NKOSI. I'll melt you down, Ma-Hlope. You'll be thinner than a reed when I've finished with you.

MA-HLOPE. Ma-Gwagwa, you're my witness.

MA-GWAGWA. Aw, shut up too.

MA-NKOSI. You must thank your lucky stars I'm no longer young, Ma-Hlope. I'm Magonso's daughter if you've forgotten; the same Magonso who used to kill lions as if they were cats. I don't take nonsense from any woman —and no man either!

MA-GWAGWA. Peace! Peace!

MA-NKOSI. What peace, peace! You stand there accusing a poor girl and then talk nonsense. Women of the church! You stink! But let me warn you, Ma-Hlope. Next time will be your last time. Stay with those words. [MA-NKOSI *moves left. She stops and looks back. Exit left.*]

MA-HLOPE. Ma-Gwagwa, tell me. What did I do to that woman?

MA-GWAGWA. Ma-Hlope, you have a memory like a fowl. Have you forgotten Ma-Nkosi to talk to her like that? You were very lucky.

MA-HLOPE. She called me a fat bitch. What's wrong if I'm fat? Her husband doesn't feed me. Let's go. Here's that witch of a girl again, but we'll deal with her. [*Spits.*]

*They walk away. Re-enter* MAPULE *with a can on her head. She crosses to* GRAN.

MAPULE. See, Gran, I told you you were imagining things. Where's Ma-Nkosi?

GRAN. She was passing on her way to the store. There was nearly a fight between Ma-Nkosi and Ma-Hlope. Ma-Hlope forgets quickly. Her fat deceives her.

MAPULE. It would have served her right.

GRAN. Right! A killing—right! Ma-Nkosi's a devil. She's Magonso's daughter, she is. She used to fight with the boys—this same Zwane and company. Ma-Hlope's playing with fire.

MAPULE. Someday I may boil down Ma-Hlope myself.

GRAN. Mapule, what are you saying! Is Ma-Hlope your equal? You touch that woman and you touch me! Where's your respect for your elders?

MAPULE. Then let them behave like grown-ups.

GRAN. Drag out the devil in your heart by its tail. I won't have you talking like that. [*Ringing of church bells.*] There goes the first bell for the evening service. I'm worried about Mfundisi. Do you know what's wrong with him, Mapule?

MAPULE. No, Gran.

GRAN. You are just like Mfundisi. I don't know what's wrong with this village. The sun and the heat are getting into people's heads. [*Sound of drumming.*] And there's Maziya starting up with his drums! Au! No wonder it won't rain.

## SCENE II

MFUNDISI'S *house. It is afternoon.* MFUNDISI *is pacing up and down and groaning.*

MFUNDISI. I'm finished. Finished! I'll write to Charity and tell her everything. Everything! How shall I tell her? Let me see. "Dear Charity, don't come back to Mzindi.

I am finished. I am ruined. I am not worthy of you. In a moment of weakness I committed an indiscretion . . ." No. No. A sin. A sin? Damn it! Oh damn it! [*He holds his head in anguish.*] I must tell her everything. "Dear Charity, I am ruined. My life has fallen in a heap, a shambles, all because of a momentary aberration . . ." No. No. Face up to your guilt like a man. [*He clenches his fists.*] Now. Try again. "Dear Charity, don't come back. I'm ruined. I . . ." Yes, Gideon?

GIDEON. Here's your dinner, Mfundisi.

MFUNDISI. I'm not hungry, Gideon.

GIDEON. Not hungry, Mfundisi?

MFUNDISI. I'm not hungry.

GIDEON. Yes, Mfundisi. [*He begins to walk away.*]

MFUNDISI. Gideon!

GIDEON. Yes, Mfundisi?

MFUNDISI. Never mind. Didn't I teach you to look people in the eyes when you talk to them? What are you looking at?

GIDEON. There's a letter under the door. I'll get it, Mfundisi. Here it is.

MFUNDISI. Thank you, Gideon. But who could have written to me? It's not stamped. [*He tears open the envelope. A moment of silence.*] Oh, God! Oh, God! It's all right, Gideon.

GIDEON. Yes, Mfundisi. [*Exit.*]

MFUNDISI. Oh, God! Oh, God! Now I'm truly finished. What's this? "Don't let Sister Mapule pull down your collar!" My God, it's out. I'm finished. It must be the girl. No. She wouldn't talk. She said so. What shall I do now? Gideon!

GIDEON. Yes, Mfundisi?

MFUNDISI. Run to Gran Shongwe and tell Sister Mapule I want to see her immediately.

GIDEON. Yes, Mfundisi.

MFUNDISI. Run! [*Exit* GIDEON.] Oh, God, it's known. What shall I do? I could confess. No, I couldn't face that. Let me prepare Charity for the blow. I must tell her everything. Everything else is lost, but I mustn't lose her. Oh, Charity, Charity, why did you have to go away? Look at the mess I'm in now! No. She's not to blame. I did it and no one else is to blame. Don't look for a scapegoat. Damn it, what a mess! Oh, God, I'm finished, finished. No, that's just self-pity. Let me think. Let me think carefully. I'm not the first man to get into this sort of trouble—and not the last. Every day thousands, perhaps millions, get into it. It's nothing new. I must get it into proportion, into perspective. Now. [*Sitting and beginning to write.*] "Dear Charity, I have walked Mzindi village full of my own importance. I saw in the hardness of the life around me the measure of my own worth. I ministered not to the sick, the bereaved, the troubled, but ministered to my own vanity. I loved sickness because it brought me to the sick bed, and death because it brought me face to face with the final agonies. My pride and arrogance have tripped me. I have fallen. I do not think I will ever rise again. . . ." [*Knocking at the door.*] Mapule!

*Enter* MAPULE.

MAPULE. You sent for me, Muruti?

MFUNDISI. Thank you, Gideon. [GIDEON *goes into the kitchen.*] You have talked, Mapule. Yes, you have! Don't deny it. Here's the proof. Read it. Go on, read it. What do you say to that? You have talked.

MAPULE. No, Muruti. I didn't say a word to anyone.

MFUNDISI. You didn't tell your gran?

MAPULE. No, Muruti. I promised you I'd tell no one.

MFUNDISI. But someone knows.

MAPULE. It's not from me, Muruti.

MFUNDISI. Someone must have seen us. Could it be the boy? Gideon!

GIDEON [*from the kitchen*]. Mfundisi?

MFUNDISI. No. Never mind!

MAPULE. May I go now, Muruti?

MFUNDISI. Don't go. Say you forgive me.

MAPULE. I forgave you the same day. In this room. I'm sorry for you, Muruti. I wish I could help you.

MFUNDISI. Are you sorry for a wretch like me? I don't deserve it.

MAPULE. I'm very, very sorry, Muruti. I weep for you. Good-bye, Muruti.

MFUNDISI. Good-bye, Mapule. [*Exit* MAPULE.] I'm alone. Alone in my night. Oh, what am I to do now? Gideon!

*Enter* GIDEON.

GIDEON. Mfundisi?

MFUNDISI. Did you see who brought the letter?

GIDEON. No, Mfundisi. I just saw it when you called me.

*Knock at the door.*

MFUNDISI. Gideon, see who it is.

GIDEON. It's Father Zwane, Mfundisi.

MFUNDISI. Tell him I'm not well.

*Enter* ZWANE.

ZWANE. Good afternoon, Mfundisi.

MFUNDISI. Good afternoon, Bro—er—Mr. Zwane. You may go, Gideon.

ZWANE. May I sit down? [*He sighs contentedly.*] Ah, your chairs are very comfortable. There are only two houses where the chairs are comfortable—here and at my house. [*With mock concern.*] Why, Mfundisi, you don't look yourself at all—untidy and unshaven. Your wife wouldn't know you.

MFUNDISI. I'm not feeling very well.

ZWANE. It's the heat—or are there other things?

MFUNDISI. What do you mean?

ZWANE. Ha! Ha! Ha! Nothing. Nothing. There are many things that can make a man ill. Surely you know that.

MFUNDISI. Yes, yes.

ZWANE. You ought to know.

MFUNDISI. What should I know, Zwane?

ZWANE. I'm just talking. I see you're writing a letter—to your wife? That's good. Some men forget their wives once they're out of sight. They start looking around for new pastures, eh? You know what we men are like! Ha! Ha! Ha! We men are dogs.

MFUNDISI. Mr. Zwane, whatever is the matter with you? You come into my house . . . Are you drunk?

ZWANE. I'm as sober as you are. There's no need to hide your letter. Don't worry—I'm raw; I'm illiterate. I can't read all you're telling her—but it should be plenty. Ha! Ha! Ha!

MFUNDISI. Mr. Zwane, what do you want here?

ZWANE. Oh, I heard you were not well, and so I came along to see an old friend. Ha! Ha!

MFUNDISI. It's nothing. I'll be well tomorrow.

ZWANE. This place is no good. How long have you been here, Mfundisi?

MFUNDISI. Five years.

ZWANE. That's a long time. Do you like it here?

MFUNDISI. Look, what's this all about?

ZWANE. Just that foreigners don't usually like Mzindi. You and Mapule are the only foreigners here. I'm glad you've enjoyed the hospitality of Mzindi. But it's not usual.

MFUNDISI. What are you trying to say, Mr. Zwane?

ZWANE. Nothing—just talking to an old friend. Have you ever thought of leaving us, Mfundisi—of asking for a transfer?

MFUNDISI. Why should I?

ZWANE. Oh, it can get very hot here.

MFUNDISI. It's hot now. I don't mind the heat.

ZWANE. Ah, but it can get hot in other ways too. Then this place can be really bad.

MFUNDISI. What are you talking about? Are you in your right senses?

ZWANE. Come, come, Mfundisi. You know. Ha! Ha! Ha!

MFUNDISI. I know nothing except that your behaviour is insulting.

ZWANE. You got a letter today.

MFUNDISI. Letter?

ZWANE. Yes. Of course, educated people like you might not call such a thing a letter exactly. But I thought it was all right.

MFUNDISI [*breathing heavily*]. I don't know what you are talking about.

ZWANE. Shame, shame, Mfundisi, your lying like this!

MFUNDISI. Zwane, I've heard enough of this nonsense. You're mad. I must finish my letter now.

ZWANE. I wouldn't tell her everything if I were you. Ha! Ha!

MFUNDISI [*angrily*]. Get out! Get out before I . . . I . . .

ZWANE. Don't touch me. If you do, I know the way to the police station. And you wouldn't like that, would you? You're a highly strung man. Get a woman. Get Sister Mapule to console you.

MFUNDISI. You're evil, Zwane. You have fouled this village.

ZWANE. And you? Didn't your collar drop to the floor?

MFUNDISI. Get out of here! I don't know what you're talking about!

ZWANE. Come now, Mfundisi. You were trying to sleep with Mapule. Don't look so shocked! I don't blame you. I wouldn't mind sleeping with her myself. I hear Basutus are very nice.

MFUNDISI. Stop it! Stop it! You're a wicked man. Oh, God!

ZWANE. She's a stingy one—that Musutu girl.

MFUNDISI. What do you want, Zwane?

ZWANE. You're a clever man, Mfundisi. You know the Bible back to front. Look at all those books you've read. You're not a raw kaffir like me!

MFUNDISI. What do you want? You're wasting my time.

ZWANE. That's it, eh? You wouldn't like your troubles to be known, would you?

MFUNDISI. I don't care! Oh, God! I don't care! You're a bad man, Zwane. A bad, bad man. And I've trusted you.

How could I? You're a snake. You've been biting my
ankles.

ZWANE. And you? Didn't you turn people against me?
Didn't you make sure I wouldn't be treasurer of the
council? The pot calling the kettle black—it that it?

MFUNDISI. You are evil, evil.

ZWANE. You're finished here, Mfundisi. We don't want
you in Mzindi. I think you'd better write your letter of
resignation now. Go somewhere else. We don't want
you. [*He rises.*] Well, that's all I came to say. I hope
you'll take my advice. Good night, Mfundisi. I hope you
sleep well. [*Exit. There is a silence.*]

MFUNDISI. Oh, my God! My God! What have I done? I'm
finished! Finished! What can I do? My letter. Yes, yes.
Where was I? Here . . . "I do not think I'll rise again.
[*He continues to write.*] I don't want to rise again. The
drought persists, and it is evil deeds like mine that have
brought God's wrath on us. I am a rain-killer. Yet I
believed once that I had been truly called. That is no
more. My soul is parched like the earth outside—too,
too dry for the rain of repentance. How can the rain of
mercy fall on me? [*Baying of a dog, the hoot of an owl,
and the sound of distant drumming.*] Perhaps I'm bewitched, for the drums are playing at Maziya's again. . . ."

## SCENE III

MAZIYA's *kraal. It is early evening.* MA-ZWANE *and* ZWANE
*approach* MAZIYA; MA-ZWANE *is carrying her sick child.
Others stand left of centre and watching.* MTSAKASI *is drumming gently.*

MAZIYA. Drum. Drum for the spirits, boy. [*Drumming for a
while.*] All right. Hoooo! Stop! Bring me that razor blade.
. . . Hurry up. The child must have cuts to protect him
against the witches. Bring the child here, Ma-Zwane.

MA-ZWANE *places the child on a mat in front of* MAZIYA.

MA-ZWANE. Don't be afraid, my boy. He's making you better. It won't hurt.

MAZIYA. The wrists first. [*He bends over the child. The child cries.*] All right, my boy. We're chasing the witches who make you ill. Now the other wrist. [*The child cries weakly and continues to cry.*] Now the chest; and last of all the temples. This one and this one. Now this powder —the defeater of witches. Rub it into the cuts. [*The child screams.*] Dare to come now, you cursed witches! It's finished. Now to smoke him. Smoke out the witchcraft. Zwane, have you a half-crown piece?

ZWANE. Here it is, Maziya.

MAZIYA. Mtsakasi, bring that horn from under the rafter. Look sharp. The bull horn of all fats—make a witch dance. And bring me that broken clay pot. Pile the fats on the half-crown. There . . . Mtsakasi, go outside and find me a piece of burning charcoal. Hurry up! Zwane, give me that blanket on the cross pole. Good. The witches are going to dance. I'll show them their mothers. Bring the child. Put it on the mat and cover it with the blanket. Now the charcoal on the fats. [*Sizzling sound. Coughing.*] Now, under the blanket. Hold it down. Don't let any smoke escape. [*The child coughs and cries.*] Hold the child down. Beat the drums, Mtsakasi. [*Drumming.*] Play for the spirits. Go away witches! Go to your mothers! [*The child is quiet.*] Go away! [*Clap! Clap!*] Get out of this child! [*The drumming continues.* MAZIYA *dances about, waving the ox-tail.*]

MA-ZWANE. He's not crying. He's not kicking. My child! Get out of the way! Take off that blanket!

MAZIYA [*wildly*]. Go away, witches! Go to the one who sent you!

MA-ZWANE. My child! He's stopped breathing! [*Screams.*]

ZWANE. Bring him here. Maziya, what's this? Maziya, this child!

MAZIYA. Go away, witches! You dirty witches! I've beaten you! Ha! Ha! Ha! I'm the gnarled tree that conquers the hurricane. I'm the black bull that roars and the sky trembles. I've conquered you—you witches. Ha! Ha! Ha!

MA-ZWANE. My child—He's dead! He's dead! [*Screams.*] My child! Maziya, my child!

MAZIYA [*demented laugh*]. Yohohohoho . . . I've conquered the witches! I'm the gnarled tree that conquers the hurricane. I'm the black bull that roars and the sky trembles. Yohohoho . . . Kill the witches. Yohoho . . . [*The drumming stops.*]

ZWANE. Hau, this child. Maziya, the child's dead. What must we do?

MA-ZWANE. Maziya, my child! My child!

MAZIYA. Yohoho . . . I've conquered the witches. I've healed your boy. I'm the gnarled tree——

MA-ZWANE. My child! My child! My child is dead!

MAZIYA. He's well. I've healed him. Play, drum for the ancestors. Drum, Mtsakasi. Drum as you've never drummed before.

*The drumming starts again.* MA-ZWANE *screams.*

MA-ZWANE. My child! I want my child! That witch must give me back my child!

MAZIYA. I'm the gnarled tree that conquers the hurricane. I'm the black bull that roars and the sky trembles. Play. Play, Mtsakasi. Thank the spirits. The ancestors. Yohohoho——

ZWANE. Maziya, you've killed my child.

MAZIYA. I've healed him. There he is. Take him away. I want a beast now.

ZWANE. You've killed my child. I'm fetching the police for you. You won't get away with this. I'll bring them now. You'll see! [*Exit.*]

## SCENE IV

*At* GRAN SHONGWE's *kraal. Sound of drumming.* GRAN
SHONGWE *is sitting on a mat outside her hut.* MAPULE *is
grinding corn.*

GRAN. Mapule, what was that? A lamentation?

MAPULE. It sounded like one, Gran. [*Wailing.*] There it is
again.

GRAN. It stabs the heart! What——

MAPULE. It's from Maziya's. The drums are playing there
again tonight.

GRAN. I don't know what's happened to this place. [*Lamentation.*] There it is again. What does it say, Mapule?

MAPULE. Wait. It sounds like "My child." Someone seems
to be laughing. I can't hear. Those drums . . . It's Maziya
in one of his frenzies.

GRAN. No. Mapule, I don't like it.

MAPULE. What, Gran?

GRAN. I don't like it.

MAPULE. There's nothing to be worried about, Gran.

GRAN. You know nothing. You were born yesterday. I don't
like it. I tell you, I don't like it.

MAPULE. Gran, Gran, there's nothing.

GRAN. You never knew the old days. It's tense tonight—
just like those nights.

MAPULE. What on earth are you talking about, Gran?

GRAN. When the soil had to be strengthened. So that the
crops stood a strong, dark green . . .

MAPULE. Dark green?

GRAN. Then a very black person—a green one in Swazi—
was chosen. You never knew except for the waiting, the
unease in the air. We knew the moment it was over,
though nobody spoke. People breathed again. Life relaxed and went on as always. . . .

MAPULE. Ritual murder! But that doesn't happen anymore.

GRAN. My Uncle Mbabane was a very black man. We don't know what happened to him to this day.

MAPULE. But that time is past!

GRAN. I know. But nothing in the human soul dies. Things change, but people are really always the same.

MAPULE. We don't do those things anymore. We have the police. We go to school. It can't happen today!

GRAN. My child, you'll learn that there are things in people —like a grinding stone—and even that wears out. To-night feels like those old days when our warriors used to go to wash their spears in the blood of the mountain people and bring back women captives. . . .

MAPULE. It's the heat and the drought. Once it rains——

GRAN. Tonight I wish there was a man in the house. My poor husband, who died many years ago . . .

MAPULE. There are people all around us. You just have to shout.

GRAN. You and Ma-Nkosi are hiding something from me. . . . Is it this?

MAPULE. Aw, Gran. You're imagining things. [*The wailing stops.*] That woman has stopped. But there's still that madman's cackle. I'll get the supper.

GRAN. I'm not hungry.

MAPULE. Not hungry after a day in the fields, Gran?

GRAN. Where is it, Mapule? Where is it?

MAPULE. Where is what, Gran?

GRAN. *Phelamaphupho*—Ender of Dreams—my father's battle spear?

MAPULE. There, in that thatch, where I wouldn't see it. But why——

GRAN [*taking spear from thatch*]. Ah, here you are, Ender of Dreams. Many dreams vanished at your thrust. These notches are the men the great Mahlosi, my father, killed in battle.

MAPULE. Aw, Gran, a whole tribe.

GRAN [*reminiscently*]. The earth eats up great and small. Your great-grandfather was a hero—a terrible man. I see

him now. The massed warriors dropping down their
spears and sitting on their haunches as he rises to *Giya*—
to shout and dance his praises before Chief Sogasa. He
eats up the ground with his maniac strides—the women
shrilling in terrible ecstasy. His song of praise was long
and terrible. Ender of Dreams, do you remember?

MAPULE. You sound as if you are longing for those days,
Gran.

GRAN. No, just remembering. Ender of Dreams, you'll look
after us, won't you?

MAPULE. Gran, look! Look in the west! Clouds are rising
over Mpakeni and racing this way. Gran! Gran! They're
rain clouds. It will rain. [*A sudden thud like that of a
heavy stone.*] What was that? [*Another thud.*] A stone!
Gran, there's a crowd outside.

GRAN. I told you. Ender of Dreams, it has come!

## SCENE V

*Outside* GRAN SHONGWE's *kraal. A mob has gathered and
there is a tumult of angry voices. The crowd surges forward
from right of stage led by* MA-HLOPE, MA-GWAGWA, *and*
MA-ZWANE, *who is carrying her dead child.*

MA-HLOPE. The witch!

MA-GWAGWA. The Musutu bitch!

MA-ZWANE. My child! My child! Killed by a witch! Come
out! Come out and take this corpse! I want my child! I
want him alive!

MA-HLOPE. Musutu witch, come out!

MA-GWAGWA. We're sick and tired of the witch!

CHORUS. The witch! The witch! Come out!

GRAN. What's this noise outside my house? What do you
want?

MA-HLOPE. Your witch of a granddaughter!

MA-GWAGWA. We have nothing against you, Gran Shongwe.

CHORUS. The witch! The witch!

MA-HLOPE. Come out, you witch! You ate Ma-Zwane's child! Come out!

GRAN. What have you people been drinking? Witch! Witch yourselves! *Voetsek*—dogs of Mzindi!

MA-HLOPE. Let's drag her out!

CHORUS. Yes! Yes!

GRAN. I'll die with the first one who comes! Just try!

MA-GWAGWA. She has a spear!

MAPULE. Do you want me? Here I am!

MA-HLOPE. The witch is cheeky.

MA-ZWANE. Come and take this! I don't want a corpse! I want my child! I tell you, I want my child or I'll do terrible things to you!

MA-HLOPE. Kill the witch!

CHORUS. Kill the witch! *Bulala umtsakatsi!*

MAPULE. Then what are you waiting for?

GRAN. Come! I'm Mahlosi's daughter! *Phelamaphupho,* Ender of Dreams, will end your nonsense for you!

MA-HLOPE. Burn down the huts!

CHORUS. Burn them! Burn them!

MA-GWAGWA. Stop! No! We have no quarrel with Gran Shongwe.

CHORUS. No. No, we have none.

*Enter* MA-NKOSI *from left, running breathlessly.*

MA-NKOSI. What's this? What are you doing here?

MA-HLOPE. The defender of witches has come!

MA-GWAGWA. Ma-Nkosi, go away!

VOICE ONE. There she is, the witch!

VOICE TWO. She's killed Zwane's child!

MA-HLOPE. And the rain!

MA-ZWANE. I want my child! Here, take your corpse!

MA-NKOSI. You want your child when you killed it on purpose! Are you mad, woman?

MA-HLOPE. She bewitched the child!

MA-NKOSI. It's you again, Ma-Hlope!

CHORUS. She bewitched the child!

MA-HLOPE. She's brought ruin on all of us!

MA-ZWANE. What are we waiting for? Deal with the witch!

CHORUS. Yes! Yes! Kill the witch!

MA-NKOSI. Then kill me first! Ma-Hlope, I die with you tonight!

CHORUS. Kill the witch!

MAPULE. Come and try!

*Enter* MFUNDISI, *running into the mob.*

MA-HLOPE. Here's Mfundisi!

MA-GWAGWA. We don't want him here!

CHORUS. We don't want him!

MA-HLOPE. There's your Musutu bitch!

MFUNDISI. [*panting and breathless*]. What's this? Brethren, good people . . .

*Uproar.*

MA-HLOPE. This isn't your church! Go away!

CHORUS. Go away! Go away!

MFUNDISI. Will you listen to me?

MA-HLOPE. Go away and pray!

CHORUS. Go and pray!

MA-NKOSI. Let him speak! Ma-Hlope, shut your fat mouth!

*Dying hubbub.*

MFUNDISI. What childishness is this? Why are you behaving like hooligans?

MA-HLOPE. We don't want to listen to you!

MA-NKOSI. Shut up, Ma-Hlope! You fat bitch!

MFUNDISI. What do you think you're doing here? What——

MA-HLOPE. We're dealing with your witch!

MA-GWAGWA. She killed Zwane's child!

MA-ZWANE. I want my child! I want my child!

MFUNDISI. So that is it. You are hunting out witches! You
are back in the past! I'll tell you who bewitched Zwane's
child—Zwane and his wife! [*Uproar.*] Let me finish. Yes,
Zwane and his wife! They refused to take the child
to the hospital. They said they knew. They wouldn't listen.
"Won't listen sees by blood." The blood is their dead
child. I'm sorry for Zwane, and his wife, but they mustn't
look for a scapegoat. And why is this scapegoat Mapule?
I'll tell you: because she's a foreigner.

MA-HLOPE. It's not that! You're lying!

CHORUS. It's not that! No!

MFUNDISI. What is it then? Although she's black like you,
she's a Musutu, not a Swazi. That's why! This is
tribalism.

MA-HLOPE. She's a bitch! She corrupts our children. We
know about you! Don't think we don't know!

MA-NKOSI. Shut up, you fat dump!

MFUNDISI. You corrupt your children yourselves. What do
your children think of this? A mob hounding a poor
defenceless girl.

MA-HLOPE. Your lover?

MFUNDISI. Is this what you teach your children? Tell me!

MA-HLOPE. The bones smelt her out! Come on, Ma-
Gwagwa . . .

MFUNDISI. The bones, eh? Now it's the bones. The bones
smelt her out, so she's a witch?

MA-HLOPE. Yes.

MA-GWAGWA. A Musutu witch.

MFUNDISI. Is it not your tribal prejudice that smelt her
out? Isn't it because she's not one of you? The bones
told you just what you wanted to be told. You went
there looking for a witch, a Musutu witch—Mapule!

CHORUS. No.

MFUNDISI. And you cry that the white man treats you
badly because you're black, because you're not like him.
You think it's a bad thing. But when you persecute this

girl, then it's all right. You people are doing just what you say the whites are doing—but you're doing it to a black like yourselves! [*Uproar.*] You don't like to hear it? Yes, it's the same thing. Don't think that because you're black you're better and can't do what the white man does. If you don't believe it, here's the proof!

MA-HLOPE. We know all about you and her. Don't think we don't! Remember the collar!

MFUNDISI. I'll come to that, Ma-Hlope. Let me finish this. So the bones told you that Sister Mapule was a witch? And you believed those bones.

MA-HLOPE. Yes.

MA-GWAGWA. They told the truth.

MFUNDISI. Clever bones! Very clever indeed! But tell me, do those bones ever tell you about joy and happiness? Do they ever say: "You must plough like this, and plant like this; the rain will fall at such a time? Do they ever tell you how to make your lives better? No. Never. The bones tell you who is a witch. They tell you whom to suspect. They are bones of strife, of accusation, of destruction. [*Murmurs of dismay.*] But I'll tell you who is the real witch. . . . [*Pause.*]

CHORUS. Who?

MFUNDISI. You!

CHORUS. No!

MFUNDISI. And me! I'm the greatest witch in Mzindi.

MA-GWAGWA. This is a miracle.

MFUNDISI. A witch is someone who is proud, intolerant, cowardly; who is always ready to see the faults in other people but never in himself! That's you! That's me!

MA-NKOSI. Not you, Mfundisi. Not you!

MFUNDISI. Yes, me! I am no better because I wear my collar back to front. Because I say "Brother," "Sister." I talk about love, but how do you know that there is not hate in my heart? I talk of purity, but how do you know I am not an adulterer? [*Murmurs.*] Good people of Mzindi, I have a confession to make to you. After I have made it and gone away, I hope you will forgive me. I have wronged Sister Mapule——

MAPULE [*shouting*]. No, Muruti! Muruti, no!

CHORUS. Hau! What's this?

MFUNDISI. Yes, I've wronged her. I sinned against her.

MAPULE [*tearfully*]. Please, please, Muruti.

MFUNDISI. Mapule, let me speak. I tried to sleep with her.

CROWD. Nooo!

MAN'S VOICE. That's nothing, Mfundisi.

MFUNDISI. Yes, my heart and eyes were full of adultery.

MAPULE [*sobbing bitterly*]. No, Muruti. No, Muruti. You can't do this.

MFUNDISI. Yes, I have wronged you, Mapule. I hope you will forgive me. I have failed you people of Mzindi. I have failed God. It is not this girl you must hound, but me! I am the witch. Me! [*Pounds his chest.*] Your Mfundisi. I hope you will forgive me. It is all over now. [*Exit MFUNDISI.*]

MA-HLOPE. She's a witch! It doesn't change anything!

CHORUS. Shut up, Ma-Hlope.

MA-NKOSI [*clapping her hands*]. A miracle!

MA-GWAGWA. The police! Zwane's brought them!

MA-HLOPE. What about them? We're doing nothing!

MA-GWAGWA. I'm going, people. I don't want to get mixed up in——

MA-HLOPE. You're a coward, Ma-Gwagwa.

MA-GWAGWA. Yes, I am. [*Exit left.*]

    *Enter police from right, running into the crowd.*

SERGEANT MABIKA. What's going on here? [*Silence.*] I said: What's happening here? Hey, you, tell me!

MA-HLOPE. We're just standing. And don't you "Hey" me!

SERGEANT. Just standing, eh! There was someone talking to you. Where is he?

MA-NKOSI. Mfundisi. Where's Mfundisi?

MA-HLOPE. He must have gone away to nurse his troubles.

SERGEANT. All right. Now you go home, all of you. There's been enough trouble from you already! That old Maziya killing Zwane's child! Go to your homes! Go on! Constable Dladla, disperse them. Home! Go home!

*There is a general movement.* MA-GWAGWA *comes running back, shrieking wildly.*

SERGEANT. What is it, woman? What is it?

MA-GWAGWA [*terrified*]. That tree! That tree!

MA-HLOPE. What tree, Ma-Gwagwa?

VOICES. What is it? What is it?

MA-GWAGWA. He's hanging . . . !

SERGEANT. Come, show us. [*Exit left with some of the crowd.*]

MA-GWAGWA. Over there. Behind that tree.

*The crowd runs to the tree.*

VOICES [*off*]. Mfundisi! It's Mfundisi!

SERGEANT [*off*]. Mfundisi! Quick, Constable Dladla, cut him down. . . . Be quick man!

DLADLA. Hold him, Sarge.

SERGEANT. I've got him! [*Carrying* MFUNDISI.] Put him down, Constable.

MA-NKOSI. Is he still alive?

*Pause.*

SERGEANT. No. Dead!

VOICES. Dead! Oh, God! Dead!

SERGEANT. He did it right under our very noses. Now, tell me, why should Mfundisi want to do a thing like this? [*Silence.*] Tell me! Now what did you do to him?

MA-HLOPE. Nothing. He tried to sleep with the Musutu girl.

SERGEANT. Well? Is that all? My God, what a fool! Aren't you all going to your homes to play *mgiqilogiqi*—the tumbling game? What a foolish man! Where's the girl?

MA-HLOPE. Here she is.

SERGEANT. Come here. What do you know about this?

MAPULE [*sobbing*]. Muruti was killed by this beastly village, by people like Zwane. He was a good man, a good man.

SERGEANT. And you, girl, why didn't you give him what he asked?

GRAN. Hey, you, Mabika. Don't talk to my granddaughter like that! Do you think this is a laughing matter!

SERGEANT. All right, Gran Shongwe. Hau, what a terrible thing to happen.

DLADLA. Suicide, Sarge?

SERGEANT [*impatiently*]. Yes, yes.

*There is a sound of mad laughter as* MAZIYA *is led in from left by* TWO CONSTABLES. ZWANE *follows.*

SERGEANT. What's that? What's happening?

MA-HLOPE. It's Maziya. He's mad.

SERGEANT. Mad? And he killed Zwane's child. Are you all mad?

MAZIYA. Yohohoho! I'm the gnarled tree that conquers the hurricane, the black bull that roars and the sky trembles. Where are you taking me, eh? Where are you taking me? There's Ma-Zwane. Ask her! I healed the child. Ma-Zwane, show them the child. Yohoho!

GRAN. Aw, God. What's this? Handcuffs on the poor thing? Sergeant Mabika, is he still a thing for handcuffs? Can a thing like that run away?

SERGEANT. Constable Ngwenya, take off the handcuffs.

NGWENYA. Yes, Sarge. Come, hold up your hands, like this.

MA-ZWANE. My child! My child! He killed my child!

ZWANE. All right, Ebenezer's mother. The law will deal with him.

MAZIYA. Yohohoho! Who's this on the ground?

MA-HLOPE. It's Mfundisi. He's dead. He hanged himself.

GRAN. And that pleases you, doesn't it, Ma-Hlope? That's just what you wanted!

MA-HLOPE. How you do talk, Gran Shongwe!

MA-NKOSI. Shut up, you fat dump!

VOICES. No, Ma-Nkosi. Please.

GRAN. Yes, that's what you wanted. All of you. Well, it's happened. Rejoice! Sing! Come on! Sing! Dance! Come on! What are you waiting for?

*There is a loud crack of thunder, which rumbles and fades far away.*

SERGEANT. It wants to rain.

MA-HLOPE. Don't say that. You'll chase it away.

MAZIYA. Wake up, Mfundisi. Wake up. Wake up and see my rain. My rain! My rain! Yohohoho! My rain! I took out the witches' pegs! I conquered the witches!

SERGEANT. Constable Dladla and Constable Nkosi, carry the Mfundisi to his house. And Constable Ngwenya, take the old madman to the van. Hurry up. I don't want to be caught in the rain.

NGWENYA. Come on, you—madman. Forward!

GRAN. Hey, you, police boy Ngwenya! Gently with Maziya. He belongs to a generation that has dried up.

SERGEANT. You heard, Constable Ngwenya!

NGWENYA. Yes, Sarge. [*Gently.*] Come on, Maziya.

SERGEANT. And you. Go to your homes. There's nothing more to see. It's over. [*Crack of thunder.*] There! And the drought's over. All things end—that which does not end, bodes ill. Good night to all of you.

*There is another crack of thunder and a flurry of raindrops.*

VOICES. Rain! It's raining! It's raining!

MAZIYA. My rain! My rain! See, Mfundisi, my rain!

NGWENYA. Come on, Maziya. Let's go.

MAZIYA. Good-bye, my people. I've given you rain. I'll be back. I don't know where they're taking me, but I'll be back. I can never die. Zwane, don't forget my beast. Yohoho! My rain! I'm the gnarled tree that conquers the hurricane, the black bull that roars and the witches tremble. . . . [*Exit right.*]

GRAN. The things of this world!

MA-NKOSI. Yes, Gran Shongwe. The things of this world.

*There is the sound of a van driving off.*

GRAN [*shouting*]. Go well, Maziya.

ZWANE. Let's go home, Ebenezer's mother. The law will deal with Maziya.

MA-ZWANE. But it won't bring back my child. Here— carry him. [*Sobs.*] My child! My child!

MA-NKOSI. We're saved, Gran Shongwe. It's raining!

GRAN. Yes, Ma-Nkosi. But what a time! What a time it's been!

MA-HLOPE. It's Maziya's rain. He defeated the rain-killers.

MA-NKOSI. You're wrong, Ma-Hlope. It's Mfundisi's rain. He prayed for it.

MAPULE. It's God's rain, Ma-Nkosi.

GRAN. What does it matter? It's raining. Come, Mapule, we're getting wet.

MAPULE. Yes, Gran.

*Exeunt. There is thunder, followed by a heavy, steady downpour.*

# EDUFA

*by*

## EFUA T. SUTHERLAND

# CHARACTERS

ABENA, *Edufa's sister*
EDUFA
SEGUWA, *a matronly member of the household*
AMPOMA, *Edufa's wife*
KANKAM, *Edufa's father*
CHORUS *of women from the town*
SENCHI, *Edufa's friend*
SAM, *an idiot servant*


SCENE: The courtyard and inner court of EDUFA's expensive house. The two areas are linked by wide steps. The inner court is the ground floor of the house. Here, towards the back, and slightly off-centre, a slim pillar stands from floor to ceiling. Back of this pillar is a back wall. There are also two flanking walls, left and right. Short flights of steps between back and side walls lead into EDUFA's rooms on the left, and guest rooms on the right. A door in the right wall, close to the courtyard steps, leads into the kitchen. There are three, long, boxlike seats, which match the colour of the pillar. Two of these are close to the courtyard steps, against the side walls; one is right of the pillar.

An atmosphere of elegant spaciousness is dominant.

For Act Three, the seats are shifted to more convenient positions, and light garden chairs, a trestle table, and a drinks trolley are moved in.

People in the audience are seated in EDUFA's courtyard. The gate by which they have entered is the same one the chorus and other characters use as directed in the play.

Music for the four songs, transcribed by Dr. E. Laing, will be found at the end of the play.

# EDUFA

## PROLOGUE

ABENA *is sitting on a side seat, her head in her lap, her cloth wrapped round her for warmth. She is gazing into a small black water-pot which stands on the step below her. Another pot, red, stands on the floor beside her. She tilts the black pot, measuring its contents with her eyes. Then she looks up, sighs wearily, and rubs her eyes as if she can no longer keep sleep away.*

ABENA [*beginning slowly and sleepily*].
   Night is long when our eyes are unsleeping.
   Three nights long my eyes have been unsleeping,
   Keeping wakeful watch on the dew falling,
   Falling from the eaves . . .

[*She glances anxiously round the inner court, rises, goes towards the steps leading to* EDUFA'S *rooms, hesitates, and turns back.*]

   And dreaming.
   Dreamlike views of mist rising
   Above too much water everywhere.
   I heard tonight
   A voice stretched thin through the mist, calling.
   Heard in that calling the quiver of Ampoma's voice.
   Thought I saw suddenly in the restless white waters
   The laterite red of an anthill—jutting
   And rocking.
   A misty figure on its topmost tip,
   Flicking her fingers like one despairing.
   I panicked, and came to this door, listening,
   But all was silence—
   Night is so deceiving when our eyes
   Are robbed too long of sleep.

[*She returns to her seat, puts her head back on her knees, and is soon singing.*]

   O child of Ama,
   Child of Ama in the night

Is wandering,
Crying, "Mm-m-m-m,
How my mother's pondering."
O child of Ama,
Why is she wandering,
Why wandering,
Why wandering in the night
Like the dying?
*Meewuo!*

[*She keeps up the last bars of the song for a while, patting
the black pot with one hand and her own arm with the
other, in a manner suggestive of self-consolation. Presently,
she looks into the sky again.*]

But my last night of wakefulness is over. [*She rises,
tipping the black pot.*] The last drop of dew has fallen.
There's enough dew water in the pot. [*She picks up the
pot and tilts the red one.*] And here is stream water from
the very eye of the spring where the red rock weeps without ceasing. [*Gesturing towards* EDUFA'S *rooms.*] My
brother Edufa, your orders are done, though I obey without understanding. . . . [*Walking about.*] Here in this
house, where there was always someone laughing, suddenly no one feels like smiling. I've never known such
silence in my brother's house. Mm? It is unnatural. From
rising until sleep claimed us again at night, people came
through our gate, for who doesn't know my brother
Edufa in this town? Benevolent one, who doesn't love
him? Old and young, they came. They brought laughter.
Those who brought sadness returned with smiles, com-
forted.

Why then does brother shut our gate to stop such
flow of friends? Mm? True that Ampoma, his wife, is unwell; but if she is unwell, should we not open our gate?
She is not mortally ill; but even so, just let it be known,
and sympathy and comforting gifts would flow in from
every home. So much does the whole town hold her dear.
[*Yawning.*] Oh well . . . I don't even know what it is
that ails her. Their door is barred, and my brother says
nothing to me. [*Yawning again.*] Ha! Tired. [*She picks*

*up the red pot also, carrying the two pressed against her body.*] Well . . . I place these at his door . . . [*She places them at the top of the steps.*] . . . and make my way . . . to . . . [*Yawning.*] sleep. I don't know why I should be so sad. [*She crosses, humming her song, and goes out through the kitchen door.*]

# ACT ONE

## SCENE I

EDUFA's *hands reach out and pick up the pots. He is heard issuing instructions urgently to someone inside.*

EDUFA. Pour first the dew water, and then the stream water, over the herbs in the bathroom. Quickly. Then bring out fire for the incense.

*Outside the courtyard walls a chorus of women is heard performing.*

CHORUS [*chanting to the rhythm of wooden clappers*].
   Our mother's dead,
   Ei! Ei—Ei!
   We the orphans cry,
   Our mother's dead,
   O! O—O!
   We the orphans cry.

*The chanting repeats. As the voices, the clack-clack accompaniment, and the thudding of running feet recede,* SEGUWA *comes hurriedly out of* EDUFA's *rooms. She listens as she crosses to the kitchen, and is clearly disturbed by the performance. Her brief absence from the court is filled in by the chanting, which becomes dominant once again as the chorus returns past the house. She comes back, carrying a brazier in which charcoal fire is burning in a small earthen pot. She hesitates by the kitchen door, still preoccupied with the performance outside. At the same time* EDUFA *rushes out in pyjamas and dressing gown. He carries a box of incense and has the air of a man under considerable mental strain.*

EDUFA. Why are they doing a funeral chant? They are not coming towards this house? [*To* SEGUWA.] You've spoken to no one?

SEGUWA [*with some resentment*]. To no one. My tongue is

silenced. [*Pause.*] It must be for someone else's soul
they clamour.

*The chanting fades.*

EDUFA [*composing himself*]. No, they are not coming here.
[*Pause.*] Put the fire down. [SEGUWA *places the fire close
to the central seat.* EDUFA *rips the box open and flings
incense nervously on the fire.*] Keep the incense burning
while Ampoma and I bathe in the herbs.

SEGUWA. It seems to me that the time has come now to
seek some other help. All this bathing in herbs and incense burning—I don't see it bringing much relief to
your wife, Ampoma, in there.

EDUFA. Doubting?

SEGUWA. I'm not saying I doubt anything. You have chosen
me to share this present burden with you, and I'm letting my mouth speak so that my mind can have some
ease. It is I myself who say I'm hardy, but how can I
help having a woman's bowels?

EDUFA. Calm yourself. I cannot give in to any thoughts
of hopelessness. Where is your faith? I thought I could
trust it.

SEGUWA. You can trust my secrecy; that I have sworn;
though what I have sworn to keep secret, now frets
against the closed walls of my skull. I  haven't sworn
to have faith against all reason. No, not in the face of
your wife's condition in that bedroom there. Let's call
for help.

EDUFA [*with indications of despair*]. From whom? We are
doing everything we can. Also, it is Ampoma's wish that
no one should be allowed to see her.

SEGUWA. And is she dead that we should be bound to honour her wishes? She is not herself. In her present state
we can expect her to say childish things. The sick are
like children. Let me call for help.
     It is almost unnatural that even the mother who bore
her should be kept ignorant of her sickness, serious as it
now is. Ah, poor mother; if we could but see her now.
She is probably pampering the children you've sent to

her, keeping them happy, thinking she is relieving her
daughter for rest and fun with you, her husband. [*Bitterly.*] How you are deceived, Mother.

EDUFA. Don't fret so much. Calm yourself, will you?

SEGUWA. It is your wife who needs calming, if I may say so.

EDUFA. You've promised to stand with me in this trouble.
You will, won't you? Your service and your courage these
last few days have given me strength and consolation.
Don't despair now. Ampoma is getting better.

SEGUWA. Better? Ho, ho. After fainting twice last night?
[*Shrugs.*] Ah, well, just as you say. I promised to stand
with you and will. But may God help us all, for the
bridge we are now crossing is between the banks of life
and the banks of death. And I do not know which way
we're facing. [*Pause.*] Where is the incense? I'll keep it
burning.

EDUFA [*relieved*]. Your kindness will not be forgotten, believe me, when we can smile again in this house. [*He
gives her the box. She sprinkles more incense on the fire.*]
See that the gate is barred.


SCENE II

AMPONA *has appeared unnoticed at the top of the steps
and is standing there unsteadily. There is a look of near
insanity about her.* SEGUWA *sees her first and lets out a
stifled scream.*

EDUFA [*hurrying to her*]. Oh, Ampoma. You shouldn't
leave your bed. You shouldn't come out here.

AMPOMA [*weakly*]. The sun is shining on the world, and I
am . . . falling. [*She totters.*]

SEGUWA. Hold her! She'll fall.

EDUFA [*only just saving* AMPOMA *from falling*]. Is the gate
barred?

SEGUWA [*with uncontrolled irritation*]. O God! I cannot understand it. [*She picks up a wrap* AMPOMA *has dropped on the steps and starts towards the gate, but gives up in confusion, and returns to the incense-burning.*]

AMPOMA [*moving and compelling* EDUFA, *who is supporting her, to move with her*]. I have come out into the bright sun. There is no warmth in my bed. And no comfort. Only darkness.

EDUFA. Sit, then. Let us sit together here. [*He urges her tenderly to the seat near the kitchen door, takes the wrap from* SEGUWA, *and arranges it round* AMPONA'S *shoulders.*] You want to be in the sun? That means you are getting well. You are. Tell yourself you are. Make your soul will your strength back again. [*Pause.*] In a little while we will bathe in the herbs, and later today, at the junction between day and night, we will bathe again, the final time. Tomorrow . . . tomorrow, you will feel much better. I promise you.

AMPOMA [*dreamily*]. Tomorrow? When . . . is tomorrow? [*She droops and quickly buries her face in the nape of* EDUFA's *neck.*]

EDUFA [*confused*]. Tomorrow . . .

AMPOMA [*breaking free*]. Oh, no! I cannot have them straying.

SEGUWA *picks up the wrap she flings away and hovers anxiously in the background.*

EDUFA [*helplessly*]. What? Who?

AMPOMA. Like two little goats. I'm leaving them. I? Two little goats struggling on the faraway hillside. I see their eyes glowing in the dark, lonely. Oh, my little boy! And you, my girl with breasts just budding! What hands will prepare you for your wedding? [*She sobs quietly.*]

SEGUWA. She is talking of her children. Thank God they are not here to see this sight.

EDUFA [*to* AMPOMA]. Don't talk as if all were ending. All is not ending. It cannot end. [*To* SEGUWA.] Put on more incense. [*He guides* AMPOMA *back to the seat.*]

AMPOMA [*on the way*]. My bed is so full of a river of my own tears, I was drowning there. [*Helplessly.*] Why do we weep so much? [*They sit.*]

EDUFA. Dreams. You only dreamed these things. Sickness plagues the mind with monstrous fantasies. Pay no heed to them. Think only of reality. . . . Think of me. Is not your bed that sunny place in which we plant our children? There has never been anything but warmth and happiness there, and never will be, as long as I live and love you so.

AMPOMA. Don't speak of it. I have strayed into the cold. Yet, how good that I should not be the one to live beyond your days. I could not live where you are not. I could not live without you, my husband.

EDUFA. Ah, loving wife.

AMPOMA. Yes. That is the truth. I have loved you.

EDUFA. You have. And I have you still to fill my days with joy. [*He puts his arm round her protectively.*]

AMPOMA [*looking at him sadly*]. I am dying too young, don't you think? Look at me. [*She rises abruptly.*] What am I saying? We knew this day could come. Am I listening to the lure of his voice at this final stage? Weakening at the closeness of his flesh? [*To EDUFA.*] Help me. Take your arm away from me. Why do you restrain me at your peril?

EDUFA. Come inside. You've been out here too long already.

AMPOMA [*more calmly, moving again, halting now and then*]. Let me talk with you a little longer in the sun before I step into the dark, where you cannot see me. Soon my pledge will be honoured. I am leaving our children motherless in your hands. Let me hear you say you love them, though I know you do.

EDUFA. I love them, Ampoma.

AMPOMA. And will you keep them from harm? Protect them?

EDUFA. How else would I be worthy of the sacred name of father? How worthy of your trust, brave woman? No harm shall come to the children that I can prevent.

AMPOMA. I fear the harm that might come to them from another woman's dissatisfied heart.

EDUFA. Ampoma, what are you saying? Another woman? I swear that in this, as in nothing else, true triumph is mine. You inspire devotion, incomparable one. There is no other woman beside you.

AMPOMA. The dead are removed. Time must, and will, soften pain for the living. If you should marry another woman, will she not envy my children because you have them with your own love and mine combined?

EDUFA. Poor Ampoma. In what unfamiliar world is your mind wandering that you speak so strangely?

AMPOMA. Promise me that you will never place them in another woman's power. Never risk their lives in the hands of another. Promise me that, and I will die without that unbearable fear here in my heart.

EDUFA. You will not die. But if it will calm you to hear it, I do promise.

AMPOMA. That you will not marry again?

EDUFA. That no other woman will cross my inner door, nor share my bed. This house will never even harbour a woman not of my own blood, at whom my eye could look without restraint.

AMPOMA. Swear it.

EDUFA. I swear it.

AMPOMA [*calmly walking away from him*]. Over me the sun is getting dark. [*With great agitation.*] My husband! Watch the death that you should have died. [*She frets from place to place as if escaping from him.*] Stay over there in the sun. Children! My children! If I could cross this water, I would pluck you back from the mountainside. Children! Hold my hand! [*She stretches out her hand to the vision that she alone can see.*]

EDUFA [*catching hold of her*]. Oh, wife of my soul. You should never have made that fatal promise.

AMPOMA. That I loved you? My love has killed me. [*Faintness comes over her. She falls into EDUFA's arms.*] Children! And . . . Mother . . . Mother.

EDUFA *takes her in, almost carrying her.* SEGUWA, *not
      quite knowing how to help, follows them.*

CHORUS [*heard again in the distance*].
    Our mother's dead,
    Ei! Ei—Ei!
    We the orphans cry,
    Our mother's dead,
    O! O—O!
    We the orphans cry.

          *The voices travel farther into the distance.*


## SCENE III

SEGUWA [*returning*]. This is what we are living with. This
    weakness that comes over her and all this meandering talk.
    Talk of water and of drowning? What calamitous talk
    is that? When will it end? How will it end? We are
    mystified. How wouldn't we be? Oh, we should ask Edufa
    some questions; that is what I say. You should all ask
    Edufa some questions. [*She goes to the fire, throws in
    more incense, and withdraws from it as if she hates it.*]
    I wish I could break this lock on my lips.
    Let those who would gamble with lives
    Stake their own.
    None I know of flesh and blood
    Has right to stake another's life
    For his own.
    Edufa! You have done Ampoma wrong,
    And wronged her mother's womb.
    Ah, Mother! Mother!
    The scenes I have witnessed in here,
    In this respected house,
    Would make torment in your womb.
    Your daughter, all heart for the man
    She married, keeps her agonies from you.
    Ah, Mother! Mother!

Edufa has done Ampoma wrong.
*Tafrakye!*
Some matters weight down the tongue,
But, Mother, I swear
Edufa does Ampoma wrong,
He does her wrong.

*She returns angrily to the incense burning.*

## SCENE IV

KANKAM *enters through the gate. Hearing his footsteps,*
SEGUWA *turns round in alarm. She is torn between surprise
and fear when she notices who has arrived.* KANKAM *stops
on the courtyard steps.*

SEGUWA [*approaching him hesitantly*]. Grandfather!

KANKAM [*quietly*]. Yes. It is me. Three years, is it? Three
years since I walked out of that same gate, a disappointed
father. Three years. Well . . . tell him I am here.

SEGUWA. Tell Edufa?

KANKAM. Yes, the man whom nature makes my son.

SEGUWA. Oh, Grandfather, do I dare? So troubled is his
mood, he has ordered his gate shut against all callers.

KANKAM [*with power*]. Call him.

SEGUWA [*nervously*]. As for me, I'm willing enough to call
him, but——

KANKAM [*an angry tap of his umbrella emphasizing his
temper*]. Call him! It was I who bore him.

SEGUWA [*on her knees, straining to confide*]. Oh, Grandfather, help him; help him. God sent you here, I'm sure. I
could tell you things—no . . . I couldn't tell you. Oh,
please forget your quarrel with him and help us all. What
shall I say? Hmm. His wife, Ampoma, is sick, sick, very
sick.

KANKAM. So he bars his door, just in case anyone looks in
to offer help. [*Calling with authority.*] Edufa! Edufa!

SEGUWA [*hurrying*]. I will call him. He was bathing. [*She
meets* EDUFA *coming out of his rooms.*]

EDUFA [*seeing his father and recoiling*]. You? What do
you want? [*His eyes shift uneasily as* KANKAM *stares hard
at him. He comes down the steps*]. What do you want?
Three years ago you declared me not fit to be your son and
left my house. Had my position not been well evaluated
in this town, you might have turned tongues against me
as the man who drove his own father out of his home.
What do you want now?

KANKAM [*walking deliberately to the seat near the kitchen*].
Yes. It has burnt down to loveless greetings between
father and son, I know. What do I want? I will tell you
presently. [*He sits.*] Don't let us fail, however, on the
sacredness of courtesy. Had I entered the house of a total
stranger, he would have given me water to drink, seeing
I'm a traveller. [EDUFA *is embarrassed, but at that moment*
SEGUWA *is already bringing water from the kitchen.*] I
happen to be your father, and you a man in whose
house water is the least of the things that overflow.

SEGUWA *gives the water to* KANKAM, *who pours a little on
the floor stylistically for libation, drinks, and thanks her.
She returns to the kitchen.*

EDUFA [*awkwardly*]. Well?

KANKAM. Sit down, son. Sit. [EDUFA *sits uneasily on the
opposite seat.*] What do I want, you say? [*Very deliberately.*] I want the courage that makes responsible men.
I want truthfulness. Decency. Feeling for your fellow-
men. These are the things I've always wanted. Have you
got them to give? [EDUFA *rises, angry.*] I fear not, since
you have sold such treasures to buy yourself the importance that fools admire.

EDUFA. If you have come only to tempt me to anger, then
leave my house.

KANKAM. Oh, stop blabbering. I left before, and will do so
again, but it isn't any absurd rage that will drive me out.

EDUFA. What do you want, I say?

KANKAM [*with terrible self-control*]. The life of your wife, Ampoma, from you.

EDUFA [*very nervous*]. And you mean by that? [KANKAM *only stares at him.*] What makes me keeper of her life?

KANKAM. Marriage . . . and her innocent love. [*A chilly pause.*] Oh, I know it all, Edufa. You cannot hide behind impudence and lies, not with me. Diviners are there for all of us to consult. [EDUFA *winces.*] And deeds done in secret can, by the same process, be brought to light.

EDUFA. You know nothing. Diviners! Ho! Diviners? What have diviners got to do with me?

KANKAM. That, you must tell me. I believe in their ancient art. I know, at least, that Ampoma is sick and could die. It has been revealed to me that she could die. And why? That you might live.

EDUFA. Absurd. It is not true. . . . Ampoma is a little ill, that's all. She has fever . . . that's all. . . . Yes . . . that's all. You are deceived.

KANKAM. Deceived. That I am. Am I not? Look at me and tell me it is not true. [EDUFA's *eyes shift nervously.*] He cannot. How could he? [*Pause.*] I went to my own diviner to consult him about my health. He spread his holy patch of sand, lit candles, and over his sacred bowl of water made incantation, and scrawled his mystic symbols in the sand.

I'll tell you what he saw in his divination, for it was all about you, my son. [*Advancing on* EDUFA.] Four years ago you went to consult one such diviner.

EDUFA. Do you want me to take you seriously? You cannot believe all this, you who educated me to lift me to another plane of living.

KANKAM. That's all right, my man. Most of us consult diviners for our protection. All men need to feel secure in their inmost hearts.

EDUFA. I am not all men. I am emancipated.

KANKAM. As emancipated as I'll show. Your diviner saw

death hanging over your life—a normal mortal condition, I would think. But what happened, coward, what happened when he said you could avert the danger by the sacrifice of another life?

EDUFA. He lies.

KANKAM. Who? Has that not been heard before? Has that not been said to many of us mortal men? Why were you not content, like all of us, to purge your soul by offering gifts of cola and white calico to the needy, and sacrificing a chicken or a sheep or, since you can afford it, a cow?

EDUFA. Are you all right, Father?

KANKAM. Beasts are normal sacrifices, but surely you know they are without speech. Beasts swear no oaths to die for others, Edufa. [*Pause.*] Were you not afraid, being husband and father, that someone dear to your blood might be the one to make the fatal oath over that powerful charm you demanded and become its victim?

EDUFA. This is intolerable. I will hear no more. [*He makes for his rooms.*]

KANKAM [*with quiet menace, barring his way*]. You will hear it all, unless you'd rather have me broadcast my story in the marketplace and turn you over to the judgement of the town. [EDUFA *stops, sensitive to the threat.*] My diviner does not lie. The very day itself when all this happened was clearly engraved in sand.

EDUFA [*huffily*]. All right, all-seeing, prove it. [*He sits.*]

KANKAM [*standing over him*]. It had been raining without relief since the night before. Dampness had entered our very bones, and no one's spirits were bright. But you were, of all of us, most moody and morose; in fact, so fractious that you snapped at your wife for merely teasing that you couldn't bear, for once, to be shut away from your precious business and society. It was as if you couldn't tolerate yourself, or us. Suddenly you jumped up and rushed out into the raging storm. That was the day you did your evil and killed your wife.

EDUFA. Great God! If you were not my father, I would call you——

KANKAM. Towards evening you returned. The rain had stopped, and we of the household were sitting here, in this very place, to catch what warmth there was in the sickly sunset. You seemed brighter then, for which change we all expressed our thankfulness. In fact, contrarily, you were cheerful, though still a little restless. How could we have known you were carrying on you the hateful charm? How could we have suspected it, when your children were playing round you with joyful cries? How could we have known it was not a joke when you suddenly leaned back and asked which of us loved you well enough to die for you, throwing the question into the air with studied carelessness? Emancipated one, how could we have known of your treachery?

EDUFA [*rising*]. Incredible drivel! Incredible. Is this the man I have loved as father?

KANKAM. You had willed that some old wheezer like me should be the victim. And I was the first to speak. "Not me, my son," said I, joking. "Die your own death. I have mine to die." And we all laughed. Do you remember? My age was protecting me. [*Pause.*] Then Ampoma spoke. [*Pause.*] Yes, I see you wince in the same manner as you did when she spoke the fatal words that day and condemned her life. "I will die for you, Edufa," she said, and meant it too, poor doting woman.

EDUFA. Father, are you mad?

KANKAM [*shocked*]. *Nyame* above! To say father and call me mad! My *ntoro* within you shivers with the shock of it!

EDUFA [*aware that he has violated taboo*]. You provoked me.

KANKAM [*moving away*]. All right, stranger, I am mad! And madness is uncanny. Have you not noticed how many a time the mad seem to know things hidden from men in their right minds? [*Rounding up on* EDUFA.] You know

you killed your wife that day. I saw fear in your eyes when
she spoke. I saw it, but I didn't understand.

I have learned that in your chamber that night you
tried to make her forswear the oath she had innocently
sworn. But the more you pleaded, the more emotionally
she swore away her life for love of you; until, driven by
your secret fear, you had to make plain to her the danger
in which she stood. You showed her the charm. You con-
fessed to her its power to kill whoever swore to die for
you. Don't you remember how she wept? She had spoken
and made herself the victim. Ampoma has lived with
that danger ever since, in spite of all your extravagant
efforts to counter the potency of the charm by washings
and rites of purification. [*With great concern.*] Edufa, I
am here because I fear that time has come to claim that
vow.

EDUFA. Leave me alone, will you? [*He sits miserably.*]

KANKAM. Confess it or deny it.

EDUFA. I owe you no such duty. Why don't you leave me
alone?

KANKAM. To kill? Say to myself, Father, your son wants to
murder, and go? All the world's real fathers would not
wish a murderer for a son, my son. Yes, in spite of my
rage there is still truth of father and son between us.

EDUFA. Rest. My wife, Ampoma, is not dying.

KANKAM. If she does not die, it will be by the intervention
of some great power alone. An oath once sworn will
always ride its swearer. But there might still be a chance
to save her.

EDUFA. Indeed, in this age there are doctors with skill
enough to sell for what's ailing her, and I can pay their
fees.

KANKAM [*pleading*]. Confess and denounce your wrong.
Bring out that evil charm. And before Ampoma and all
of us whose souls are corporate in this household, denounce it. Burn it. The charm may not be irrevocably
done if we raise the prayer of our souls together.

EDUFA. Will it help you if I swear that there is no ground
for all your worry? And now will you let me go?

KANKAM [*with anguish*]. Hush! You swear? Oh, my son, I
have finished. I can do no more. Have you sunk so low
in cowardice? If you must lie, don't swear about it in a
house in which death is skirmishing and the ancestral
spirits stand expectantly by. A man may curse himself
from his own lips. Do not curse the house in which your
children have to grow.

Spirits around us, why don't you help him save himself? When he went to consult the diviner, he was already doing well. You could tell. If you looked at his
new clothes, you could tell; if you looked at his well-
appointed house in whose precincts hunger wouldn't dwell.

Already, the town's pavements knew when it was he
who was coming. Nudging announced him. Eyes pivoted
to catch his smile. [*With disgust.*] You could see all the
ivory teeth and all the slimy way down the glowing gul-
lets of those who were learning to call him sir. For he was
doing well in the art of buying friends by street benevo-
lence.

EDUFA [*seizing on a diversion*]. Now you betray yourself.
It has taken me all these years to probe the core of your
antagonism. From what you say, it is clear at last that
you envied me. Oh! What lengths a man will go to hide
his envy.

KANKAM. Pitiful.

EDUFA. Fathers are supposed to share with pride in their
sons' good fortune. I was not so blessed. My father envied me and turned enemy—even while he ate the meat
and salt of my good fortune.

KANKAM. Pitiful.

EDUFA. And there was I, thinking that enemies could only
be encountered outside my gates.

KANKAM. Pitiful. At my age a man has learned to aim his
envy at the stars. [*Suffering.*] Pity him, you spirits. He
grew greedy and insensitive, insane for gain, frantic for
the fluff of flattery. And I cautioned him. Did I not warn
him? I tried to make him stop at the point when we

men must be content or let ourselves be lured on to our
doom. But he wouldn't listen. He doesn't listen. It makes
me ill. Violently ill. I vomit the meat and salt I ate out
of ignorance from his hand.

I have finished. [*Pause.*] It wouldn't be too much to
ask to see the lady before I leave?

EDUFA. She mustn't be disturbed.

KANKAM [*picking up his umbrella from the seat*]. Well . . .
as you wish, noble husband. There are enough women, I
suppose, ready to fall for your glamour and line up to
die for you. I am leaving. Forever now. [*He steps into
the courtyard.*]

EDUFA. One moment. [KANKAM *turns to him hopefully.*] I
hope you haven't talked like this to anyone. You could
do so much harm. Unjustly.

KANKAM [*with a rage of disappointment*]. Worm. Coward.
You are afraid for your overblown reputation, aren't
you? You are afraid that if the town got to know, they
would topple you. No. I am tied by my fatherhood, even
though I am not proud that my life water animated you.
It is not my place to disillusion your friends. I'll let them
bow to a worm. In time they are bound to know they're
bowing too low for their comfort. Were this matter a
simple case of crime, I would perhaps seek solution by
bringing you to secular justice. As it is, to try still to
save the woman's life, our remedy is more probable in the
paths of prayer, which I now go to pursue away from your
unhelpful presence. [*He leaves.*]

EDUFA.
Alone.
Tears within me that I haven't had the privilege to shed.
Father!
Call him back that I may weep on his shoulder.
    Why am I afraid of him? He would stand with me
even though he rages so.
    Call him back to bear me on the strength of his faith.
    He knows it all. I can swear he is too true a man to
play me foul. But I could not risk confirming it. I dread
the power by which he knows, and it shall not gain ad-

mission here to energise that which all is set this day to exorcise.

No, a man needs to feel secure! But, oh, how I am stormed.

Don't ask me why I did it; I do not know the answer. If I must be condemned, let me not be charged for any will to kill, but for my failure to create a faith.

Who thought the charm made any sense? Not I. A mystic symbol by which to calm my fears—that was all I could concede it.

It still doesn't make any sense. And yet, how it frets me, until I'm a leaf blown frantic in a whirlwind.

If only I hadn't been so cynical. I bent my knee where I have no creed, and I'm constrained for my mockery.

Hush, O voice of innocence! Still your whining in the wind. Unsay it. Do not swear, for I am compromised.

She who lies there must recover if ever I'm to come to rest. I love my wife, I love her. My confidence is her hope and her faith in me, mine.

So are we locked.

# ACT TWO

## SCENE I

*The* CHORUS *is heard approaching* EDUFA'S *house.*

CHORUS.
Ei! Ei—Ei!
We the orphans cry,
Our mother's dead,
O! O—O!
We the orphans cry.

*They enter through the gate at a run. Their exuberance and gaiety would belie the solemn nature of their ritual observance. They stop below the courtyard steps.*

CHORUS ONE [*calling*]. May we enter? Are there no people in this beautiful house?

CHORUS TWO. In the house of the open gate?

CHORUS THREE. In the house of He-Whose-Hands-Are-Ever-Open?

CHORUS.
Open Face
Open Heart
Open Palm,
Edufa.

CHORUS FOUR. Come, scratch our palms with a golden coin.

CHORUS FIVE. With a golden nugget.

CHORUS. For luck and good fortune.

CHORUS ONE [*stepping up*]. And Ampoma the beautiful; where is she? Woman of this house of fortune. Singing your husband's praise is singing your praises too. Tender heart who nurses him to his fortune. Stand side by side while we beat envious evil out of your house.

CHORUS. Are there no people in this beautiful house?

SEGUWA [*entering from the kitchen*]. Who let you in?

CHORUS [*cheerfully*]. The gate of this house is always open.

SEGUWA [*uneasily*]. Well . . . greeting . . .

CHORUS. We answer you.

SEGUWA [*still hesitating at the kitchen door*]. And you have come . . . ?

CHORUS ONE. We have come to drive evil away. Is the man of the house in? And the lady? We are driving evil out of town.

CHORUS.
From every home
From street and lane
From every corner of our town.
Ei! Ei—Ei!
We the orphans cry.

CHORUS TWO [*steps up, sniffing and trying to locate the scent*]. Incense.

SEGUWA [*moving quickly forward*]. Whose funeral sends you out in ceremony?

CHORUS. Another's, and our own. It's all the same. While we mourn another's death, it's our own death we also mourn.

SEGUWA [*touched*]. True. [*She wipes away a tear.*]

CHORUS [*crowding near her*]. Oh, don't let us sadden you.

SEGUWA. There is so much truth in what you say. I would say, Do your rite and go in peace, for it is most necessary here. I would say, Do your rite and do it most religiously, for it is necessary here. I would say it, but I am not owner of this house.

CHORUS ONE. Why do you hesitate? Is Edufa not in?

SEGUWA. I am trying to make up my mind whether he should be in or out.

CHORUS TWO. Well, if a man is in, he's in; and if he is out, he's out. Which is it?

CHORUS ONE. Make up your mind, for soon, noon will be handing over its power to the indulgent afternoon, and our ritual is timed with the rigours of high noon. Which is it? Is he in or out?

SEGUWA. For driving evil out, he is in, I suppose.

CHORUS. Aha! Then call him.

SEGUWA. I will do my best to bring him out.

CHORUS TWO. Do your best?

SEGUWA. Well . . . I mean . . . Ampoma, his wife, is lying down . . . and . . .

CHORUS ONE. And it is hard for him to tear himself away. . . . Aha!

SEGUWA. Yes . . . No . . . Well . . . let me go and find out. I can make up my mind better away from your questioning eyes. [*With a gesture of invitation as she makes for* EDUFA's *rooms.*] Wait.

CHORUS. We are waiting. [*They surge into the court.*]

CHORUS ONE. What's her trouble? There was a riot in her eyes.

CHORUS TWO. We haven't come to beat her. [*Showing her clappers.*] These aren't cudgels to chastise our fellow men. These are for smacking the spirits of calamity.

CHORUS ONE [*snidely*]. Ampoma is lying down, she said.

CHORUS TWO [*laughing*]. Sick, or lying down in the natural way?

CHORUS THREE. I would say, Simply rich. Would you not do the same in her place? Let her enjoy her ease.

CHORUS FOUR. Imagine the fun of it. [*She goes to the seat, right, and mimes lying down luxuriously, much to the enjoyment of her friends.*] O lady, lady lying in a bed of silk! What kind of thighs, what kind of thighs must a woman have to earn a bed of silk? A bed of silk, O! If I had her life to live, I wouldn't be out of bed at eleven o'clock in the morning either. Never, O!

*In the middle of this fun-making,* EDUFA *rushes out. He stops short at the sight. But the mood of hilarity there compels him to a show of humour.*

CHORUS [*running up to crowd round him*]. Husband!

CHORUS ONE. Aha! The giver himself.

CHORUS. Greeting.

EDUFA. I answer. Well? . . . Well?

CHORUS ONE. We would not dream of passing up your house while we do our rite.

EDUFA. Whose death is it? Is the rite for a new funeral?

CHORUS ONE. No. It's for an old sorrow out of which time has dried the tears. You can say that we are doing what gives calamity and woe the final push in the back—which is a manner of speaking only, as you know——

EDUFA. And you have come here . . .

CHORUS ONE. To purge your house also in the same old manner, for calamity is for all mankind and none is free from woe.

EDUFA. Thank you. You may proceed.

CHORUS TWO [*in fun*]. Then cross our palms with the gleam of luck. And give us a welcome drink. [EDUFA *motions to* SEGUWA, *who goes to the kitchen to get drinks, taking the brazier away with her.*] And let the beautiful one, your wife, know that we are here.

EDUFA. She is not very well today.

CHORUS [*genuinely*]. Oh! Sorry.

EDUFA. Nothing serious. In fact she is getting better.

CHORUS [*relaxing*]. Good. We greet her and wish her well.

EDUFA. She thanks you. Welcome in her name, and from myself as well. [*He takes a big gold ring off his finger and touches the palm of each of the women with it, saying:*] Good luck and good fortune to you, friends. [SEGUWA *brings drinks on a tray, which she places on the seat near the kitchen.*] And here are your drinks.

CHORUS ONE [*solemnly*]. Come, friends. Let's do the ceremony for the benevolent one.

CHORUS [*becoming formal*]. Evil has no place here. Nor anywhere. Away, away. [*Moving rhythmically at a slow running-pace through the court and courtyard, they perform their ritual with solemnity. Chanting.*]
Our mother's dead,
Ei! Ei—Ei!
We the orphans cry,
O! O—O!
We the orphans cry.

*[Speaking, at a halt.]*

Crying the death day of another
Is crying your own death day.
While we mourn for another,
We mourn for ourselves.
One's death is the death of all mankind.
Comfort! Comfort to us all,
Comfort!

Away evil, away.
Away all calamity,
Away!

*[Chanting, on the move.]*

Our mother's dead,
Ei! Ei—Ei!
We the orphans cry,
Our mother's dead,
O! O—O!
We the orphans cry.

*During this ritual* SEGUWA *stands attentively in the background.* EDUFA *remains just above the courtyard steps, intensely quiet, eyes shut in private prayer. The* CHORUS *finish up on the steps below, facing him.*

CHORUS ONE. There now. We have done. Health to you. *[*EDUFA *is too removed to hear her.]* Health to you, Edufa, and to your wife and all your household. *[To her companions.]* See how he is moved. We have done right to come to the house of one as pious as he.

CHORUS TWO. Such faith must surely bring him blessing.

EDUFA *[stirring].* Your drinks await you.

*The mood of the* CHORUS *changes to lightheartedness again.*

CHORUS ONE *[as her companions collect their drinks, her own glass in hand].* That's right. Tears and laughter. That's how it is. It isn't all tears and sorrow, my friends. Tears and laughter. It isn't all want and pain. With one hand we wipe away the unsweet water. And with the other we raise a cup of sweetness to our lips. It isn't all tears, my friends, this world of humankind.

CHORUS [*drinks in hand*]. May you be blessed, Edufa.

EDUFA [*hurrying them up nicely*]. Drink up. Day is piling up its hours, and you must be eager to attend the business of your own homes. It was good of you to come. [*He contrives to draw* SEGUWA *aside.*] Go in there. Ampoma was sleeping. It would not do for her to walk out into this. [SEGUWA *hurries into* EDUFA's *rooms.*] You did well to come. A man needs friendship. But it's late in the morning, and you are women . . . with homes to feed.

CHORUS ONE. We will come again to greet your wife.

EDUFA [*skilfully herding them out*]. Yes, yes——

CHORUS TWO. Would you sit us at your generous table? Eat with us?

CHORUS THREE. Charm us?

EDUFA. Yes. All in good time . . . some day soon.

SEGUWA [*running out happily*]. Edufa! Edufa! She has asked for food.

EDUFA [*excitedly*]. For food. She has?

SEGUWA [*making fast for the kitchen*]. For soup. She says, I would like some fresh fish soup. Thank God.

EDUFA. Thank God. Get it.

SEGUWA. After three days without interest——

EDUFA. Get it quickly.

SEGUWA. Thank God. [*She enters the kitchen.*]

EDUFA [*calling after her*]. Is there fish in the house? If not, send out instantly. Thank God. [*Stretching out his hands to the* CHORUS.] Victory, my friends.

CHORUS ONE [*puzzled*]. So relieved. Ampoma must be more ill than he cared to let us know. Thank God.

CHORUS TWO. He is wise not to spill the troubles of his house in public.

EDUFA [*on his way in*]. Thank you, friends. I must leave you now.

## SCENE II

*As* EDUFA *and the* CHORUS *are leaving,* SENCHI, *carrying a small battered leather case, swings in flamboyantly, whistling to announce himself.*

SENCHI. . . . and the wanderer . . . the wanderer . . . the wanderer comes home. [*Seeing the* CHORUS.] Comes in the nick of time, when everything he loves is together in one place. Friends, women, bottles . . . [*His laughter is all-pervasive.*]

EDUFA [*thrilled*]. Senchi!

SENCHI [*airily to the* CHORUS]. Good afternoon. My name is Senchi, and I'm always lucky. I love women and always find myself right in the middle of them. Welcome me.

CHORUS FOUR [*quite pleased*]. He's quite a fellow.

SENCHI. She's right.

EDUFA. Senchi. What brings you here?

SENCHI [*stepping up to him*]. Life . . . brings me here. Welcome me.

EDUFA. Indeed. You've come in excellent time.

SENCHI. And what are you doing here? Practising polygamy? Or big-mammy? Or what? Anyone you choose to declare will be against the law. I'm in transit, as usual. May I spend the night with you?

EDUFA. But certainly. Do me the favour. It's very good to see you, and my privilege to house one as lucky as you obviously are.

SENCHI [*to* CHORUS]. Now he flatters.

EDUFA. I only wish we were better prepared to receive you.

SENCHI. Impossible. [*His eyes on the* CHORUS.] You couldn't improve on this welcome here. All good stock, by their looks. Local breed? They're not dressed for fun and games, though, are they? Pity.

CHORUS THREE [*approvingly*]. He's quite a fellow.

SENCHI [*sniffing*]. And I smell—what is that I smell? Incense? [*To* EDUFA.] Say, have you changed your religion

again? What are you practising now? Catholicism,
spiritualism, neo-theosophy, or what? Last time I passed
through here, you were an intellectual atheist or something in that category. I wouldn't be surprised to see you
turned Buddhist monk next time. [*The* CHORUS *are leaving.*] Don't go when I've only just come. [*To* EDUFA.]
What are they going away for?

CHORUS. Our work is finished here.

EDUFA. They've been doing a ceremony here. Don't delay
them any longer.

SENCHI. Why, I smelled something all right. What are they?
Your acolytes? Wait a minute. They're in mourning. Is
someone dead? [*To* EDUFA.] None of your own, I hope.

EDUFA. No.

CHORUS. This was an old sorrow, friend.

SENCHI. Ah! I understand. One of those "condolences"
rites. Why do you people prolong your sorrows so? [*To*
CHORUS.] Though, I must observe, you have a funny way
of going about it—drinking and sniggering. [*Very playfully.*] Come on, give me those confounded sticks. I'll
show you what they are good for. [*He snatches the clappers from the* CHORUS, *and a mock chase follows, during
which he tries to smack them. He flings the clappers in
a heap below the steps near the kitchen.*] Now, embrace
me, and be done with sorrow.

CHORUS [*delighted*]. Oh! Oh! We were on our way.

SENCHI. To me. [SEGUWA, *entering, sees the romping, and
her single exclamation is both disapproving and full of
anxiety.* SENCHI *turns to her.*] What's the matter with the
mother pussy cat? Come over, lady, and join the fun.

EDUFA [*sensitive to* SEGUWA's *disapproval*]. Let the women
go now, Senchi.

SENCHI. Why? That's no way to treat me.

SEGUWA [*ominously*]. Edufa.

EDUFA. They can come back some other time.

SENCHI. Tonight? All of them?

SEGUWA. Edufa.

EDUFA. Let them go now. Tonight? Very well, tonight.

CHORUS THREE [*eagerly*]. To eat?

SEGUWA. Edufa.

EDUFA. Yes. Why not?

SENCHI. You mean that?

EDUFA. A bit of a party, since my wife recovers . . . and——

SENCHI. Oh, how thoughtless of me. Has Ampoma been ill? And I haven't asked of her. . . . Though I've brought her a song. It's all your fault for distracting me. Sorry.

EDUFA. . . . and you too have come, my friend, and brought us luck. It seems to me that we are permitted to celebrate my good fortune——

CHORUS ONE. Expect us.

CHORUS TWO. We will be glad to help you celebrate.

EDUFA [*to* CHORUS]. And to you also I owe my gratitude——

CHORUS. Expect us. [*They leave cheerfully through the gate.*]

SENCHI. Wonderful. [*He joins* EDUFA *in the court.*]

EDUFA [*with a great sigh*]. Oh, Senchi! This has been quite a day.

SENCHI [*suddenly serious*]. Tired? Between you and me, my friend, I'm downright weary in my b-o-n-e-s, myself. I've become quite a wanderer, you know, tramping out my life. It isn't as if I didn't know what I'm looking for. I do. But, oh, the bother and the dither. And the pushing and the jostling. Brother, if you meet one kind, loving person in this world who will permit a fellow to succeed at something good and clean, introduce me, for I would wish to be his devotedly and positively forever. Amen. But of that, more later. I'm worn out with travel. Lead me to a bed in a quiet corner for some sweet, friendly, uncomplicated sleep.

EDUFA. Won't you eat?

SENCHI. No food. Only peace, for a while.

EDUFA. As you wish. [*To* SEGUWA.] Take my friend to the

guest rooms overlooking the river. It's quiet there. We'll talk when you awake. No luggage?

SENCHI [*showing his battered leather case*]. This is all I care about.

EDUFA [*to* SEGUWA]. See that he has all he needs. And after, arrange a meal for tonight. Spare nothing. [*He hurries into his rooms.*]

SEGUWA [*grimly*]. This way. [*She strides ahead to the steps leading into the guest rooms.*]

SENCHI [*catching up with her*]. For the sake of a man's nerves, can't you smile? I can't stand gloom.

SEGUWA. You should have your fun another day.

SENCHI. What particular brand of fun is this you're recommending?

SEGUWA. The party tonight.

SENCHI. That? Don't call that a party, woman. Call it something like Senchi's Temporary Plan for the Prevention of Senchi from Thinking Too Hard. You don't grudge me a small relief like that, surely. [SEGUWA *wipes away a tear.*] Come on. Now what have I said? Are you one of those women who enjoy crying? I'll make a bargain with you, then. Allow me to have my rest. When I awake, I promise to make you cry to your heart's content—by singing, merely. I make songs, you know. [*Patting his leather case.*] Songs for everything; songs for goodness, songs for badness; for strength, for weakness; for dimples and wrinkles; and, for making you cry. But I'll tell you a secret. I never make songs about ugliness, because I simply think it should not exist.

SEGUWA [*exasperated*]. This way, please. [*She leads* SENCHI *up the steps.*]

ABENA *enters from the kitchen with a smart tray on which is a hot dish of soup. She is on her way to* EDUFA'S *rooms, looking decidedly happy.*

ABENA [*stopping halfway up the steps, proudly smelling the soup*]. She will like it. I used only aromatic peppers—

the yellow—and the mint smells good. [EDUFA *comes out.*] Dear brother. [*She raises the tray for him to smell the soup.*]

EDUFA [*smelling*]. Lovely. Little one, are you well? We haven't talked much of late.

ABENA. I'm glad she's better.

EDUFA. Oh . . . yes. You did your work well, it seems.

ABENA. My work?

EDUFA [*quickly changing the subject*]. How is your young man? [*He takes the tray.*]

ABENA [*shyly*]. I will see him today.

EDUFA. Good. You haven't had much of a chance lately, have you?

ABENA. No . . . er . . . Can't I take the soup in to her? I've had such thoughts. I miss her. We were so happy before all this began, stringing beads and looking through her clothes. She's going to let me wear her long golden chain of miniature barrels at my wedding— right down to my feet.

EDUFA. Let's get her up strong, then. You can see her to-night. We have guests.

ABENA [*appreciatively*]. Yes. I've heard him singing.

EDUFA. It's very good to have him here.

ABENA. He sings well.

EDUFA. Some women from town are coming to eat with us tonight.

ABENA [*with childlike joy*]. People here again. Laughter again.

EDUFA [*smiling, but compelling her down the steps*]. Sister, come. [*Intimately.*] Did you mind staying up nights? Was it very hard?

ABENA [*unburdening*]. Not . . . too . . . hard. I didn't mind it inside the house, though it got so ghostly quiet at times, I almost saw my lonely thoughts taking shape before my eyes . . . becoming form in the empty air. And then, collecting the stream water . . . that . . . that in the night, and the forest such a crowd of unfamiliar presences.

EDUFA. Hush! It's over. All over. Thank you. Go out now.
  Enjoy yourself. Can you give us a nice meal tonight?

ABENA. Delighted.

*As she goes through the kitchen door,* SAM *enters through
the gate, running, dodging, like one pursued. He carries a
bird cage and a small tin box.*

SAM [*to an imaginary crowd towards the gate*]. Thank
  you. Thank you. [*Gloatingly.*] They didn't get me.
  [*Speaking to no one in particular.*] An idiot's life isn't so
  bad. There are always people to stop children throwing
  stones at us. They only do that for idiots, I find. [*To the
  cage.*] Let us tell my master that. [*Paying tender attention
  to what is inside the cage, he walks up a step, crosses to
  left, and puts the cage and the box down.*]

SEGUWA [*entering from the kitchen*]. You're back.

SAM. Are you pleased to see me? [*Lifting up the cage.*]
  Look, he is my bird.

SEGUWA [*horrified*]. Don't bring it near me. It's an owl.

SAM [*blithely*]. Of course. An owl is a bird.

SEGUWA. What's it doing here?

SAM. It came with me. It was an owl before; but now it's
  with me, it's no longer itself. It's the owl of an idiot.
  What we get, we possess. I caught it in a tree.

SEGUWA. Take it outside. [SAM *sulks, turning his back on
  her.*] Did everything go well? Did you find the place?
  Did you see the man? [SAM, *moving his bird cage aside,
  merely nods his affirmatives.*] And what's the news?
  [SAM's *back stiffens stubbornly.*] It's no good; he won't
  talk to me. I'll let your master know you're back. [*She
  goes into* EDUFA's *rooms, while* SAM *pays fussy attention
  to his owl. She returns with* EDUFA, *who is in a state of
  high expectancy.*] There he is . . . back.

EDUFA [*coaxingly*]. Sam, are you back?

SEGUWA. I don't know what he's doing with that thing. Let
  him take it away.

EDUFA. What is it, Sam?

SEGUWA. An owl.

EDUFA [*terrified*]. Take it out. [SAM *sulks.*] We would do well not to disturb him before we've heard what he has to say. He can get very stubborn. [*Sweetly.*] Sam, come here. [SAM *doesn't budge.*] You may keep your bird. [SAM *turns to him, grinning broadly.*]

SAM [*pointing to the owl*]. My owl and I had a nice thought for you on the way. When you are born again, Master, why don't you come back as an idiot? There are always people to stop children throwing stones at us. They only do that for idiots, I find.

EDUFA [*smiling in spite of himself*]. All right. Now tell me quickly what I want to know. [*Anxiously.*] Did you find the place?

SAM. It's an awful place. What do you send me to places like that for? Not the village itself. That is beautiful, floating in blue air on the mountain top, with a climb-way in the mountain's belly going zig-zag-zig, like a game. [*He thoroughly enjoys his description.*]

SEGUWA [*impatiently*]. He's so tiresome with his rambling.

EDUFA [*trying to be patient*]. Good, you found the village. And the man?

SAM. He is a nice man, tall as a god. And he fed me well. You don't give me chicken to eat, but he did. [*Thinks a bit.*] What does such a nice man live in an awful house like that for? That's the awful part.

EDUFA [*very anxiously*]. Never mind. What did he say?

SAM. Ah! [*Secretively.*] Let me fetch my box of goods. [*He fetches the tin box and sets it down before* EDUFA.] First, three pebbles from the river. [*He takes out these pebbles.*] Catch them. [*He throws them one by one to* EDUFA.] One. Two. Three. [EDUFA *catches them all.*] Good! They didn't fall.

EDUFA [*intensely*]. I understand that. We mustn't let Ampoma fall to the ground.

SAM [*taking out a ball of red stuff*]. With this, make the sign of the sun on your doorstep where your spirit walks in and out with you. Come, I know you are not much of

an artist. I'll do it for you the way the man showed me.
[*He walks importantly to the steps leading to* EDUFA's
*rooms, and as he draws a raying sun boldly on the riser of
the first step:*] Rays! Everywhere . . . you . . . turn.

SEGUWA [*with awe*]. Ampoma talks so much of the sun.

EDUFA. Yearningly.

SAM [*returning to the box*]. And then came the part I
didn't understand.

EDUFA [*hoarsely*]. Yes . . . quickly, where is it?

SAM. Here it is in this bag. [*He produces an old leather
pouch which is spectacularly designed and hung with
small talismans.*]

EDUFA [*trembling*]. Give it to me.

SAM. Now listen. He says burn it.

EDUFA *snatches the pouch from him.*

EDUFA [*to* SEGUWA]. Get fire—in the back courtyard.
Quickly.

SEGUWA *leaves in haste.*

SAM [*with emphasis*]. The man says, Burn it with your own
hands, before you bathe in the herbs for the last time.

EDUFA [*with eyes shut*]. We're saved. [*Then he becomes
aware again of the waiting* SAM.] Well done, Sam. You
may go.

SAM. I won't go to that awful house again.

EDUFA. No. Get something to eat. And rest. You are tired.
[SAM *picks up the box and walks eagerly to the bird
cage.*] But . . . Sam. You must let that bird go.

SAM [*aggrieved*]. My owl? Oh, Master, he is my friend. He's
the bird of an idiot. He likes us. He and I had a nice
thought for you on our way——

EDUFA [*threateningly*]. Take it out of here! Out.

SAM. Oh . . . [*He picks up the bird cage and goes out of
the gate muttering sulkily.*] We'll stay outside. . . . If they
won't have us in, we won't eat. . . . We will starve ourselves. . . . We . . .

EDUFA [*gripping the pouch in his fists with violence*]. This is the final act. I will turn chance to certainty. I will burn this horror charm and bury its ashes in the ground: the one act that was still hazard if left undone.

# ACT THREE

## SCENE I

*A trestle table covered with a fresh white cloth is moved into the court, close to the central seat. So is a loaded drinks trolley. The seats left and right are shifted in. Wicker garden chairs provide additional seating.*

*ABENA and SEGUWA are preparing for the party, obviously enjoying doing it with some taste. They move in plates, cutlery, serviettes, wine glasses, etc., pursuing their work without paying more than momentary attention to any distractions.*

*SENCHI and EDUFA appear from the guest rooms. EDUFA is in evening dress but has yet to put on his jacket. SENCHI looks noticeably absurd in a suit that is not his size. He brings his leather case, which he soon places carefully against the trestle table.*

SENCHI. I'm grateful to you for listening to all my talk.

EDUFA. If it helps, I'm happy to listen. What can I do more?

SENCHI. Every now and then I feel this urge to talk to some-body. It helps me to dispose of the dust of my experiences. And that's when I come here. There are not many people with enough concern to care about what accumulates inside a man. [*He indicates his heart.*] You and Ampoma both listen well, though I must say that you, being so solid and so unemotional, lack the rain of her sympathy.

EDUFA. That's your secret, then. I've never told you I admire you although you can't show a balance in the bank, have I?

SENCHI. No.

EDUFA. I do. You're so relaxed and normally so convincing with your laughter. Yet, you do puzzle me somewhat.

Don't you think it is important to have solidity? Be something? Somebody? Is being merely alive not senseless?

SENCHI. What is this something, this somebody that you are? Give it name and value. I'm not being disparaging; I'm seeking.

EDUFA. I don't know. I thought I did until it got so confusing, I . . . Ask the town. They know who Edufa is and what he's worth. They can count you out my value in the homes that eat because I live. Yes, my enterprises feed them. They rise in deference from their chairs when they say my name. If that isn't something, what is? And can a man allow himself to lose grip on that? Let it go? A position like that? You want to maintain it with substance, protect it from ever-present envy with vigilance. And there's the strain that rips you apart! The pain of holding on to what you have. It gives birth to fears which pinch at the heart and dement the mind, until you needs must clutch at some other faith. . . . Oh, it has driven me close to horror . . . and I tell you, I don't know what to think now.

SENCHI [who has been listening with concern]. We make an odd pair of friends, to be sure. You, with your machines growling at granite in your quarries to crumble and deliver to you their wealth; and I, trying to pay my way in the currency of my songs. But perhaps that, like many statements we are capable of expressing, is merely grasping at extremes of light and dark, and missing the subtle tones for which we haven't yet found words.

EDUFA. Yes, I do have my moments when I'm not quite as solid as you think, when solidity becomes illusory.

SENCHI. But you do give an impression of being settled and satisfied, which is what I'm not.

EDUFA. I wish I could, like you, dare to bare myself for scrutiny. [Pause.] I'm being compelled to learn however, and the day will come, I suppose.

SENCHI. Ah, yes. We commit these thoughts to the wind and leave it to time to sift them. [Snapping out of his *serious mood.*] I'm ready for immediacy, which is this evening's light relief. Where are the ladies?

EDUFA. Don't worry; they will not miss this chance to dine at Edufa's house.

SENCHI [*preening*]. Do I look noticeable? [*Making much of his ill-fitting suit.*] I've never gone hunting in fancy dress before.

EDUFA [*really laughing*]. Oh, Senchi, you're so refreshing, you ass.

SENCHI. Yes, call me ass. Always, it's "You're an ass!" Seldom does a man say, "I am an ass." That takes courage. But you're right. I am an ass, or I would be wearing my own suit.

EDUFA. Come on. You don't mind wearing my suit?

SENCHI. I do. It's the same as a borrowed song, to me. Singing other people's songs or wearing other people's suits, neither suits me.

EDUFA [*teasing*]. Well, you're in it now.

SENCHI. Being an ass, I am. However, it will serve for an evening of foolery. [*A flash of seriousness again.*] Tell me, do you understand, though?

EDUFA. What, Senchi?

SENCHI [*earnestly*]. You see, it's like this. My own suit may be shabby, but its shabbiness is of my making. I understand it. It is a guide of self-evaluation. When I stand in it, I know where I stand and why. And that, strangely, means to me dignity and security.

EDUFA. There, you're getting very serious. Have a drink.

SENCHI. A drink. Ah, yes. [*Stopping short at the trolley.*] Oh, no, not before I have greeted Ampoma with breath that I have freshened in my sleep.

*He sits.* EDUFA *serves himself a drink.*

## SCENE II

EDUFA. Our guests will soon arrive. Before they do, I have
an act of love that I must make tonight.

SENCHI. You surprise me. Can't you wait? You?

EDUFA. It is a gesture of pure pleasure such as my heart has
never before requested.

SENCHI. I don't need telling about the pleasure of it. What
I'm saying is, Can't you wait? You?

EDUFA. Just now you judged me unemotional.

SENCHI. Don't worry; after this confessional, I absolve you
of the charge.

EDUFA. You see, I've never stinted in giving my wife gifts.
Gold she has and much that money can buy. But tonight
I'm a man lifted up by her love, and I know that nothing
less than flowers will do for one such as she is.

SENCHI. Applause. Talk on.

EDUFA [to ABENA]. Fetch the flowers, sister. [She goes into
the kitchen.]

SENCHI [watching her go]. You make me feel so unmarried,
confusing Senchi's Plan for the Ruination of Women.
You're driving me to sell my freedom to the next girl
that comes too near me.

EDUFA. Don't do that. Learn to love, my friend.

ABENA returns with a beautiful bouquet of fresh flowers and
hands it to EDUFA.

SENCHI. Lovely.

EDUFA [to ABENA]. Little one, you who are soon to marry,
I'm giving you a chance to look at love. Take these
flowers in to Ampoma. [He speaks emotionally into the
flowers.] Tell her that I, her husband, send them, that it
is she who has so matured my love. I would have pre-
sented them myself, but I have learned the magic of
shyness and haven't the boldness to look into her eyes
yet.

ABENA *embraces him happily and takes the flowers from him.*

SENCHI. Applause! Standing ovation! This is the first grace-ful act I've ever seen you do. [*As* ABENA *walks away.*] Keep the door open as you go, and let my song keep tune to this moment of nobility. [*He sings.*]
Nne
Nne Nne
Nne
Nne Nne
O Mother
Nne
Nne Nne

ABENA, *turning in appreciation of the song, drops the flowers, which fall on the step with the sign of the sun on it.*

ABENA. Oh! [*She quickly retrieves the flowers.*]

EDUFA [*becoming tense*]. For God's sake, be careful.

SENCHI [*continuing after the incident*].
If I find you
Nne
Nne Nne
I'll have to worship you
Nne
Nne Nne
I must adore you
Nne
Nne Nne
O Mother
Nne
Nne Nne

[EDUFA, *enchanted by the song, attempts to join quietly in the refrain.*]
She's wonderful
She's wonderful
O Mother
She's wonderful
Yes, if I find you
Nne

Nne Nne
I'll have to worship you
Nne
Nne Nne
I must adore you
Nne
Nne Nne
O Mother
Nne
Nne Nne

EDUFA. Very good, Senchi.

SEGUWA *is so affected by the song that she is sobbing quietly behind the table.*

SENCHI [*noticing her*]. That is the wettest-eyed woman I've ever seen. [*He goes to her.*] Oh, sorry; I promised to make you cry, didn't I? There now, are you happy?

SEGUWA. That's a song after my own heart.

SENCHI. After mine also.

*There is a sudden ripple of laughter from* EDUFA's *rooms.*

EDUFA [*elatedly*]. That is her laughter. That is Ampoma. I love her. [ABENA *returns.*] Is she happy?

ABENA. Radiant. She was standing before the mirror when I entered, looking at her image, her clothes laid out on the bed beside her. Seeing the flowers mirrored there with her, she turned to greet their brightness with her laughter. Then she listened to your song with her eyes shut and sighed a happy sigh. She listened to your message attentively and said, "Tell my husband that I understand."

EDUFA [*glowing*]. She does. I know. She loves. I know.

ABENA. "Tell Senchi," she said, "that all will be left to those who dare to catch in song the comfort of this world."

SENCHI. That, I have understood.

ABENA. And she will join you later, she says.

EDUFA. Yes, she is able to, tonight. Great heart-beat of

mine, it is good to be alive. [*Briskly.*] Senchi, a drink
now?

*They go to the drinks.*

ABENA. Everything is ready to serve, brother. And I am
awaited.

EDUFA [*affectionately*]. Go; you have earned your moment.

ABENA *hurries out.*

SENCHI [*watching her approvingly*]. Little sister, buxom
sister. I ought to think of marrying that girl.

EDUFA [*smiling*]. Too late. You have lost her to another.

SENCHI. Too bad. I'm always ending up blank. But, never
mind now. [*Declaiming.*] I will make do with ephemerals.
Turn up the next page in Senchi's chronicle of uncer-
tainties. [*He gets a drink.*]

# SCENE III

SENCHI [*at the trolley, his back to the courtyard*]. They are
coming.

EDUFA [*turning round and seeing nobody*]. How do you
know?

SENCHI [*also turning round*]. I'm highly sensitised, that's
all. I can feel women twenty miles away, minimum range.

*The CHORUS enter through the gate, talking. They are
dressed, even overdressed, for the evening.*

CHORUS ONE. That was exciting, dodging those prying
eyes in town.

EDUFA [*to SENCHI*]. You win. They are here.

CHORUS TWO. Won't they be surprised tomorrow when
they learn that we too have been invited here.

CHORUS THREE. There they are, waiting for us.

SENCHI [*to EDUFA, meaning his suit*]. Do I look noticeable?

EDUFA [*sharing the fun*]. I don't stand a chance beside you.

CHORUS ONE. How do I look?

CHORUS FOUR. Fine. [*With relish.*] Look at that table. It is good simply to see.

CHORUS TWO [*also impressed*]. Ei!

SENCHI. Is there a roadblock there? Come on; I never allow women to keep me waiting.

CHORUS [*in fun below the courtyard steps*]. Is there anybody in this beautiful house?

SENCHI [*pleased*]. A lively flock, eh? They have a sense of humour. That's a good beginning.

EDUFA [*coming forward*]. Good evening.

CHORUS. We answer you.

SENCHI [*meeting them*]. Embrace me.

CHORUS ONE [*flirtatiously*]. Do you always do things in such a hurry?

SENCHI. That's a good one. That is a rollicking good one. Lady, for that much perkiness, I'm yours . . . momentarily.

EDUFA [*enjoying it*]. Senchi. Ladies, it's very good of you to come, and thank you for this morning's kindness.

CHORUS ONE. We trust your wife keeps well. Shall we be seeing her this evening?

EDUFA. Certainly. She will join you presently.

CHORUS ONE. Accept this little gift for her from all of us here. [*She hands the gift to him.*]

CHORUS TWO. We were making so much noise here this morning; we hope we didn't disturb her in any serious way.

EDUFA. Oh, no. On her behalf, I thank you. Sit wherever you like. [*The* CHORUS *choose seats.* CHORUS FOUR *sits close to the set table, eyeing everything.*] This is indeed most pleasant. I'll get you drinks. [*He places the gift on the table and gets busy with drinks.*]

SENCHI [*startling* CHORUS FOUR *at the table*]. We are not quite eating yet, you know.

CHORUS FOUR [*naïvely*]. It looks so pretty.

SENCHI. You look prettier than forks and knives and stiff-backed serviettes; that is sure.

CHORUS FOUR [*uncomprehending*]. Serviettes?

SENCHI. Yes, these things. [*Taking her by the hand to the seat near the kitchen.*] Sit over here with me. I have other things I rather think it will be interesting to try to negotiate with you. May I hold your hand? Or is that considered adultery in these parts? [*They sit.*] I always try to get the local customs straight before I begin negotiations.

EDUFA [*handing out drinks*]. Senchi, give the lady a drink at least.

SENCHI *assists him.*

CHORUS FOUR. Lady! Ei, that's nice.

SENCHI [*pleased with her*]. She is positively c-u-t-e.

CHORUS TWO [*confidentially to* CHORUS THREE]. This is all as we imagined it. Better even.

CHORUS THREE [*full of curiosity*]. Who is his friend?

SENCHI [*at the trolley*]. Aha! I have ears like a hare, you know. Before a woman can say "Senchi," I come to the summons of her thought. I'm accutely sensitive. Edufa, she wants to know who I am. Tell her I'm a neo-millionaire in search of underdeveloped territories. [*The* CHORUS *respond with laughter.*] They applaud. They do have a sense of humour. Fine. [*Fussily.*] Drinks all round, and who cares which is what. [*He hands a drink to* CHORUS FOUR.]

EDUFA. I do. Everyone gets exactly what she wants.

*The drinks are settled.* SENCHI *sits in a central position.*

SENCHI [*raising his glass ceremoniously*]. We have it in hand. [*A moment of awkward silence as people drink.*] Now, what's the silence for? This is a party. Shall we play games?

CHORUS ONE. What games?

SENCHI. Party games.

EDUFA. Excuse me. I'll see if Ampoma is ready. [*He goes to his rooms.*]

SENCHI [*rising promptly*]. That's kind of you, Edufa. [*To* CHORUS.] He is a most considerate, kindhearted man when I'm around.

　　Let's make the best of our opportunities. Now, let me see. We will not play Musical Chairs; that, being a little colonial, is somewhat inappropriate here. But I'm open to suggestion . . . and . . . if you like, inspection too. [CHORUS *laugh heartily as he strikes poses.*] They merely laugh, which is no way to encourage me. Hm . . . [*He plays at thinking seriously.*] Do you like songs?

CHORUS [*enthusiastically*]. Yes.

SENCHI [*liking this*]. That means I can entertain you in songs, eh?

CHORUS. Yes.

SENCHI. Do you like stories?

CHORUS. Yes.

SENCHI. That means I must tell them, eh?

CHORUS. Yes.

SENCHI. What do I get for all of this, from you?

CHORUS ONE. We laugh for you.

SENCHI. And with me?

CHORUS. Oh, yes.

SENCHI. Yes. Yes. Do you never say No?

CHORUS. No.

SENCHI. Brilliant conversation. Senchi, you must make better headway. [*Pauses reflectively.*] Oh, yes, you are. They say they don't ever say No.

CHORUS ONE. Isn't he funny!

*She and the others have been enjoying a private joke centred on* SENCHI'*s ill-fitting suit.*

SENCHI. Oh, madam, that's unkind.

CHORUS ONE. It's your suit . . . pardon me . . . but your suit . . .

SENCHI. That kind of joke should thoroughly frustrate a

man. But I must admit it is most intelligent of you. I
don't know whether you realise how positively brilliant
your observation is. Well now, what next? I have an
idea. I sing a bit, you know.

CHORUS [*eagerly*]. Ah!

SENCHI. Does that mean, Sing?

CHORUS. Yes.

SENCHI. Yes! We will all sing my song. Listen; it's easy.

*He sings snatches of the song for* AMPOMA, *encouraging the*
CHORUS *to participate. They try.*

CHORUS ONE. It's sad.

SENCHI. So it is. But, quickly before you start crying all
over me, here is a rumpus song all right. We will have
the foolery for which I'm fitly suited tonight. Here is the
story of it. A traveller's tale. I'm a bit of a traveller, you
know. [*He poses for effect.*]
    And I came to this city called Bam, and there was
this man; whether he is mad or simply stark raving poor,
I couldn't ascertain. But he impressed me; I can tell you
that. Wait a minute; I've written his story down. [*He
takes some sheets of paper out of his leather case.*] I'm
a bit of a writer, you know. [*The* CHORUS *nudge each
other.*]
    A man claimed insane walks through the city streets.
No prophet nor priest costumed in fancy gown is he; but
he too, afire with zeal, feels that men must heed his creed
—or at the least applaud the wit with which he calls
them sons of a bitch. [*He looks round for approval. The
faces round him are getting blank with incomprehension.
He becomes more declamatory.*]
    He raves through the city streets at sane passers-by.
And what does he say? He feels that heed ought to be
given to his preaching, or at the least, applause must greet
his singular screeching:
    "Gentlemen, show me a thought you've thought
through, and I'll bow to you right low and grant you a
master's due.

"Feather-fine ladies with hips that rhyme, who the blazes minds your children's manners at this time?

"Left, right, left, does not feed a nation. I'd rather have you roaring drunk at a harvest celebration."

Oh, he is a character, an absolute word-exhibitor. But, Ladies, where is your laughter? Aren't you amused?

CHORUS [*quite blank*]. We are listening.

SENCHI. Good. I thought myself that his words should sound good on a trumpet. [*He takes a small trumpet out of his leather case.*] Come on, procession! [*He begins to blow a tune to the words in quotation above. The* CHORUS *are swept into the fun. They are dancing round after him, procession style, when* EDUFA *enters, now in his jacket.*] Join up, Edufa. Procession.

EDUFA *complies.* SENCHI *alternates between the trumpet and singing the words. Presently, the whole group is singing to his accompaniment.* AMPOMA *appears unnoticed at the top of the steps. She is tastefully dressed in a delicate colour, looking very much like a bride. She watches the romping scene briefly, with a mixture of sadness and amusement, before she descends at a point when the group is taking a turn in the courtyard.*

EDUFA [*seeing her*]. Ah, friends, my wife!

*The singing and dancing comes to an abrupt halt.*

SENCHI [*with profound admiration*]. Ampoma. Mother.

CHORUS. Beautiful.

AMPOMA [*graciously*]. I'm sorry I was not up to welcome you, Senchi.

SENCHI. You are here now, Ampoma, and well. I couldn't wish for more.

AMPOMA. That was your singing. It is a lovely song.

SENCHI. Yes, for such as you a man must sing. The song is yours, made in the strain of your name, my gift to you. [*He takes a sheet of music out of his pocket.*] Take it. [*She does.*] And accept me as yours, devotedly and positively forever. . . . Amen!

*The* CHORUS *practically applaud.*

CHORUS ONE. Isn't he a character!

AMPOMA [*to the* CHORUS]. I didn't know about the women being here. Thank you for your company. I hope my husband is honouring your presence here.

CHORUS. We are most happy to be here.

EDUFA. There is a gift they brought for you.

AMPOMA. How kind. [*Pensively.*] So many rays of kindness falling on me, each with its own intensity . . . [*Brightening.*] I respond with warm heart . . . and hand. [*She shakes hands hurriedly and nervously with the* CHORUS.]

EDUFA [*whispering to her*]. Your hand is trembling. You're sure you're not cold? I'll fetch you a wrap.

AMPOMA [*with cheerfulness*]. No, I'm well wrapped in your affection, and that is warm enough. My friends, you see I have a most affectionate husband.

SENCHI. We will have to name this the night of fond declarations.

EDUFA [*a little nervously*]. Had we better eat now?

AMPOMA. Yes, our friends must be hungry . . . and it is getting late.

SENCHI. Escort her to her chair there. [*He starts the* CHORUS *singing again and moving in mock procession into the court.* AMPOMA *joins in the game. Suddenly she loses her balance and barely avoids a fall. Only her hand touches the ground as she steadies herself.* SENCHI *springs to her support.*] Oh, sorry.

EDUFA [*worried*]. Be careful with her. [*He escorts her to a chair by the pillar.*] Sit down, Ampoma, please. [SE-GUWA, *who sees the fall as she is bringing in a dish of food, is frozen in her tracks. This so unnerves* EDUFA *that he speaks harshly to her.*] Where's the food? Why are you standing there? Bring it. [*He gives attention to* AMPOMA.]

AMPOMA. I'm all right. Please don't shout at her. She has nursed me well.

SENCHI. No, Edufa, don't. That woman's tears are too ready to fall.

*From this stage, a strange mood develops in* AMPOMA. *She
   frequently talks like one whose mind is straying.*

AMPOMA [*fast*]. Friends, eat. My husband provides well.
   I hope you're happy here. Why am I sitting down? [*She
   rises.*] I must feed you. [*As she quickly passes plates of
   food served by* SEGUWA.] Eat. We must eat to keep the
   body solidly on its feet. I wasn't able to cook for you myself. [*Pause.*] That's sad. A woman must serve her husband well. But I'm sure the food is good. We never serve
   anything but the best to our friends. Eat. You don't know
   how good it was to hear you fill this house with merri-
   ment. Eat.

*Everyone is served.* AMPOMA *sits down and receives a plate
   from* EDUFA, *who has been watching her anxiously.*

SENCHI [*to* CHORUS FOUR]. You may eat now. [EDUFA *sits
   down beside* AMPOMA, *but his mind is not on his food.*]
   Ampoma, I need your rare counsel. Which of these
   five women shall I take to wife, lawfully?

AMPOMA [*laughing gaily*]. Oh, Senchi, bless you. Which
   one catches your eye everywhere you turn, like I catch
   Edufa's eye? That's the one you should have.

*The women avert their eyes, eating busily.*

SENCHI [*looking round*]. No hope.

EDUFA [*at the table*]. Here is wine. [*Like one about to pro-
   pose a toast.*] This evening is a celebration unpremedi-
   tated.

SENCHI [*sitting up*]. Speak, husband, speak.

EDUFA. There is nowhere I would rather be, nothing more
   than this I would rather be doing. Join with me in drinking to the health of my lovely wife, whom I publicly
   proclaim a woman among women and friend among
   friends.

SENCHI. Applause. Vote of thanks!

EDUFA. Drink. To her health.

CHORUS *and* SENCHI [*rising, each with glass in hand*]. To
   your health, Ampoma.

CHORUS ONE [*instinctively formal*]. In all directions we let our libation pour. Your husband is true and rare. Live together blessedly to the end of your days. Health to you.

CHORUS. Health to your children. Health to your house.

AMPOMA [*deeply shaken*]. I will have some wine now. Thank you, my friends.

EDUFA [*serving her*]. Here.

SENCHI. And enough of solemnity. You're making her pensive.

*They all sit.*

EDUFA [*with unconcealed concern*]. Ampoma.

AMPOMA. I'm all right. [*She rises. She is not all right.*] It is a moving thing to feel a prayer poured into your soul. But now it's over. [*Pause.*] Give me some wine. [*Now straining for a diversion, she moves forward to gaze into the sky above the courtyard.*] The night is usually full of stars. Where are they all tonight? Senchi, can't you sing them out in a riot?

SENCHI [*beside her, parodying*]. Little stars; little, colossal, little stars. How I wonder where you are. How I wonder why you are. How I wonder which one of you is my star, and why you fizzle.

AMPOMA [*very pleased*]. That's good. Oh, Senchi.

CHORUS ONE. He is never at a loss for things to say.

CHORUS TWO. It's extraordinary.

EDUFA. If he could settle down, he could become a poet.

AMPOMA [*seriously*]. He is one already, no matter how he roams.

SENCHI [*touched*]. Thank you, Ampoma.

AMPOMA [*returning to her chair*]. Eat, friends, it's late.

CHORUS TWO. But you are not eating.

AMPOMA. I have fed all I need. And there is no time. Very soon I must embrace my husband before you all, answering the affection into which he draws me. [*She rises hastily and loses her balance again, just avoiding a fall, steadying herself with her hand.*]

EDUFA [*supporting her, and very disturbed*]. Don't trouble, I implore you.

SENCHI [*to* AMPOMA]. Sorry. [*Trying to relax the tensing atmosphere.*] But, come on, Edufa. Let her embrace you. I haven't ever seen Ampoma breaking through her shyness. Besides, if she embraces you, then I can embrace all the others; and so the night makes progress swingingly.

AMPOMA [*embracing* EDUFA]. Women, I hope you don't think me without modesty. [*Taking up a position.*] We spend most of our days preventing the heart from beating out its greatness. The things we would rather encourage lie choking among the weeds of our restrictions. And before we know it, time has eluded us. There is not much time allotted us, and half of that we sleep. While we are awake, we should allow our hearts to beat without shame of being seen living. [*She looks magnificent and quite aloof. Then she speaks more quietly.*] My husband, you have honoured me by your words and by your precious gift of flowers. I wish to honour you in return, in language equally unashamed. [*She beckons to* SEGUWA, *who, since* AMPOMA's *near fall, has been expressing her alarm in the background.*]

Go to my room. On my bed there is a casket. Bring it to me. [SEGUWA *complies.*]

CHORUS TWO. Many women would like to be in a position to say what you have said here, Ampoma.

SENCHI. Therefore, I should not neglect to pay attention to my preliminary surveys which will prepare the way for such contracts to be signed. [*He eyes the* CHORUS *playfully.*] Shall we change seats? [*As he changes seats to sit by another woman.*] I have been camping too long in one place and getting nowhere.

SEGUWA *returns with the casket.*

EDUFA [*confused and uncomfortable*]. What's this?

AMPOMA [*opening the casket and taking out some smart waist beads*]. Waist beads, bearing the breath of my tenderness.

CHORUS [*nonplussed, eyes popping, but laughing*]. Oh! Oh!

EDUFA [*astounded, embarrassed, but not displeased*]. Ampoma!

SENCHI [*beside himself*]. Great! Whew!

AMPOMA [*inscrutable*]. Women, you understand, don't you, that with this I mean to claim him mine? And you are witnesses. My husband, wear this with honour. [*She surprises* EDUFA *by slipping the beads round his neck. His first reaction is shock.*] With it I declare to earth and sky and water, and all things with which we shall soon be one, that I am slave to your flesh and happy so to be. Wear it proudly, this symbol of the union of our flesh.

*The* CHORUS *and* SENCHI *are making the best of a most astonishing situation by laughing at* EDUFA's *discomfiture.*

EDUFA [*attempting to hide his embarrassment behind a smile*]. Why, Ampoma . . . Well . . . what can I say . . . [*He removes the beads as soon as she lets go.*]

SENCHI. That's rich. Oh, Ampoma, you are the most terrific woman I have ever seen. Don't stand there so foolishly, Edufa. Do something. Say something. I would sweep her up in my arms, take wings, and be gone.

AMPOMA [*very abruptly*]. Excuse me, friends, I must leave you. I hope you will tell the town what I have done without considering it gossip. If I had wished it not to be known, I would not have done it here before you. Take my hand in yours quickly. [*She shakes hands with the women in great haste.*] I am happy that you came. . . . I do not know you well, but you are women and you give me boldness to commit my deepest feelings to your understanding. [ *She is hurrying away.*] Sleep well when you return to your own homes.

CHORUS [*chilled*]. Good night, Ampoma. Good night.

EDUFA [*miserably*]. I must see her in. [*He catches up with her before she reaches the steps.*] Are you all right?

AMPOMA [*brightly*]. Oh, yes. It's such a relief to feel so well at last.

*She takes his hand, looks round, and seems to be wanting to linger.* EDUFA *attempts to lead her away.*

SENCHI [*to* CHORUS]. You have seen truth.

CHORUS ONE. I couldn't have believed it if my own eyes hadn't witnessed it. Ampoma?

SENCHI. Just do what she recommends, that's all.

EDUFA *and* AMPOMA *are going up the steps.*

AMPOMA. Thank you, but don't leave our friends. I want to go in alone.

EDUFA. As you wish, my dear, but——

AMPOMA. I want to; please don't leave them now.

EDUFA [*reluctantly*]. I'll make it very brief and join you presently. [*He comes down.*] Ah, Senchi, she's all but taken my breath away. [AMPOMA *falls on the step with the sign of the sun on it, causing* SEGUWA *to scream.* EDUFA *runs to his wife, yelling with horror.*] No! Ampoma! No!

SENCHI [*helping to lift up* AMPOMA]. Why didn't you take her up the steps?

CHORUS TWO. She's been unsteady all the time. She's not recovered yet, is she?

EDUFA [*unaware of anyone else's presence*]. There, Ampoma, there. You didn't fall all the way to the ground. I will not let you fall. No! No! No! Not to the ground. To the ground? No! Lean on me. You shouldn't have come out. I shouldn't have permitted it. Oh! No! [*He is taking her up.*]

SENCHI [*with great concern*]. Take her in. It wasn't a big fall, fortunately. [*Helplessly.*] Sleep well, Ampoma. [AMPOMA *turns to look at him with a wistful smile. He is left standing alone on the steps, deeply puzzled.*] That's strange. . . . [*He comes down.*] Well, sit down, ladies. [*Obviously trying to pretend the atmosphere of panic doesn't exist.*] I don't blame Edufa for overdoing his concern. He's a man caught in the spell of high romance. Why, if I were in his shoes, I would be even more wildly solicitous. [*He thinks this over, forgetting the presence of the* CHORUS *meanwhile.*] In his shoes? No, not that. I'm wearing his suit, I openly confess, but his shoes I wouldn't wear. I, Senchi, must at all times maintain a genuine contact with the basic earth in my own shoes. [*Shaking himself out of his reflection.*] Have a drink. [*But he cannot move.*] She didn't fall too badly, did she? Perhaps she shouldn't be up yet.

CHORUS ONE. I'm thinking the same, remembering her action here.

CHORUS TWO. You saw it? The tension beneath the smile?

CHORUS THREE. She was unhappy.

CHORUS ONE. But she was happy also, strangely.

*It is now that* SEGUWA *is noticed wandering in the court-yard with gestures of desperation.*

SENCHI [*unnerved*]. Woman, you are too excitable. What are you fussing around for like a hen wanting somewhere to lay an egg? [SEGUWA *looks at him as if she's afraid he'll hit her.*] Control yourself.

SEGUWA. I cannot any more. She fell. Did you count? Oh! The thought! She fell three times, and each time she touched the ground. Oh! Oh!

*The* CHORUS *converge on her.*

CHORUS ONE. What do you mean?

SENCHI. Oh, come off it. My goodness, she didn't break any bones. Ampoma wouldn't forgive you for making her seem so fragile.

SEGUWA. She fell off the sign of the sun; and the sun itself is blanked, and it is dark.

CHORUS [*with urgency*]. What sign?

SEGUWA [*out of control*]. Bad signs. They would pose no menace if no oath had been sworn and we were free to read in her present condition normal disabilities for which remedy is possible. As it is, the reality of that oath makes Edufa for all time guilty, no matter how or when she meets her end.

SENCHI. Don't talk to us in fragments, woman.

SEGUWA. I thought we could cancel out the memory. [*Rushing towards the steps.*] But I see the sign of the

three pebbles, and on the third fall she fell on the sign
of the sun, to the ground. [*She points out the sign of
the sun.*]

CHORUS [*crowding round*]. What is it?

SENCHI. What is this, woman?

SEGUWA [*hiding her face in her hands and turning away*].
It shouldn't be there to plague our memory, deluding us
from the path of reason.

SENCHI. This woman is unstable. I wouldn't have her running about my house if I had one. But . . . what is this
sign?

SEGUWA [*terrified*]. I don't know. I have told you nothing.
Get out. I know nothing about it. Why did you come
feasting here tonight? Get out! Get out, all of you. [*She
rears up against the wall, pointing at the* CHORUS.] Or are
you eager to take Ampoma's place? Can you pay the
price of sharing Edufa's bed? Nothing less than your
lives? Oh, he is most dangerous.

*She dashes off into* EDUFA'S *rooms. The* CHORUS *and* SENCHI
*hover round the steps, staring at the sign of the sun.*

CHORUS [*several voices*]. She's terrified.

SENCHI. So is Edufa. Does a fall call for these flights of
terror? Such hysteria? [*He scrutinises the sign, and his
distress increases.*] I should break in there and demand
explanation.

CHORUS ONE. Do you remember this morning, at our ceremony, that woman's haunted look, her strangeness?

CHORUS TWO. Her fighting to say whether Edufa was in or
out?

CHORUS ONE. And Edufa himself. If there wasn't something terribly wrong, would he have been so conspicu-
ously relieved when Ampoma asked for food?

SENCHI. Do you mean that all this happened here?

CHORUS THREE. Yes, this morning, in our presence.

SENCHI [*grimly to himself*]. To me, also, he has shown
some strange disturbances of spirit this day. . . . And
then, Ampoma's wandering mind tonight, her . . . But

let's not run on so. We know nothing until I go in there.
[*He is about to force his way into* EDUFA'*s rooms when*
SEGUWA *rushes out. She cringes when she sees him and
flees into the courtyard, her fist in her mouth as if to
stifle an outcry.*] Where's Edufa? Woman, speak. What's
happening here?

CHORUS. Talk to us. Tell us.

*They and* SENCHI *press in on* SEGUWA *as she roams with
her hand pressed against her mouth. She suddenly notices
the clappers that the* CHORUS *used in the mourning rite,
seizes them, and thrusts them impulsively at the* CHORUS.

SEGUWA [*bursting out*]. Don't ask me to talk. Help me. You
have come to do the rite, have you not? Do it quickly, I
implore you.

SENCHI [*at the top of the step*]. Edufa!

SEGUWA. What is there left of sacredness?

CHORUS. By the souls of our fathers, speak.

SEGUWA. It is that evil charm on which the oath was sworn.
We cannot ever forget it. We cannot reason without it
now.

SENCHI. What? Charms in Edufa's house?

CHORUS. What charm?

SENCHI. Edufa! It's Senchi.

SEGUWA. And yet he burned it. But the deed was done. He
buried it, but it was her he buried.

CHORUS. Buried?

SEGUWA. Oh, speak, tongue! Women, you did your ceremony here, but you left the evil one himself behind you.
Edufa. He is in there with his victim. This is the day
when Edufa should have died. Another has died for
him: his wife, Ampoma. She loved him, and she has
died to spare his life.

CHORUS ONE. Died? For him? People don't die that kind
of death.

CHORUS. Died? No. We have eaten here with her, laughed
with her.

SENCHI [*helplessly*]. Groans in there . . . like one who
    stifles agony lest he shed unmanly tears. I fear it is the
    worst, my friends.

SEGUWA. Coward! Coward! Coward! He is a cursed man.
    Go. Tell the town about the man who let his wife die
    for him. [*She breaks down.*] Then go and tell her mother.
    Oh, Mother! Will someone go and tell her mother, for I
    cannot look her in the face. I cannot look those motherless
    children in the face.

CHORUS. You lie. We will not believe you.

SEGUWA. Come, I'll show you where he buried it.

*She strides ahead to take them to the back courtyard. Just
at this point* EDUFA *comes out, a man clearly going out of
his mind. The* CHORUS *run up to crowd below the steps.*

CHORUS ONE. Oh, Edufa. Has this woman fed from your
    hand, who now maligns you so?

SEGUWA *has fled at sight of* EDUFA.

CHORUS. We implore you, tell us she lies. We do not
    believe her, pious one. Tell us she lies.

SENCHI. Friend, what is this?

EDUFA [*dejectedly on the steps*]. If you see my father, call
    him back that I may weep on his shoulder.

CHORUS. Great God, is it true that she is dead?

SENCHI [*shaking him*]. Edufa. Friend. What's all this about
    charms?

EDUFA [*violent, his voice unnatural*]. I burned it. [*He
    slouches helplessly on the steps.*]

SENCHI. Stand up, man. What in the name of mystery is
    it all about?

CHORUS ONE. Do you hear him? He buried it, he says.
    There was something then? Edufa, is it true what this
    woman says? That Ampoma is dead, and in your place?

EDUFA. . . . and buried . . . [*Wildly.*] I told her not to
    swear. I did not know that harm could be done. I did not
    know it. [*Looking belligerently at* SENCHI, *and not recog-
    nising him.*] Who are you? Why are you looking at me?

SENCHI [*sadly*]. Senchi.

CHORUS ONE. He is raving.

EDUFA. I told her not to swear. I didn't know that harm could be done.

CHORUS. Not to swear, or harm could be done. Alas!

SENCHI [*seizing hold of him*]. Tell me all, Edufa.

*The owl hoots outside.*

EDUFA [*wildly*]. Didn't he take that bird away? [*He looks at* SENCHI *dangerously.*] Who are you? Don't restrain me. [*Straining with more than natural strength.*] Where is my leopard skin? I'll teach Death to steal my wives. [*So strong that* SENCHI *can no longer restrain him.*] Death, I will lie closely at the grave again, and when you come gloating with your spoil, I'll grab you, unlock her from your grip, and bring her safely home to my bed. And until then, no woman's hand shall touch me.

CHORUS. She is dead. [*They rush into* EDUFA's *rooms.*]

SENCHI [*with infinite sadness*]. There, Edufa, there . . . don't rave so. No . . . not this. [*He attempts to hold him again.*]

EDUFA [*wrenching himself free*]. The last laugh will be mine when I bring her home again. I will bring Ampoma back. Forward, to the grave. [*He moves in strength towards the back courtyard, roaring.*] I will do it. I am conqueror! [*His last word, however, comes as a great questioning lament.*] Conqueror . . . ?

*He runs out by way of the back courtyard. The* CHORUS *return mournfully.* SENCHI *makes his way past them into* EDUFA's *rooms.*

CHORUS [*several voices together, and a single voice every now and then, as they make their way out through the gate; rendered at a slow dirge tempo*].
Calamity.
That we should be the witnesses.
Do not restrain your tears,
Let them stream,
Make a river of sorrow, for Ampoma is dead.

We do not know how,
We do not understand,
But she is dead.

Will someone go and tell her mother!
Edufa! Edufa!
How is it possible
That she is dead?

*They can be heard beating their clappers after the chanting.*
SENCHI *returns. He stands alone on the steps.*

SENCHI. Blank. I have ended up blank once again. All that
is left, the laughter of the flowers in her lifeless arms and
the lingering smell of incense. [*He descends.*]
     And over me, the taut extension of the sky—to which
I raise my song.
     Will someone go and tell her mother? [*He sings.*]
And if I find you
I'll have to worship you
I must adore you
Nne
Nne Nne
O Mother
Nne
Nne Nne

*The End.*

# THE JEWELS OF THE SHRINE

*A Play in One Act*

*by*

JAMES ENE HENSHAW

# CHARACTERS

OKORIE, *an old man*
AROB ⎱ *Okorie's grandsons*
OJIMA ⎰
BASSI, *a woman*
A STRANGER


SCENE: An imaginary village close to a town in Nigeria. All the scenes of this play take place in OKORIE's mud-walled house. The time is the present.

# THE JEWELS OF THE SHRINE

## SCENE I

*The hall in* OKORIE's *house. There are three doors. One leads directly into* OKORIE's *room. The two others are on either side of the hall. Of these, one leads to his grandsons' apartment, whilst the other acts as a general exit.*

*The chief items of furniture consist of a wide bamboo bed, on which is spread a mat; a wooden chair, a low table, and a few odds and ends, including three hoes.*

OKORIE, *an old man of about eighty years of age, with scanty grey hair, and dressed in the way his village folk do, is sitting at the edge of the bed. He holds a stout, rough walking-stick and a horn filled with palm wine.*

*On the wooden chair near the bed sits a* STRANGER, *a man of about forty-five years of age. He, too, occasionally sips wine from a calabash cup. It is evening. The room is rather dark, and a cloth-in-oil lantern hangs from a hook on the wall.*

OKORIE. Believe me, Stranger, in my days things were different. It was a happy thing to become an old man, because young people were taught to respect elderly men.

STRANGER [*sipping his wine*]. Here in the village you should be happier. In the town where I come from, a boy of ten riding a hired bicycle will knock down a man of fifty years without any feeling of pity.

OKORIE. Bicycle. That is why I have not been to town for ten years. Town people seem to enjoy rushing about doing nothing. It kills them.

STRANGER. You are lucky that you have your grandchildren to help you. Many people in town have no one to help them.

OKORIE. Look at me, Stranger, and tell me if these shabby clothes and this dirty beard show that I have good grandchildren. Believe me, Stranger, in my younger days things were different. Old men were happy. When they died, they were buried with honour. But in my case, Stranger, my old age has been unhappy. And my only fear now is that when I die, my grandsons will not accord me the honour due to my age. It will be a disgrace to me.

STRANGER. I will now go on my way, Okorie. May God help you.

OKORIE. I need help, Stranger, for although I have two grandsons, I am lonely and unhappy because they do not love or care for me. They tell me that I am from an older world. Farewell, Stranger. If you call again and I am alive, I will welcome you back.

*Exit* STRANGER. BASSI, *a beautiful woman of about thirty years, enters.*

BASSI. Who was that man, Grandfather?

OKORIE. He was a stranger.

BASSI. I do not trust strangers. They may appear honest when the lights are on. But as soon as there is darkness, they creep back as thieves. [OKORIE *smiles and drinks his wine.* BASSI *points to him.*] What has happened, Grandfather? When I left you this afternoon, you were old, your mind was worried, and your eyes were swollen. Where now are the care, the sorrow, the tears in your eyes? You never smiled before, but now——

OKORIE. The stranger has brought happiness back into my life. He has given me hope again.

BASSI. But don't they preach in town that it is only God who gives hope? Every other thing gives despair.

OKORIE. Perhaps that stranger was God. Don't the preachers say that God moves like a stranger?

BASSI. God moves in strange ways.

OKORIE. Yes, I believe it, because since that stranger came, I have felt younger again. You know, woman, when I worshipped at our forefathers' shrine, I was happy. I knew what it was all about. It was my life. Then the preachers came, and I abandoned the beliefs of our fathers. The old ways did not leave me; the new ways did not wholly accept me. I was therefore unhappy. But soon I felt the wings of God carrying me high. And with my loving and helpful son, I thought that my old age would be as happy as that of my father before me. But death played me a trick. My son died and I was left to the mercy of his two sons. Once more unhappiness gripped my life. With all their education my grandsons lacked one thing—respect for age. But today the stranger who came here has once more brought happiness to me. Let me tell you this——

BASSI. It is enough, Grandfather. Long talks make you tired. Come, your food is now ready.

OKORIE [*happily*]. Woman, I cannot eat. When happiness fills your heart, you cannot eat.

*Two voices are heard outside, laughing and swearing.*

BASSI. Your grandchildren are coming back.

OKORIE. Don't call them my grandchildren. I am alone in this world.

*Door flings open. Two young men, about eighteen and twenty, enter the room. They are in shirt and trousers.*

AROB. By our forefathers, Grandfather, you are still awake!

BASSI. Why should he not keep awake if he likes?

AROB. But Grandfather usually goes to bed before the earliest chicken thinks of it.

OJIMA. Our good grandfather might be thinking of his youthful days, when all young men were fond of farming and all young women loved the kitchen.

BASSI. Shame on both of you for talking to an old man like that. When you grow old, your own children will laugh and jeer at you. Come, Grandfather, and take your food.

OKORIE *stands up with difficulty and limps with the aid of his stick through the exit, followed by* BASSI, *who casts a reproachful look on the two men before she leaves.*

AROB. I wonder what Grandfather and the woman were talking about.

OJIMA. It must be the usual thing. We are bad boys. We have no regard for the memory of our father, and so on.

AROB. Our father left his responsibility to us. Nature had

arranged that he should bury Grandfather before thinking of himself.

OJIMA. But would Grandfather listen to Nature when it comes to the matter of death? Everybody in his generation, including all his wives, have died. But Grandfather has made a bet with death. And it seems that he will win.

OKORIE [*calling from offstage*]. Bassi! Bassi! Where is that woman?

OJIMA. The old man is coming. Let us hide ourselves. [*Both rush under the bed.*]

OKORIE [*comes in, limping on his stick as usual*]. Bassi, where are you? Haven't I told that girl never——

BASSI [*entering*]. Don't shout so. It's not good for you.

OKORIE. Where are the two people?

BASSI. You mean your grandsons?

OKORIE. My, my, well, call them what you like.

BASSI. They are not here. They must have gone into their room.

OKORIE. Bassi, I have a secret for you. [*He narrows his eyes.*] A big secret. [*His hands tremble.*] Can you keep a secret?

BASSI. Of course I can.

OKORIE [*rubbing his forehead*]. You can, what can you? What did I say?

BASSI [*holding him and leading him to sit on the bed*]. You are excited. You know that whenever you are excited, you begin to forget things.

OKORIE. That is not my fault. It is old age. Well, but what was I saying?

BASSI. You asked me if I could keep a secret.

OKORIE. Yes, yes, a great secret. You know, Bassi, I have been an unhappy man.

BASSI. I have heard it all before.

OKORIE. Listen, woman. My dear son died and left me to the mercy of his two sons. They are the worst grandsons in the land. They have sold all that their father left. They do not care for me. Now when I die, what will they do to me? Don't you think that they will abandon me in dis-

grace? An old man has a right to be properly cared for.
And when he dies, he has a right to a good burial. But
my grandchildren do not think of these things.

BASSI. See how you tremble, Grandfather! I have told you
not to think of such things.

OKORIE. Why should I not? But sh! . . . I hear a voice.

BASSI. It's only your ears deceiving you, Grandfather.

OKORIE. It is not my ears, woman. I know when old age
hums in my ears and tired nerves ring bells in my head,
but I know also when I hear a human voice.

BASSI. Go on, Grandfather; there is no one.

OKORIE. Now, listen. You saw the stranger that came here.
He gave me hope. But wait, look around, Bassi. Make
sure that no one is listening to us.

BASSI. No one, Grandfather.

OKORIE. Open the door and look.

BASSI [*opens the exit door*]. No one.

OKORIE. Look into that corner.

BASSI [*looks*]. There is no one.

OKORIE. Look under the bed.

BASSI [*irritably*]. I won't, Grandfather. There is no need; I
have told you that there is nobody in the house.

OKORIE [*pitiably*]. I have forgotten what I was talking about.

BASSI [*calmly*]. You have a secret from the stranger.

OKORIE. Yes, the stranger told me something. Have you
ever heard of the "Jewels of the Shrine"?

BASSI. Real jewels?

OKORIE. Yes. Among the beads which my father got from
the early white men, were real jewels. When war broke
out and a great fever invaded all our lands, my father
made a sacrifice in the village shrine. He promised that if
this village were spared, he would offer his costly jewels
to the shrine. Death roamed through all the other villages,
but not one person in this village died of the fever. My
father kept his promise. In a big ceremony the jewels
were placed on our shrine. But it was not for long. Some
said they were stolen. But the stranger who came here

knew where they were. He said that they were buried somewhere near the big oak tree on our farm. I must go out and dig for them. They can be sold for fifty pounds these days.

BASSI. But, Grandfather, it will kill you to go out in this cold and darkness. You must get someone to do it for you. You cannot lift a hoe.

OKORIE [*infuriated*]. So, you believe I am too old to lift a hoe. You, you, oh, I . . .

BASSI [*coaxing him*]. There now, young man, no temper. If you wish, I myself will dig up the whole farm for you.

OKORIE. Every bit of it?

BASSI. Yes.

OKORIE. And hand over to me all that you will find?

BASSI. Yes.

OKORIE. And you will not tell my grandsons?

BASSI. No, Grandfather, I will not.

OKORIE. Swear, woman, swear by our fathers' shrine.

BASSI. I swear.

OKORIE [*relaxing*]. Now life is becoming worthwhile. Tell no one about it, woman. Begin digging tomorrow morning. Dig inch by inch until you bring out the jewels of our forefathers' shrine.

BASSI. I am tired, Grandfather. I must sleep now. Good night.

OKORIE [*with feeling*]. Good night. God and our fathers' spirits keep you. When dangerous bats alight on the roofs of wicked men, let them not trouble you in your sleep. When far-seeing owls hoot the menace of future days, let their evil prophecies keep off your path. [BASSI *leaves.* OKORIE, *standing up and trembling, moves to a corner and brings out a small hoe. Struggling with his senile joints, he tries to imitate a young man digging.*]

Oh, who said I was old? After all, I am only eighty years. And I feel younger than most young men. Let me see how I can dig. [*He tries to dig again.*] Ah! I feel

aches all over my hip. Maybe the soil here is too hard.
[*He listens.*] How I keep on thinking that I hear people
whispering in this room! I must rest now.

*Carrying the hoe with him, he goes into his room.* AROB *and*
OJIMA *crawl out from under the bed.*

AROB [*stretching his hip*]. My hip, oh my hip!

OJIMA. My legs!

AROB. So there is a treasure in our farm! We must waste
no time; we must begin digging soon.

OJIMA. Soon? We must begin tonight—now. The old man
has taken one hoe. [*Pointing to the corner.*] There are
two over there. [*They fetch two hoes from among the heap
of things in a corner of the room.*] If we can only get the
jewels, we can go and live in town and let the old man
manage as he can. Let's move now.

*As they are about to go out, each holding a hoe,* OKORIE
*comes out with his own hoe. For a moment the three stare
at each other in silence and surprise.*

AROB. Now, Grandfather, where are you going with a hoe
at this time of night?

OJIMA [*impudently*]. Yes, Grandfather, what is the idea?

OKORIE. I should ask you; this is my house. Why are you
creeping about like thieves?

AROB. All right, Grandfather, we are going back to bed.

OKORIE. What are you doing with hoes? You were never
fond of farming.

OJIMA. We intend to go to the farm early in the morning.

OKORIE. But the harvest is over. When everybody in the
village was digging out the crops, you were going around
the town with your hands in your pockets. Now you say
you are going to the farm.

OJIMA. Digging is good for the health, Grandfather.

OKORIE [*re-entering his room*]. Good night.

AROB *and* OJIMA. Good night, Grandfather.

*They return to their room. After a short time* AROB *and*

OJIMA *come out, each holding a hoe, and tiptoe out through the exit. Then, gently,* OKORIE *too comes out on his toes, and placing the hoe on his shoulder, warily leaves the hall.*

*Curtain.*

## SCENE II

*The same, the following morning.*

BASSI [*knocking at* OKORIE'S *door; she is holding a hoe*]. Grandfather, wake up. I am going to the farm.

OKORIE [*opening the door*]. Good morning. Where are you going so early in the morning?

BASSI. I am going to dig up the farm. You remember the treasure, don't you?

OKORIE. Do you expect to find a treasure whilst you sleep at night? You should have dug at night, woman. Treasures are never found in the day.

BASSI. But you told me to dig in the morning, Grandfather.

OKORIE. My grandsons were in this room somewhere. They heard what I told you about the Jewels of the Shrine.

BASSI. They could not have heard us. I looked everywhere. The stranger must have told them.

OKORIE [*rubbing his forehead*]. What stranger?

BASSI. The stranger who told you about the treasure in the farm.

OKORIE. So it was a stranger who told me! Oh, yes, a stranger! [*He begins to dream.*] Ah, I remember him now. He was a great man. His face shone like the sun. It was like the face of God.

BASSI. You are dreaming, Grandfather. Wake up! I must go to the farm quickly.

OKORIE. Yes, woman, I remember the jewels in the farm. But you are too late.

BASSI [*excitedly*]. Late? Have your grandsons discovered the treasure?

OKORIE. They have not, but I have discovered it myself.

BASSI [*amazed*]. You? [OKORIE *nods his head with a smile on his face.*] Do you mean to say that you are now a rich man?

OKORIE. By our fathers' shrine, I am.

BASSI. So you went and worked at night. You should not have done it, even to forestall your grandchildren.

OKORIE. My grandsons would never have found it.

BASSI. But you said that they heard us talking of the treasure.

OKORIE. You see, I suspected that my grandsons were in this room. So I told you that the treasure was in the farm, but in actual fact it was in the little garden behind this house, where the village shrine used to be. My grandsons travelled half a mile to the farm last night for nothing.

BASSI. Then I am glad I did not waste my time.

OKORIE [*with delight*]. How my grandsons must have toiled in the night! [*He is overcome with laughter.*] My grandsons, they thought I would die in disgrace, a pauper, unheard of. No, not now. [*Then boldly.*] But those wicked children must change, or when I die, I shall not leave a penny for them.

BASSI. Oh, Grandfather, to think you are a rich man!

OKORIE. I shall send you to buy me new clothes. My grandsons will not know me again. Ha—ha—ha—ha!

OKORIE *and* BASSI *leave.* AROB *and* OJIMA *crawl out from under the bed, where for a second time they have hidden. They look rough, their feet dirty with sand and leaves. Each comes out with his hoe.*

AROB. So the old man fooled us.

OJIMA. Well, he is now a rich man, and we must treat him with care.

AROB. We have no choice. He says that unless we change, he will not leave a penny to us.

*A knock at the door.*

AROB *and* OJIMA. Come in.

OKORIE [*comes in, and seeing them so rough and dirty, bursts out laughing; the others look surprised*]. Look how dirty you are, with hoes and all. "Gentlemen" like you should not touch hoes. You should wear white gloves and live in towns. But see, you look like two pigs. Ha—ha—ha—ha—ha! Oh what grandsons! How stupid they look! Ha—ha—ha! [AROB *and* OJIMA *are dumbfounded.*] I saw both of you a short while ago under the bed. I hope you now know that I have got the Jewels of the Shrine.

AROB. We, too, have something to tell you, Grandfather.

OKORIE. Yes, yes, "gentlemen." Come, tell me. [*He begins to move away.*] You must hurry up. I am going to town to buy myself some new clothes and a pair of shoes.

AROB. New clothes?

OJIMA. And shoes?

OKORIE. Yes, grandsons, it is never too late to wear new clothes.

AROB. Let us go and buy them for you. It is too hard for you to——

OKORIE. If God does not think that I am yet old enough to be in the grave, I do not think I am too old to go to the market in town. I need some clothes and a comb to comb my beard. I am happy, grandchildren, very happy. [AROB *and* OJIMA *are dumbfounded.*] Now, "gentlemen," why don't you get drunk and shout at me as before? [*Growing bolder.*] Why not laugh at me as if I were nobody? You young puppies, I am now somebody, somebody. What is somebody? [*Rubbing his forehead as usual.*]

AROB [*to* OJIMA]. He has forgotten again.

OKORIE. Who has forgotten what?

OJIMA. You have forgotten nothing. You are a good man, Grandfather, and we like you.

OKORIE [*shouting excitedly*]. Bassi! Bassi! Bassi! Where is that silly woman? Bassi, come and hear this. My grand-

children like me; I am now a good man. Ha—ha—ha—
ha!

*He limps into his room.* AROB *and* OJIMA *look at each
other. It is obvious to them that the old man has all the
cards now.*

AROB. What has come over the old man?

OJIMA. Have you not heard that when people have money,
it scratches them on the brain? That is what has happened to our grandfather now.

AROB. He does not believe that we like him. How can we
convince him?

OJIMA. You know what he likes most: someone to scratch
his back. When he comes out, you will scratch his back,
and I will use his big fan to fan at him.

AROB. Great idea. [OKORIE *coughs from the room.*] He is
coming now.

OKORIE [*comes in*]. I am so tired.

AROB. You said you were going to the market, Grandfather.

OKORIE. You do well to remind me. I have sent Bassi to
buy the things I want.

OJIMA. Grandfather, you look really tired. Lie down here.
[OKORIE *lies down and uncovers his back.*] Grandfather,
from now on, I shall give you all your breakfast and your
midday meals.

AROB [*jealously*]. By our forefathers' shrine, Grandfather,
I shall take care of your dinner and supply you with wine
and clothing.

OKORIE. God bless you, little sons. That is how it should
have been all the time. An old man has a right to live
comfortably in his last days.

OJIMA. Grandfather, it is a very long time since we scratched
your back.

AROB. Yes, it is a long time. We have not done it since we
were infants. We want to do it now. It will remind us of
our younger days, when it was a pleasure to scratch your
back.

OKORIE. Scratch my back? Ha—ha—ha—ha. Oh, go on, go

on; by our fathers' shrine you are now good men. I wonder what has happened to you.

OJIMA. It's you, Grandfather. You are such a nice man. As a younger man you must have looked very well. But in your old age you look simply wonderful.

AROB. That is right, Grandfather, and let us tell you again. Do not waste a penny of yours any more. We will keep you happy and satisfied to the last hour of your life.

OKORIE *appears pleased.* AROB *now begins to pick at, and scratch,* OKORIE's *back.* OJIMA *kneels near the bed and begins to fan the old man. After a while a slow snore is heard. Then, as* AROB *warms up to his task,* OKORIE *jumps up.*

OKORIE. Oh, that one hurts. Gently, children, gently.

*He relaxes and soon begins to snore again.* OJIMA *and* AROB *gradually stand up.*

AROB. The old fogy is asleep.

OJIMA. That was clever of us. I am sure he believes us now.

*They leave.* OKORIE *opens an eye and peeps at them. Then he smiles and closes it again.* BASSI *enters, bringing some new clothes, a pair of shoes, a comb and brush, a tin of face powder, etc. She pushes* OKORIE.

BASSI. Wake up, Grandfather.

OKORIE [*opening his eyes*]. Who told you that I was asleep? Oh! you have brought the things. It is so long since I had a change of clothes. Go on, woman, and call those grandsons of mine. They must help me to put on my new clothes and shoes.

BASSI *leaves.* OKORIE *begins to comb his hair and beard, which have not been touched for a long time.* BASSI *re-enters with* AROB *and* OJIMA. *Helped by his grandsons and* BASSI, OKORIE *puts on his new clothes and shoes. He then sits on the bed and poses majestically like a chief.*

*Curtain.*

## SCENE III

*The same, a few months later.* OKORIE *is lying on the bed.*
*He is well dressed and looks happy, but it is easily seen that*
*he is nearing his end. There is a knock at the door.* OKORIE
*turns and looks at the door but cannot speak loudly. An-*
*other knock; the door opens, and the* STRANGER *enters.*

OKORIE. Welcome back, Stranger. You have come in time.
Sit down. I will tell you of my will.

*Door opens slowly.* BASSI *walks in.*

BASSI [*to* STRANGER]. How is he?

STRANGER. Just holding on.

BASSI. Did he say anything?

STRANGER. He says that he wants to tell me about his will.
Call his grandsons.

BASSI *leaves.*

OKORIE. Stranger.

STRANGER. Yes, Grandfather.

OKORIE. Do you remember what I told you about my fears
in life?

STRANGER. You were afraid your last days would be miserable
and that you would not have a decent burial.

OKORIE. Now, Stranger, all that is past. Don't you see how
happy I am? I have been very well cared for since I
saw you last. My grandchildren have done everything for
me, and I am sure they will bury me with great ceremony
and rejoicing. I want you to be here when I am making
my will. Bend to my ears; I will whisper something to
you. [STRANGER *bends for a moment.* OKORIE *whispers.*
*Then he speaks aloud.*] Is that clear, Stranger?

STRANGER. It is clear.

OKORIE. Will you remember?

STRANGER. I will.

OKORIE. Do you promise?

STRANGER. I promise.

OKORIE [*relaxing on his pillow*]. There now. My end will be more cheerful than I ever expected.

*A knock.*

STRANGER. Come in.

AROB, OJIMA, *and* BASSI *enter. The two men appear as sad as possible. They are surprised to meet the* STRANGER, *and stare at him for a moment.*

OKORIE [*with effort*]. This man may be a stranger to you, but not to me. He is my friend. Arob, look how sad you are! Ojima, how tight your lips are with sorrow! Barely a short while ago you would not have cared whether I lived or died.

AROB. Don't speak like that, Grandfather.

OKORIE. Why should I not? Remember, these are my last words on earth.

OJIMA. You torture us, Grandfather.

OKORIE. Since my son, your father, died, you have tortured me. But now you have changed, and it is good to forgive you both.

STRANGER. You wanted to make a will.

OKORIE. Will? Yes, will. Where is Bassi? Has that woman run away already?

BASSI [*standing above the bed*]. No, Grandfather, I am here.

OKORIE. Now there is my family complete.

STRANGER. The will, Grandfather, the will.

OKORIE. Oh, the will; the will is made.

AROB. Made? Where is it?

OKORIE. It is written out on paper.

AROB *and* OJIMA *together:*

AROB. Written?

OJIMA. What?

OKORIE [*coolly*]. Yes, someone wrote it for me soon after I had discovered the treasure.

AROB. Where is it, Grandfather?

OJIMA. Are you going to show us, Grandfather?

OKORIE. Yes, I will. Why not? But not now, not until I am dead.

AROB *and* OJIMA. What?

OKORIE. Listen here. The will is in a small box buried somewhere. The box also contains all my wealth. These are my wishes. Make my burial the best you can. Spend as much as is required, for you will be compensated. Do not forget that I am the oldest man in this village. An old man has a right to be decently buried. Remember, it was only after I had discovered the Jewels of the Shrine that you began to take good care of me. You should, by carrying out all my last wishes, atone for all those years when you left me poor, destitute, and miserable.

[*To the* STRANGER, *in broken phrases.*] Two weeks after my death, Stranger, you will come and unearth the box of my treasure. Open it in the presence of my grandsons. Read out the division of the property, and share it among them. Bassi, you have nothing. You have a good husband and a family. No reward or treasure is greater than a good marriage and a happy home. Stranger, I have told you where the box containing the will is buried. That is all. May God . . .

AROB *and* OJIMA [*rushing to him*]. Grandfather, Grandfather——

STRANGER. Leave him in peace. [BASSI, *giving out a scream, rushes from the room.*] I must go now. Don't forget his will. Unless you bury him with great honour, you may not touch his property.

*He leaves.*

*Curtain.*

SCENE IV

*All in this scene are dressed in black.* AROB, OJIMA, *and* BASSI *are sitting around the table. There is one extra chair.*

*The bed is still there, but the mat is taken off, leaving it bare. The hoe with which* OKORIE *dug out the treasure is lying on the bed as a sort of memorial.*

AROB. Thank God, today is here at last. When I get my own share, I will go and live in town.

OJIMA. If only that foolish stranger would turn up! Why a stranger should come into this house and——

BASSI. Remember, he was your grandfather's friend.

OJIMA. At last, poor Grandfather is gone. I wonder if he knew that we only played up just to get something from his will.

AROB. Well, it didn't matter to him. He believed us, and that is why he has left his property to us. A few months ago he would rather have thrown it all into the sea.

OJIMA. Who could have thought, considering the way we treated him, that the old man had such a kindly heart!

*There is a knock. All stand.* STRANGER *enters from Grandfather's room. He is grim, dressed in black, and carries a small wooden box under his arm.*

AROB. Stranger, how did you come out from Grandfather's room?

STRANGER. Let us not waste time on questions. This box was buried in the floor of your grandfather's room. [*He places the box on the table;* AROB *and* OJIMA *crowd together.* STRANGER *speaks sternly.*] Give me room, please. Your grandfather always wanted you to crowd around him. But no one would, until he was about to die. Step back, please.

*Both* AROB *and* OJIMA *step back.* OJIMA *accidentally steps on* AROB.

AROB [*to* OJIMA]. Don't you step on me!

OJIMA [*querulously*]. Don't you shout at me!

STRANGER *looks at both.*

AROB. When I sat day and night watching Grandfather in his illness, you were away in town, dancing and getting drunk. Now you want to be the first to grab at everything.

OJIMA. You liar! It was I who took care of him.

AROB. You only took care of him when you knew that he had come to some wealth.

BASSI. Why can't both of you——

AROB [*very sharply*]. Keep out of this, woman. That pretender [*pointing to* OJIMA] wants to bring trouble today.

OJIMA. I, a pretender? What of you, who began to scratch the old man's back simply to get his money?

AROB. How dare you insult me like that!

*He throws out a blow.* OJIMA *parries. They fight and roll on the floor. The* STRANGER *looks on.*

BASSI. Stranger, stop them.

STRANGER [*calmly looking at them*]. Don't interfere, woman. The mills of God, the preachers tell us, grind slowly.

BASSI. I don't know anything about the mills of God. Stop them, or they will kill themselves.

STRANGER [*clapping his hands*]. Are you ready to proceed with your grandfather's will, or should I wait till you are ready? [*They stop fighting and stand up, panting.*] Before I open this box, I want to know if all your grandfather's wishes have been kept. Was he buried with honour?

AROB. Yes, the greatest burial any old man has had in this village.

OJIMA. You may well answer, but I spent more money than you did.

AROB. No, you did not. I called the drummers and the dancers.

OJIMA. I arranged for the shooting of guns.

AROB. I paid for the wine for the visitors and the mourners.

OJIMA. I——

STRANGER. Please, brothers, wait. I ask you again, Was the old man respectably buried?

BASSI. I can swear to that. His grandsons have sold practically all they have in order to give him a grand burial.

STRANGER. That is good. I shall now open the box.

*There is silence. He opens the box and brings out a piece of paper.*

AROB [*in alarm*]. Where are the jewels, the money, the treasure?

STRANGER. Sh! Listen. This is the will. Perhaps it will tell us where to find everything. Listen to this.

AROB. But you cannot read. Give it to me.

OJIMA. Give it to me.

STRANGER. I can read. I am a schoolteacher.

AROB. Did you write this will for Grandfather?

STRANGER. Questions are useless at this time. I did not.

AROB. Stop talking, man. Read it.

STRANGER [*reading*]. Now, my grandsons, now that I have been respectably and honourably buried, as all grandsons should do to their grandfathers, I can tell you a few things.

First of all, I have discovered no treasure at all. There was never anything like the "Jewels of the Shrine." [AROB *makes a sound as if something had caught him in the throat.* OJIMA *sneezes violently.*] There was no treasure hidden in the farm or anywhere else. I have had nothing in life, so I can only leave you nothing. The house which you now live in was my own. But I sold it some months ago and got a little money for what I needed. That money was my "Jewels of the Shrine." The house belongs now to the stranger who is reading this will to you. He shall take possession of this house two days after the will has been read. Hurry up, therefore, and pack out of this house. You young puppies, do you think I never knew that you had no love for me, and that you were only playing up in order to get the money which you believed I had acquired?

When I was a child, one of my first duties was to respect people who were older than myself. But you have thrown away our traditional love and respect for the elderly person. I shall make you pay for it. Shame on you, young men, who believe that because you can read and write, you need not respect old age as your forefathers did! Shame on healthy young men like you, who let the land go to waste because they will not dirty their hands with work!

OJIMA [*furiously*]. Stop it, Stranger, stop it, or I will kill you! I am undone. I have not got a penny left. I have used all I had to feed him and to bury him. But now I have not even got a roof to stay under. You confounded Stranger, how dare you buy this house?

STRANGER. Do you insult me in my own house?

AROB [*miserably*]. The old cheat! He cheated us to the last. To think that I scratched his back only to be treated like this! We are now poorer than he had ever been.

OJIMA. It is a pity. It is a pity.

STRANGER. What is a pity?

OJIMA. It is a pity we cannot dig him up again.

*Suddenly a hoarse, unearthly laugh is heard from somewhere. Everybody looks in a different direction. They listen. And then again . . .*

VOICE. Ha—ha—ha—ha! [*They all look up.*] Ha—ha—ha —ha! [*The voice is unmistakably Grandfather* OKORIE'*s voice. Seized with terror, everybody except* BASSI *runs in confusion out of the room, stumbling over the table, box, and everything. As they run away, the voice continues.*] Ha—ha—ha—ha! [BASSI, *though frightened, boldly stands her ground. She is very curious to know whether someone has been playing them a trick. The voice grows louder.*] Ha—ha—ha—ha! [BASSI, *too, is terrorised, and runs in alarm off the stage.*] Ha—ha—ha —ha!!!

*Curtain.*

# THE LITERARY SOCIETY

*by*

## HENRY OFORI

# CHARACTERS

Narrator
Nkansa
Asante
Sokportie
Osafo
Addo
Secretary
Kublenu

# THE LITERARY SOCIETY

NARRATOR. The story takes place in a little town in the interior of the country. In such places, well-known in Ghana, people from other parts—because of their various occupations—are compelled to live in this town, Akutuase, and pursue their daily duties under the most austere conditions. The literate folk in the town find it necessary, in order to make life more pleasant, to run a social and literary club. The club, in fact, is the academy of learning in this little community. To show how earnest the members are in the deliberations, we present to you one—just one—incident in the club-room.

It is evening in Akutuase, and as that day happens to be a club-meeting day, we find a group of the members in front of the cocoa shed (which is used as the clubhouse), waiting for the President in order that the day's business may begin.

NKANSA. I wonder what is keeping the President at home. I am sure he is still drying his cocoa beans . . . ha . . . ha . . . ha.

ASANTE. You cannot say anything about anybody without making fun of him. I wonder what is wrong with you.

NKANSA. You mean what is right with me. There is nothing wrong with me, but there is everything wrong with you, my dear Asante.

ASANTE. Don't call me "my dear Asante"; you are not even half my age, yet you think you are my equal.

NKANSA. God forbid! Imagine me being of such a mental disposition as you are.

ASANTE. What do you mean by that, eh . . . what?

NKANSA. If you don't understand the language, I am afraid I am not going to teach you now.

*Laughter.*

ASANTE. So you are laughing, are you? You always encourage this boy to be proud. I must warn you that if he abuses

me again and I decide to beat him, no one should interfere.

SOKPORTIE. I cannot understand why you two people are
always at the point of fighting. I shall recommend to the
President that we buy some boxing gloves for those who
want to try out their strength . . . ha . . . ha . . . ha . . . !

*Conversation lapses and a Mammy truck passes by.*

ASANTE. Honestly, these drivers are at times reckless. Look
at how that fellow drove past, and he is passing through
a town too. That is how they come to knock down our
goats.

SOKPORTIE. Last week four sheep and one goat were
killed by passing Mammy trucks. I wish the police would
make a law to make killing sheep a crime.

NKANSA. The police have better things to do than make
such unnecessary laws. Sometimes it is the fault of the
sheep and goats.

ASANTE. Which reminds me that some human beings behave like sheep.

NKANSA. By which you mean . . . ?

ASANTE. Have I mentioned your name? Are you the only
human being here? Why are you always so proud?

NKANSA. I think I am a human being, and I think that you
are not mad to talk to the wind and that you were addressing yourself to us.

ASANTE. And if I was addressing myself to you all, are you
the spokesman of the group? [*He moves threateningly
towards* NKANSA, *and* SOKPORTIE *comes between them.*]
You must be careful, you hear? You must be very, very
careful.

SOKPORTIE. Oh, Mr. Asante, don't do that. What are you
two doing; are you small boys?

OSAFO, *the President, arrives and moves up to them.*

OSAFO. What is happening here; are they fighting?

NKANSA. No, President, Mr. Asante and I disagreed to
agree, and we were actually trying to show each other
who was the wiser.

*Laughter.*

OSAFO. Is everybody here? We should go in and do business, you know; time is far spent.

NKANSA [*aside*]. As if we have been delaying the meeting and not himself.

*They all troop into the club-room and seat themselves. A bolt is drawn and gates clang open; furniture is dragged— then silence.*

OSAFO [*clearing his throat*]. I declare the meeting open. The Secretary may read the minutes of the last meeting.

ADDO. On point of order, Mr. President, you forgot to say prayers.

OSAFO. Oh, I'm sorry, gentlemen—shall we pray, gentlemen?

*Chairs creek.*

OSAFO. O Lord, who has brought us into this little bush town in order that we may gain our daily bread in order to get strength to do thy good work, we pray you to bless our little club and keep us all along the path of righteousness, so that we may learn something from our meetings. Bless this meeting tonight, so that everybody ends well. . . . Amen.

CHORUS. A A A A-men!!!

OSAFO. I would like to advise members that though this is not a church, we must learn to respond to prayers in the proper manner. What was the use of saying "A A A A-men"?

I now call upon the Secretary to read the minutes of our last meeting.

SECRETARY. Minutes of the meeting of the Akutuase Literary and Social Club held in the club-room on September tenth, 1957, under the chairmanship of the Vice President, Mr. Akosa. The minutes of the previous meeting was read, and after necessary corrections had been made, it was approved and adopted. The main matter of the evening was a lecture by Mr. Osafo, President of the club and manager of the Providence Cocoa Syndicate Limited. His topic was China.

As Mr. Osafo said at the beginning of the lecture, "No one could talk about China without talking about Japan, for the two," he maintained, "are like Siamese twins." In fact, he continued, the last time he saw a Chinese and a Japanese (during the first world war, in East Africa), he could hardly tell one from the other.

Mr. Osafo said that as the two countries had the same people, it was much easier to describe life in Japan, as the Japanese were the same as Chinese. He said that both countries write their literature in the same manner—that is from right to left and upside-down. This made it difficult for other people, like us, to understand them. He said Japan had an Emperor but the Chinese had none; but that did not make much difference, since the Chinese had their first Emperor, called Jino Teno, about 6000 B.C., long before the Japanese had any.

Mr. Osafo said that because Japan is an island, most of the inhabitants are sailors, but China was one large land mass, and as a result most of the people are farmers. Touching upon the question of education, he said that the Japanese were more clever than the Chinese, for they could make aeroplanes out of bamboo sticks. He said he himself bought in the year 1933 a Japanese bicycle made out of bamboo for fifteen shillings at Accra and that the machine served him for about ten years. The Chinese, on the other hand—he said—being farmers, were only concerned with the production of farm products and were not interested in the manufacture of articles. He said that it was the Chinese who first discovered how to make pork. He said that there were two brothers in China called Bobo and Oti, who kept pigs as domestic animals. He said, one day the pig-sty caught fire and before they could save the poor animals, the animals had been killed by the fire. He said that Bobo and Oti were sad that their pets had died; and so they went into the pig-sty after the fire to have a look at them. There they saw that their flesh had been roasted to a very appetising brown hue. Oti then tore off a piece of the flesh of one of the roasted pigs and ate it. He found it very tasteful and therefore asked Bobo to try it

too. Bobo tried it and liked it, and soon the whole village grew to like the taste of pork. In concluding his talk
on China, the President said that what always reminded
him of China was the discovery of the palatability of
roast pork.

In thanking the President for his brilliant exposition
of life in China, the Vice President said that it was true
that knowledge is powerful but experience is more powerful, for as he maintained, the President, Mr. Osafo,
had never been to a secondary school but yet was capable
of meeting any secondary school scholar in any field of
study.

The meeting was brought to a close at 7:45 P.M.

OSAFO. Well, gentlemen, you have heard the minutes read;
if anyone has any correction or amendments to make,
let him say so.

NKANSA. Mr. President, I have two corrections to make.

ASANTE. He always has corrections to make; as for this
boy——

NKANSA. Will you please shut up! If you have anything to
say, address the chair.

ASANTE. Are you talking to me?

NKANSA. Of course, yes. Who are you?

ASANTE. And who are you, too?

OSAFO. Please, gentlemen, I resent any such exchange of
bad words. You must remember we are all big men in
our houses. I don't understand why you, Mr. Asante,
should interrupt when someone is on his feet speaking.

NKANSA. That is what he always does when I get up to
speak. I don't understand it at all.

ASANTE. When did I interrupt your speech, eh, when?

OSAFO. All right, all right, go on, Mr. Nkansa.

NKANSA. Thank you, sir. As I was saying, I have two corrections to make in the minutes. I was not here myself
during the lectures, for I was on holiday, but I know that
the Japanese never make aeroplanes out of bamboo. In
the second place, neither the Japanese nor the Chinese

write upside-down. It is rather the Russians who write upside-down.

SECRETARY. I remember very well the President saying that the Japanese make aeroplanes and bicycles out of bamboo and that both the Japanese and Chinese write upside-down. I therefore see no reason why I should change the statements. If——

ADDO. I very well remember the President making such remarks.

OSAFO. I do not remember ever making these statements which you now put in my mouth. I remember saying that the Chinese were the first to discover that pork was good to eat, especially with rice.

SOKPORTIE. Yes, I also remember the President saying that thing about the pork.

SECRETARY. So you people mean to say that I imagined what I wrote down in the minutes book? If that is the case, then I am not suitable to be the Secretary, and you can ask someone else to take the office.

ASANTE. As for me, I shan't say anything. Whenever I say something, they say I am interrupting.

NKANSA. You don't happen to talk at the right time. This is the time for you to say something, for you were here on that day.

ASANTE. Was I addressing you, eh? . . . Be very careful, you Nkansa. What you want to see, you will soon see.

NKANSA. Prpprppprpprpp. What can you do?

OSAFO. Not again, Mr. Nkansa. If you and Mr. Asante continue like this, I shall have to use my powers as President to ask you to leave this room. Why are you two always quarrelling like women? [*Pause.*] And now about this China thing, I never said those things, so they may be deleted.

SECRETARY. But, Mr. President, I distinctly heard you say that when you saw a Chinese and a Japanese during the world war, in Burma, you could hardly tell the difference.

OSAFO. Of course I said that, but what had that got to do

with bamboo aeroplanes? I was just referring to the physical features of the two peoples. Any more corrections?

ASANTE. If people are going to say one thing today and change their minds tomorrow because a small boy just out of college thinks it is wrong, then this club is not going to have any future.

OSAFO. Mr. Asante, I strongly resent your statement. It is in fact a deliberate attempt to discredit my integrity and character. It is good that I am the President, otherwise I would have considered it so personal that we would have had to settle the case outside this house. I gave the lecture and know what I said. Why try to baffle me by putting things that are not true in my mouth, eh? . . . Why?

SECRETARY. Is it the general wish of the house that I delete those two statements made by the President?

NKANSA. You should not say "those two statements made by the President," because he denies ever having made them.

SECRETARY. I suppose you would be a better secretary than myself? All along I have noticed how you have intentionally tried to discredit me, so that you may be offered the post. I am not being paid to do this, and if you want to take over, you can take over right now.

NKANSA. Of course, I would be a better secretary. For one thing, I shall not put fictitious statements to the credit of people who haven't made them.

SECRETARY. All right then, come and take over the post right now. [SECRETARY *gets up as if to leave the room.*]

ADDO. Mr. Secretary, don't do that. You know we have in our constitution how secretaries may be appointed, removed, or may resign. What you are trying to do now is not in the constitution. If therefore you feel you have been offended so much that you want to resign, you have to go through the proper formalities. You don't just get up and say, I have resigned.

SECRETARY. So I am not being constitutional? All right. I shall hand in my resignation to the President after the meeting.

OSAFO. If there are no more corrections or amendments, will somebody please move for the minutes to be accepted as the correct proceedings of the last meeting.

*Silence.*

NKANSA. I move that the minutes as corrected be accepted by the house.

ADDO. I second the motion.

OSAFO. Those in favour, say Aye.

VOICES. Aye Aye Aye [*About five voices.*]

OSAFO. Those against . . . ? Since no one seems to be against the motion, I shall sign the minutes book. Well, to today's business. The Treasurer has to give us a report on the state of our finance.

SECRETARY. On point of order, I think it is the duty of the Financial Secretary.

KUBLENU. No, it is not the Financial Secretary who should give such a report. It is the duty of the Treasurer. After all, he keeps the money. How can I give a report on our finance if I don't know how much we have in our coffers?

NKANSA. I think he is right, gentlemen.

ASANTE. I think he is wrong.

NKANSA. Of course, you always think wrongly.

*Laughter.*

SOKPORTIE. I don't mind if you ask me to give the financial report. I know how much we have in the coffees.

OSAFO. In the what fees?

SOKPORTIE. In the coffees, Mr. President.

OSAFO. Oh, coffers.

SOKPORTIE. Yes, coffees. We have three pounds sixteen shillings and ninepence halfpenny. We at first had four pounds.

NKANSA. What do you mean by "at first"?

SOKPORTIE. I mean, this morning we had four pounds. But this morning the Secretary came for three shillings and threepence. The three shillings was for a writing pad and a minutes book. The threepence was for the bottle of ink you see on the Secretary's table.

ASANTE. If that is the situation, then how came the halfpenny in the account?

SOKPORTIE. Well, this morning when I opened the tin box in which I keep the money for the club, I saw a halfpenny in it. I asked my wife whether she put it in, but she said, No. I was not able to find out where it came from.

ASANTE. In other words, your wife knows where we keep our money?

NKANSA. And why not? They both live in the same house, and if he does not tell her about it, she may go and take some money out of it.

SOKPORTIE. In fact, she gave me the tin box, which used to contain chocolates.

ASANTE. Then I suppose one of your five children went and put in the halfpenny.

OSAFO. Mr. Asante, I don't understand why you are making all this fuss about such a small matter. The Treasurer is not short of money. In fact, we have made a profit of a halfpenny. I personally don't see anything wrong with that.

ASANTE. I see a lot wrong with that. Today he is halfpenny surplus, tomorrow he will be two pounds short. What sort of accounting system is he using? If I find a halfpenny in my pocket, I certainly would know how it got there.

NKANSA. Everybody here knows that.

*Laughter.*

ASANTE. It is important that our Treasurer should know how to keep our money so that it does not mix with other people's.

OSAFO. All right, Mr. Asante, we shall tell the Treasurer not to mix our money with other people's. Mr. Sokportie, you may continue with the report.

SOKPORTIE. Unfortunately, not all members have paid their dues up to now.

ADDO. How many have not paid?

SOKPORTIE. Two have not paid. One member has been on trek since a month ago, but he wrote to me that he will pay as soon as he gets back here.

ADDO. And is the other man who has not paid here in town?

SOKPORTIE. Yes, in fact he is in this room.

NKANSA. This is a shame. Even I have paid.

ASANTE. What do you mean by, even you? Are you not working like everyone else?

NKANSA. And what about you? Are you not working? Have you paid your dues?

ASANTE. I have not paid, but that is not my fault. I told Mr. Sokportie that at the end of the month he should come and collect it.

OSAFO. But, Mr. Asante, as a responsible adult and a gentleman, you do not have to wait for the Treasurer to come to you for your dues. You should have brought the money with you to this meeting. I would advise members not to give too much trouble to our Treasurer. He is not being paid for this job. Members should always help him by sending their dues to him. He is a very busy man indeed, as you may all know.

ASANTE. We are all very busy men.

ADDO. Don't say that, Asante. I am a busy man too, but I always send my dues to Mr. Sokportie in his house.

OSAFO. I think the matter is settled and Mr. Asante should bring his dues to the next meeting. [*Laughter.*] We shall get on to the next item on the agenda: membership. I regret to say that the membership over the last two years has been dropping gradually. At the beginning of 1955 we were fifty strong. Now we are only nineteen. I know several people have been transferred from this town to other parts of the country, but others have come here to take their places. I cannot understand why we have not been able to attract these people into our club.

ASANTE. I know why. We do not plan interesting activities; on the other hand, when we come here, the meetings develop into a discussion of personal matters. No one would like to come into a club of equals only to be laughed at or abused by small boys.

ADDO. Your reasons, Asante, are not sensible.

ASANTE. You see what I was saying . . . abuses . . . that is all we hear at these meetings.

ADDO. Perhaps I used the wrong word, but what I was trying to say was that your reasons for the refusal of other gentlemen in this town to join us are not realistic at all. I think the reason is that these people are more interested in getting drunk every night than in coming here for intelligent discussion. Here is the storekeeper of the U.A.C. shop; ask him how many times these people call on him to buy drinks. When a man is interested in getting drunk, nobody but a missionary can make him put a stop to the practice. I personally do not see why we should worry because these people refuse to become members. In such matters, I think it is the quality of the members and not the quantity that matters.

NKANSA. Hear, hear!

ADDO. We may have seventy members, but if they are of the wrong type, you will soon see that this will become not a Social and Literary Club but a boozemen club.

ALL. Hear, hear, hear!

SOKPORTIE. I agree in toto with what the last speaker said. Even with our small number of members, you all know the amount of trouble I find for myself when it comes to collecting dues.

ASANTE. This has nothing to do with dues. We want more members and you get up to talk about dues. I bet if someone else becomes the Treasurer, you will give the same amount of trouble if he comes to collect the dues from you.

*Laughter.*

OSAFO. Do I take it that it is the wish of members to restrict the number to what it is at present?

VOICE. Yes!

OSAFO. On the other hand, I had in my mind a bright idea for making our membership balanced. What I mean is this: You see all the members are males. Every time we hold a dance, we always have to ask a lady (my wife) to act as the M.C. with one of our members. I think it would be a good idea if we had some female members. What do you think?

ADDO. I think it is a good idea, but from where are we going to get the ladies?

OSAFO. I was coming to that. Fortunately, this year we have had the fortune of being blessed with three female teachers in the primary school. Apart from these, a midwife has come to set up her practice in this town. The Government has kindly sent a telephone operator here too.

NKANSA. But I understand the postmaster wants to marry her.

ASANTE. Marry who?

NKANSA. The telephone operator.

ASANTE. What has that to do with us? We want female members, and the telephone operator is a female; that is all that should concern us.

OASFO. I don't think in this particular respect the problem is as simple as all that. You all know how antagonistic the postmaster is towards this club. When we want to bank our money in the Post Office Savings Bank, he is always insulting us because he says he knows we would constantly be coming to him to withdraw part of the amount. What is more, ever since we refused to allow him to come to our last dance without a ticket, he has stopped talking to me. In that case, I shall not be surprised at all if he refuses to allow the woman to become a member.

ASANTE. But the woman is not married to the postmaster yet.

NKANSA. But they are friends. He is always in her house.

ASANTE. He is always in her house and so what? You are

always in the house of one of the female teachers, but does that mean you are her friend?

NKANSA. You see how he is trying to twist everything to suit his evil mind! We are talking about the telephone operator, and you come in with this accusation. If we are to make accusations and allegations about some of us here in relationship with these female teachers, some people here will be having trouble with their wives in the house.

*Laughter. . . . Uproar.*

OSAFO. Gentlemen, the matter is an important one that concerns all of us, and I will not allow personal remarks to be made. You two, Nkansa and Asante, seem to be great rivals at something. I hope it is not about one of the female teachers. [*Laughter.*] Gentlemen, I think the best thing to be done in the case of the telephone operator, whom I am sure we all find very charming, is for one of the younger men to cultivate her friendship and draw her into the club.

NKANSA. And what about the postmaster?

ASANTE. What has the postmaster got to do with it? We want the girl, not the man.

*Prolonged laughter.*

OSAFO. Seriously, gentlemen, I think that is the best way to get the young woman into the club. I have been in this sort of thing in several towns, and every time, I found that we had female members only when the women were interested in some of the men.

ADDO. May I suggest, sir, that Mr. Nkansa, who is the youngest and most handsome among us, be asked to make it his task to woo the young woman.

ASANTE. You couldn't have suggested a better man.

*Laughter.*

NKANSA. President, I resent the statement made by the last speaker, and I am asking him to withdraw it.

OSAFO. Oh, Mr. Nkansa, but that was a compliment. We

are all aware of the immensity of your attraction and amorous propensities. [*Laughs.*] In fact, I am sure you will not be surprised to know that I think you have been experimenting with your talents on my eldest daughter. [*Uproar in the house.*] It is bound to happen in the life of every young man, especially when he is as intelligent as he is handsome. We all did that when we were young.

ASANTE. Tell him more, oh, Father, tell him more.

NKANSA. Tell who more? You are happy that I am being labelled as a lady follower. What about you?

ASANTE. What about me?

OSAFO. All right, all right, let us stop there. What about the lady teachers? I am sure, being teachers, we shall not find it difficult to get them in as members. I hesitate to suggest who should contact them on the point, but as Mr. Nkansa is also a teacher in the same school, I am sure he will find the task easy.

NKANSA. On the other hand, Mr. President, there are some people in this room here who are more intimately connected with the ladies in question. There is one man here who, though he is married, can be found always hanging around the houses of these lady teachers.

*The club-room becomes uneasily quiet, only broken by the distant titter of one or two members.*

ASANTE. There is a Twi proverb which says, Words fear the beard. Mr. Nkansa, if he is really a man, should come out with the facts of the case instead of casting insinuations.

NKANSA. If the cap fits you, wear it; so says another popular proverb.

ASANTE. You are a coward; why don't you mention the name of this married man?

NKANSA. I have said what I have said. In fact, I will say more. This married gentleman in question was on one night thrown out of the room of one of the female teachers [*Laughs.*], and not only that but the gentleman in question knocked his forehead against the door and had a deep cut. So let us see who in this room has bandaged his head. [*Laughter . . . as* ASANTE *rushes to where*

NKANSA *stands and slaps him.*] So you have slapped me!

ASANTE. And I am going to slap you again.

OSAFO. Mr. Asante, stop that childish behaviour. [NKANSA *slaps him back and the two get into a huddle.*] Mr. Asante, stop that.

ASANTE. But didn't you see him slap me?

ADDO. But you slapped him first.

OSAFO. Separate them, somebody! This is very disgraceful, two grown-ups. . . . Hey, mind what you are doing; you are overturning my table. [*The two men struggle while the other members try in vain to separate them.* MR. NKANSA *lifts* ASANTE *up and throws him on the President's table, thus overturning the bottle of ink on the President's clothes. Pause.*] Look what you have done. You have ruined my white trousers with this ink.

SECRETARY. We just bought this bottle of ink, and look what you have done to it. Overturned it all into the President's trousers.

OSAFO. This is no laughing matter. You know how much these trousers cost me? I ordered the suit from England; now look what you have done. What am I going to tell my wife? This is very disgraceful. Two grown-ups fighting like market women. The club should suspend you two gentlemen now.

ADDO. Yes, I think they should be suspended.

SOKPORTIE. And be made to pay for the bottle of ink. But, Mr. President, I think they should be made to shake hands, so as to forget what has happened.

NKANSA. I am not going to shake hands with that ass.

ASANTE. Who is an ass? Hey, look sharp, you see. [*Rushes towards* NKANSA *again.*]

KUBLENU. You are being foolish, Asante. The mere fact that you give me eggs from your station farm does not mean that I should back you when even I think you are in the wrong. After all, don't I pay for the eggs and vegetables you send to my wife?

ASANTE. So I am foolish; all right, I'll say nothing. I leave everything in the hands of the Father above . . . what I have done to you people to merit this hostility from you all!

OSAFO. That is a very stupid statement, Asante, and I am saying this not only as the President of this club but as your uncle as well. You have behaved very disgracefully today, and I wish you would do what everybody expects of you; that is, apologise. After all, you were the first to slap Nkansa, against whom you had already made allegations similar to what he made against you. You must be ashamed of yourself.

SECRETARY. Mr. President, I suggest that we appoint a committee to go into the matter and suggest the measures we as the members of the club should take.

ADDO. I think that is a good idea.

OSAFO. Now that order has been restored, may I suggest that we deal with the last item on the agenda: the salary of the watchman and caretaker. The caretaker came to see me this morning to lay a complaint. He said he had not received his monthly salary of one pound ten shillings for the last three months. I know we have not enough money in the coffers, but we must all the same pay him, for an agreement is an agreement. What do members suggest?

NKANSA. I suggest we all pay a special levy of five shillings per head for the purpose.

VOICES. That is a good idea.

OSAFO. All right, then, I shall empower the Treasurer to collect the amount from you, starting from today. In the meanwhile I am going to pay the caretaker myself and shall collect the money we contribute into my pocket. Has anyone anything to be discussed before we adjourn the meeting?

ADDO. Yes. May I suggest that we buy two pairs of boxing gloves so that the next time any members want to fight, we let them do it in the proper manner.

*Loud laughter and fade.*

# NOTES ON THE AUTHORS

LEWIS NKOSI, the author of *The Rhythm of Violence*, was born in Durban, South Africa, in 1936, and attended Zululand public schools. He spent a year at the M. L. Sultan Technical College in Durban, and in 1955 joined the Zulu-English weekly *Ilanga lase Natal* (*Natal Sun*). In 1956 he started work for *Drum* magazine, also serving as chief reporter on the Sunday paper *The Golden City Post* in Johannesburg. He accepted a Nieman Fellowship in Journalism at Harvard for 1961–62, and due to this he has been barred from returning to South Africa. Living in London as a free-lance writer, Nkosi is the literary editor of *The New African* and has published articles in *The Spectator, The Guardian, The Observer,* and *The New Statesman.* A collection of his essays, *Home and the Exile* (London: Longmans, 1965), won a prize at the Dakar World Festival of Negro Art. More recently Nkosi was the moderator-interviewer for a National Educational Television (U.S.) series of programs on African writers. *The Rhythm of Violence* is said to be the first play in English by a black South African since 1936. It has also been favorably compared to John Arden's *Serjeant Musgrave's Dance.* It is a violent drama about a subject some consider worthy of violence. Nkosi is one of the few angry young dramatists in or exiled from Africa today.

JOHN PEPPER CLARK, the author of *Song of a Goat*, was born on April 6, 1935, in Kiagbodo, Western Ijaw, Delta Province, Nigeria. Educated at schools in Okrika and Jeremi, he attended Warri Government College, Ughelli (1948–54), and the University of Ibadan (1955–60), and took his B.A., Honours English, in 1960. He was an information officer for the Nigerian government in 1960–61, and became head of features and editorial writer for the Express Group of Newspapers (Lagos) in 1961–62. In the following year he accepted a Parvin Fellowship at Princeton University. Out of this experience came a book-length essay severely critical of American customs and values, *America, Their America* (London: Andre Deutsch, 1964). He returned to Nigeria to become a research fellow in the Institute of African Studies, University of Ibadan, 1963–64, and since then has been a lecturer in the Department of English, University of Lagos. His published works include: *Poems* (Ibadan: Mbari Publications, 1962); *Three Plays* (*Song of a Goat, The Raft, Masquerade*; London: Oxford University Press, 1964); *Ozidi*, a play based on Nigerian folklore (London: Oxford University Press, 1965); and *A Reed in the Tide* (poems, 1956–64; London: Longmans, 1965).

Clark is married and has one child, and is presently at work on *A Companion Dictionary to Nigerian Literature*, a volume of Urhobo poetry, a monograph called "A Writer on Writing," and the chapter on culture for a United Nations report entitled *The Effects of the Policy of Apartheid in the Fields of Education, Science, Culture, and Information*. He has made a documentary film, under University of Ibadan and Ford Foundation sponsorship, of *The Ozidi of Atazi*, the ancient Ijaw performed-epic, and has in progress another documentary film, *The Ghost Town*, based on Forcados, once an important Nigerian port. A founding editor of *The Horn*, a magazine of student poetry at the University of Ibadan, Clark was also a founding member of the Society of Nigerian Authors. Most critics of African literature in English agree that Clark "may well be not only the best African poet but perhaps one of the major contemporary poets writing in English today."

ALFRED HUTCHINSON, the author of *The Rain-Killers*, was born in Hectorspruit, the Eastern Transvaal, South Africa, in 1924. His maternal grandfather was a Swazi chief; his other grandfather was English. After obtaining his B.A. degree and Diploma in Education at Fort Hare University College, he taught for a while before losing his position due to a prison sentence arising from his connection with the 1952 Defiance Campaign. He then taught at the Central Indian High School in Johannesburg until he was arrested in 1956 in the first mass group of South Africans charged with high treason. Jumping bail, he escaped to East Africa, and then to Ghana, where he married Hazel Slade, an Englishwoman. In 1960 he moved to England, his present country of residence, where he is a free-lance writer. See his autobiography, *Road to Ghana* (London: Gollancz, 1960; New York: John Day, 1960).

EFUA THEODORA SUTHERLAND, the author of *Edufa*, was born in Ghana in 1924 and educated there at Saint Monica's School and the Training College. In England she studied at Homerton College, Cambridge, and the School of Oriental and African Studies, University of London. She taught school in Ghana from 1951 to 1954, when she married William Sutherland. She now has three children. Mrs. Sutherland was the founder of the Ghana Drama Studio and of the Ghana Society of Writers, now the Writers' Workshop in the Institute of African Studies, University of Ghana, Legon. She helped establish the magazine *Okyeame* as an outlet for new writing in Ghana. One of Ghana's leading authors, she has written numerous poems and short stories and two books for children. Her plays, produced at the Drama Studio and elsewhere, include *You Swore an Oath* (a one-act play), *Odasani* (a Ghanaian interpretation of *Everyman*), and *Foriwa* (a three-act community play). Among her plays ready for production are *The Marriage of Anansewa* (a one-act play), *The Pineapple Child* (a fantasy), *Ananse and the Dwarf Brigade* (a children's play), *Two Rhythm Plays* (for children), and *Nyamekye* (a drama of speech, music, and dance). *Edufa* was first performed at the Ghana Drama Studio in Accra in November and December, 1964.

JAMES ENE HENSHAW, the author of *The Jewels of the Shrine*, was born in Calabar in 1924, a member of a well-known family of Eastern Nigeria. He attended Christ the King College in Onitsha and took a medical degree from the National University of Ireland in Dublin. A physician who, as he puts it, only "strayed into play-writing," his *The Jewels of the Shrine* won the Henry Carr Memorial Cup (first prize) in the All-Nigerian Festival of the Arts in Lagos in 1952. The play was published in the mid-1950's in his collection of dramas, *This Is Our Chance, Plays from West Africa* (London: University of London Press, 1957), and such was its popularity among African drama groups and schools and colleges, that the volume had its ninth impression in 1966. Dr. Henshaw is married and has five children, to whom he dedicated his seventh play, *Medicine for Love* (London: University of London Press, 1964). His other published dramas include *Children of the Goddess and Other Plays* (*Companion for a Chief, Magic in the Blood*; London: University of London Press, 1964) and *Dinner for Promotion* (London: University of London Press, 1967).

HENRY OFORI, the author of *The Literary Society*, was born in Ghana in 1925. After graduating from Achimota College in 1949, he lived in a little rural township in the forest belt, an experience that provided the incident on which *The Literary Society* is based. From 1951 to 1955, he taught physics at the Government Secondary Technical School at Takoradi. Since that time he has been working as an editor and journalist. He has written a twice-weekly column for the *Ghanaian Times* for the past ten years. His book *Tales From Dodora Forest*, published by Waterville Press, will soon be followed by a collection of essays and stories, *Life Gets Tedious*. (His total output of short pieces now numbers over two thousand.) He is currently writing memoirs of his travels through Europe, the Caribbean, Asia, America, and Africa—a book to be entitled *One Short Boy*—as well as working in the Ghana Information Service in Accra. His delightful satire on the amateur literary club in a small town was originally written for radio.

*The Editor*

FREDRIC M. LITTO was born in New York City in 1939, received his B.A. in Theatre Arts from UCLA, and will receive his Ph.D. in Theatre History this year from Indiana University. Besides being the editor of the *Afro-Asian Theatre Bulletin*, he has written numerous articles and reviews for other journals, and in April, 1964, directed a performance of Clark's *Song of a Goat* at Indiana University. He is Associate Director of the International Theatre Studies Center and is an Assistant Professor at the University of Kansas, Lawrence, Kansas.